Reformed Church in the United States

An Order of Worship

for the Reformed Church

Reformed Church in the United States

An Order of Worship
for the Reformed Church

ISBN/EAN: 9783337291570

Printed in Europe, USA, Canada, Australia, Japan

Cover: Foto ©Lupo / pixelio.de

More available books at **www.hansebooks.com**

AN

ORDER OF WORSHIP

FOR

The Reformed Church.

PHILADELPHIA:
S. R. FISHER & CO., PUBLISHERS, 54 N. SIXTH STREET.
1867.

Entered according to Act of Congress, in the year 1866, by
S. R. FISHER & CO.,
in the Clerk's Office of the District Court for the Eastern District of Pennsylvania.

JAS. B. RODGERS,
PRINTER AND STEREOTYPER,
PHILADELPHIA.

TABLE OF CONTENTS.

I. THE CHURCH FESTIVALS 5
II. A TABLE OF SCRIPTURE LESSONS 7
III. THE REGULAR SERVICE ON THE LORD'S DAY . 9
IV. THE EVENING SERVICE 18
V. THE LITANY 24
VI. PRAYERS AND THANKSGIVINGS FOR SPECIAL OCCASIONS 28
VII. THE GOSPELS, EPISTLES, AND COLLECTS . . . 37
VIII. THE HOLY COMMUNION 158
IX. HOLY BAPTISM 188
X. CONFIRMATION 203
XI. MARRIAGE 208
XII. ORDINATION AND INSTALLATION 214
XIII. EXCOMMUNICATION AND RESTORATION . . . 238
XIV. THE VISITATION AND COMMUNION OF THE SICK 247
XV. THE BURIAL OF THE DEAD 264
XVI. A SERVICE TO BE USED AT SEA 279
XVII. THE RECEPTION OF IMMIGRANTS 289
XVIII. THE LAYING OF A CORNER-STONE 293
XIX. THE CONSECRATION OF A CHURCH 298
XX. THE CONSECRATION OF A BURIAL-GROUND . . 305
XXI. AN ORDER OF SCRIPTURE READINGS FOR THE FAMILY 312
XXII. PRAYERS FOR THE FAMILY 325
XXIII. THE CANTICLES, PSALMS, AND ANCIENT HYMNS 358

THE CHURCH FESTIVALS.

The movable festivals, with the exception of Advent Sunday, are determined by Easter, which is the first Sunday next after the full-moon that follows the twenty-first of March, but if this full-moon happen on a Sunday, Easter will be the next Sunday after.

Septuagesima is nine weeks, Sexagesima eight weeks, Quinquagesima seven weeks, and the first week in Lent six weeks, respectively, *before* Easter. Ash-Wednesday is the Wednesday after Quinquagesima, Ascension Day is forty days, Whitsunday seven weeks, and Trinity Sunday eight weeks, respectively, *after* Easter.

Advent Sunday is always the nearest Sunday to the thirtieth day of November, whether before or after.

Christmas always falls on the twenty-fifth of December, Epiphany on the sixth of January, and Good Friday in the week preceding Easter.

All days appointed, by proper Ecclesiastical or Civil authority, for fasting or thanksgiving, are to be duly respected and observed.

RULE FOR DETERMINING EASTER IN ANY YEAR.

1. Divide the number of the year by 19, and call the remainder a.
2. ,,   ,,   ,, by 4,   ,,   ,, b.
3. ,,   ,,   ,, by 7,   ,,   ,, c.
4. ,, $(19a + M.)$ by 30,   ,,   ,, d.
5. ,, $(2b + 4c + 6d + N)$ by 7,   ,,   ,, e.

In the Gregorian Calendar, M and N will have the following values:—

	M.	N.
From 1582 to 1699	22	3
1700 to 1799	23	3
1800 to 1899	23	4
1900 to 1999	24	5
2000 to 2099	24	5
2100 to 2199	24	6
2200 to 2299	25	0
2300 to 2399	26	1
2400 to 2499	25	1

6. Easter will be $(22 + d + e)$ of March, or $(d + e - 9)$ of April.

If a number is obtained beyond the 24th of April, seven days must be subtracted to get the correct time of Easter.

A TABLE OF THE MOVABLE FESTIVALS FROM 1867—1890

	SUNDAYS AFTER EPIPHANY.	SEPTUAGESIMA.	ASH WEDNESDAY.	EASTER.	ASCENSION DAY.	WHITSUNDAY.	SUNDAYS AFTER TRINITY.	ADVENT.
1867	5	Feb. 17	Mar. 6	April 21	May 30	June 9	23	Dec. 1
1868	4	" 9	Feb. 26	" 12	" 21	May 31	24	Nov. 29
1869	2	Jan. 24	" 10	Mar. 28	" 6	" 16	26	" 28
1870	5	Feb. 13	Mar. 2	April 17	" 26	June 5	23	" 27
1871	4	" 5	Feb. 22	" 9	" 18	May 28	25	Dec. 3
1872	2	Jan. 28	" 14	Mar. 31	" 9	" 19	26	" 1
1873	4	Feb. 9	" 26	April 13	" 22	June 1	24	Nov. 30
1874	3	" 1	" 18	" 5	" 14	May 24	25	" 29
1875	2	Jan. 24	" 10	Mar. 28	" 6	" 16	26	" 28
1876	5	Feb. 13	Mar. 1	April 16	" 25	June 4	24	Dec. 3
1877	3	Jan. 28	Feb. 14	" 1	" 10	May 20	26	" 2
1878	5	Feb. 17	Mar. 6	" 21	" 30	June 9	23	" 1
1879	4	" 9	Feb. 26	" 13	" 22	" 1	24	Nov. 30
1880	2	Jan. 25	" 11	Mar. 28	" 6	May 16	26	" 28
1881	5	Feb. 13	Mar. 2	April 17	" 26	June 5	23	" 27
1882	4	" 5	Feb. 22	" 9	" 18	May 28	25	Dec. 3
1883	2	Jan. 21	" 7	Mar. 25	" 3	" 13	27	" 2
1884	4	Feb. 10	" 27	April 13	" 22	June 1	24	Nov. 30
1885	3	" 1	" 18	" 5	" 14	May 24	25	" 29
1886	6	" 21	Mar. 10	" 25	June 3	June 13	22	" 28
1887	4	" 6	Feb. 23	10	May 19	May 29	24	" 27
1888	3	Jan. 29	" 15	" 1	" 10	" 20	26	Dec. 2
1889	5	Feb. 17	Mar. 6	" 21	" 30	June 9	23	" 1
1890	3	" 2	Feb. 19	" 6	" 15	May 25	25	Nov. 30

A TABLE OF SCRIPTURE LESSONS

FOR ALL THE SUNDAYS IN THE CHURCH YEAR.

SUNDAYS.	MORNING.		EVENING.	
	First Lesson.	Second Lesson.	First Lesson.	Second Lesson.
In Advent.				
1	Isaiah —— 1	Luke 1 to v. 39	Isaiah —— 2	Romans —— 10
2	—— 5	—— 1 v. 39	—— 24	—— 12
3	—— 25	—— 3 to v. 19	—— 28 to v. 23	—— 14
4	—— 30	Matt. 3 to v. 13	—— 32	1 Corinthians 1
After Nativity.				
1	—— 35	Luke — 2 v. 25	—— 40	—— 2
2	—— 41	Mark 1 to v. 16	—— 42	Hebrews — 2
After Epiphany				
1	—— 44	Matthew 2 v. 13	—— 45	1 Corinthians 3
2	—— 51	John — 1 v. 29	—— 52 to v. 13	—— 13
3	—— 54	Matthew 4 v. 12	—— 55	2 Corinthians 4
4	—— 57	Luke 4 v. 14 to 33	—— 59	—— 5
5	—— 61	Matthew — 5	—— 62	Galatians — 2
6	—— 65	—— 6	—— 66	—— 3
Septuagesima.	Jeremiah —— 5	—— 7	Jeremiah — 22	Ephesians — 1
Sexagesima.	—— 35	Luke — 7 v. 19	—— 36	—— 2
Quinquagesima.	Lamentations 1	Mark 6 to v. 30	Lam. 3 to v. 37	—— 3
In Lent.				
1	Jeremiah — 7	Matthew — 10	Jeremiah — 9	—— 4
2	Ezekiel — 14	Luke 10 to v. 25	Ezekiel — 18	—— 5
3	—— 20 to v. 27	Mark 9 to v. 30	—— 20 v. 27	—— 6
4	Micah — 6	Luke — 19 v. 28	Habakkuk - 3	Philippians — 1
5	Haggai 2 to v. 10	—— 21	Zechariah — 13	—— 3
6	Daniel — 9	Matthew — 26	Malachi 3 and 4	Hebrews 5 to v. 11
Easter Day.	Exod. 12 to v. 37	Romans —— 6	Exodus 12 v. 37	Acts — 2 v. 22
After Easter.				
1	Isaiah —— 43	Acts —— 1	Isaiah —— 48	1 Corinthians 15
2	Hosea —— 13	—— 3	Hosea —— 14	Colossians — 1
3	Joel —— 3 v. 9	—— 5	Micah —— 4	—— 3
4	Micah —— 5	—— 6	Nahum —— 1	1 Thessalon. 3
5	Zechariah — 8	—— 8 v.	Zechariah — 10	—— 4
After Ascension	Joel —— 2	John —— 17	Zephaniah - 3	2 Thess. 3 to v. 17
Whit-Sunday.	Deut. 16 to v. 18	Acts 4 to v. 36	Isaiah —— 11	Acts 19 to v. 21
Trinity.	Genesis —— 1	Matthew —— 3	Genesis —— 2	1 John —— 5
After Trinity.				
1	—— 3	Acts 9 to v. 32	—— 6	1 Timothy — 6
2	—— 9 to v. 20	—— 10	—— 16 to v. 19	2 Timothy — 2
3	—— 37	—— 11	—— 42	—— 3 and 4 to v. 9
4	—— 43	—— 14	—— 45	Titus 2 & 3 to v. 10
5	—— 49	—— 15	—— 50	Hebrews — 10
6	Exodus —— 3	—— 17	Exodus —— 5	—— 11
7	—— 9	—— 20	—— 10	—— 12
8	—— 14	—— 24	—— 15	—— 13
9	Numbers —— 16	—— 26	Numbers —— 22	James —— 1
10	—— 23	—— 28	—— 24	—— 2
11	Deut. 4 to v. 41	Matthew —— 18	Deuteronomy 5	—— 3
12	—— 6	—— 20	—— 7	—— 4
13	—— 8	—— 23	—— 9	—— 5
14	—— 33	—— 25	—— 34	1 Peter — 1
15	Joshua —— 23	Mark —— 4	Joshua —— 24	—— 2
16	Judges —— 4	—— 13	Judges —— 5	—— 3
17	1 Samuel — 12	Luke —— 13	1 Samuel — 17	—— 4
18	2 Samuel — 12	—— 15	2 Samuel — 19	—— 5
19	1 Kings 8 to v. 22	—— 20	1 Kings 8 v. 22 to 62	2 Peter — 1
20	—— 17	John —— 3	—— 18	—— 2
21	2 Kings —— 5	—— 7	2 Kings — 19	—— 3
22	Daniel —— 6	—— 8	Daniel —— 7	1 John —
23	Proverbs — 1	—— 9	Proverbs — 2	—— 2
4	—— 3	—— 10	—— 8	—— 3
3	—— 11	—— 11	—— 12	Jude ——
2	—— 13	—— 15	—— 14	Rev. —— 1
1	—— 15	—— 16	—— 16	—— 22
Before Advent.				

THE REGULAR SERVICE

ON

THE LORD'S DAY.

Having taken his place on the right of the altar, the Congregation also standing up, the Minister shall say as follows:

In the name of the Father, and of the Son, and of the Holy Ghost. *Amen.*

DEARLY BELOVED IN THE LORD: If we say that we have no sin, we deceive ourselves, and the truth is not in us; but if we confess our sins, God is faithful and just to forgive us our sins, and to cleanse us from all unrighteousness. Let us, therefore, humble ourselves before the throne of Almighty God, our heavenly Father, and confess our manifold sins and transgressions with lowly and contrite hearts, that we may obtain forgiveness of the same through the merits of our Lord Jesus Christ.

Then the Minister and Congregation shall kneel, and repeat the following Confession.

ALMIGHTY and most merciful God, our heavenly Father, we cast ourselves down before Thee, under a deep sense of our unworthiness and guilt. We have grievously sinned against Thee, in thought, in word, and in deed. We have come short of Thy glory. We have broken Thy commandments, and turned aside every one of us from the way of life; and in us there is no soundness nor health. Yet now, O most merciful Father, hear us when we call upon Thee with penitent hearts; and for the sake of Thy Son, Jesus Christ, have mercy upon us. Pardon our sins, and grant us Thy peace. Take away our guilt. Purify us, by the inspiration of Thy Holy Spirit, from all inward uncleanness; and make us able and willing to serve Thee in newness of life to the glory of Thy holy name, through Jesus Christ our Lord. Amen.

Then shall the Minister rise, and pronounce to the Congregation, still kneeling, the following *Declaration of Pardon*.

HEARKEN now unto the comforting assurance of the grace of God, promised in the Gospel to all that repent and believe: As I live, saith the Lord God, I have no pleasure in the death of the wicked, but that the wicked turn from his way and live. God so loved the world, that He gave His only begotten Son, that whosoever believeth in Him should not perish, but have everlasting life.

Unto as many of you, therefore, beloved brethren, as truly repent of your sins, and believe in the Lord Jesus Christ, with full purpose of new obedience, I announce and declare, by the authority and in the name of Christ, that your sins are forgiven in heaven, according to His promise in the Gospel, through the perfect merit of Jesus Christ our Lord.

<small>Here, and at the end of every Collect and Prayer, the Congregation shall say:</small>

Amen.

<small>The Congregation shall now rise, and join with the Minister in repeating the *Apostles' Creed;* immediately after which shall be sung, chanted or recited, the *Gloria in Excelsis;* all in the following order.</small>

I BELIEVE in God the Father Almighty, Maker of heaven and earth:

And in Jesus Christ His only begotten Son our Lord; who was conceived by the Holy Ghost, born of the Virgin Mary; suffered under Pontius Pilate, was crucified, dead, and buried; He descended into hades; the third day He rose from the dead; He ascended into heaven, and sitteth at the right hand of God the Father Almighty; from thence He shall come to judge the quick and the dead.

I believe in the Holy Ghost; the holy catholic Church; the communion of saints; the forgiveness of sins; the resurrection of the body, and the life everlasting. Amen.

Minister. Praise ye the Lord.
Congregation. The Lord's name be praised.

GLORY be to God on high, and on earth peace, good will toward men. We praise Thee, we bless Thee, we worship Thee, we glorify Thee, we give thanks to Thee for Thy great glory, O Lord God, heavenly King, God the Father Almighty.

O Lord, the only begotten Son, Jesus Christ; O Lord God, Lamb of God, Son of the Father, that takest away the sin of the world, have mercy upon us. Thou that takest away the sin of the world, have mercy upon us. Thou that takest away the sin of the world, receive our prayer. Thou that sittest at the right hand of God the Father, have mercy upon us.

For Thou only art holy; Thou only art the Lord; Thou only, O Christ, with the Holy Ghost, art most high in the glory of God the Father. Amen.

Then shall the Minister read the proper Gospel and Epistle for the day; adding, so far as he may see fit, other portions of Scripture.

After the reading, the service shall proceed thus, the Congregation rising:

M. Glory be to the Father, and to the Son, and to the Holy Ghost:

C. As it was in the beginning, is now, and ever shall be, world without end. Amen.

M. The Lord be with you.
C. And with thy spirit.

M. Let us pray.

Then shall be offered the Collect for the day, and after this the following General Prayer; except that, on Festival days, the first two Collects of the same shall be omitted and the proper Festival Prayer used in their stead.

[During Lent, or in other seasons of humiliation, the *Litany* may take the place of the General Prayer.]

ALMIGHTY GOD, Father of all mercies, we, Thine unworthy servants, do give Thee most humble and hearty thanks for all Thy goodness and loving kindness to us, and to all men. We praise Thee for our creation, preservation, and all the blessings of this life; but above all, for Thine inestimable love in the redemption of the world by our Lord Jesus Christ; for the means of grace, and for the hope of glory. And, we beseech Thee, give us such due sense of all Thy mercies, that our hearts may be unfeignedly thankful, and that we may show forth Thy praise, not only with our lips, but in our lives; by giving up ourselves to Thy service, and by walking before Thee in holiness and righteousness all our days; through Jesus Christ our Lord, to whom, with Thee and the Holy Ghost, be all honor and glory, world without end. *Amen.*

GOD of all power and glory, who hast not appointed us unto wrath, but to obtain salvation by our Lord Jesus Christ, perfect and fulfill in us, we beseech Thee, the work of Thy redeeming mercy; that, being delivered more and more from our sins, we may be able to serve Thee in newness of life. Sanctify us in body, soul, and spirit; and guide us evermore in the way of peace. Help us to overcome the world. Beat down Satan under our feet. Give us courage to confess Christ always; and patience to endure in His service unto the end; that having finished our course with joy, we may rest in hope, and attain finally to the resurrection of the just, through the infinite merits of our Saviour Jesus Christ. *Amen.*

O Thou God and Father of our Lord Jesus Christ, of whom the whole family in heaven and earth is named, cause Thy blessing, we beseech Thee, to rest upon the Church, which He has purchased with His most precious blood. Illuminate her ministers with true knowledge and understanding of Thy word. Send down the healthful dew of Thy grace upon all her congregations. Deliver her from false doctrine, heresy and schism; and clothe her with the beauty of holiness and peace. Establish and reveal Thy glory among all nations. By the tranquil working of Thy perpetual Providence, confound and destroy all wicked devices formed against Thy holy Word, and bring in speedily the full victory of Thine everlasting kingdom, through Jesus Christ our Lord. *Amen.*

Almighty God, King of kings and Lord of lords, from whom proceedeth all power and dominion in heaven and on earth, most heartily we beseech Thee to look with favor upon Thy servants, the President of the United States, the Governor of this Commonwealth, and all others in authority. Imbue them with the spirit of wisdom, goodness, and truth; and so rule their hearts, and bless their endeavors, that law and order, justice and peace may every where prevail. Preserve us from public calamities; from pestilence and famine; from war, privy conspiracy, and rebellion; but especially from national sins and corruption. Make us strong and great in the fear of

God, and in the love of righteousness; so that being blessed of Thee, we may become a blessing to all nations, to the praise of the glory of Thy grace through Jesus Christ. *Amen.*

O GOD, The Creator and Preserver of all mankind, we implore Thy mercy in behalf of all classes and conditions of men; that it may please Thee to visit them with Thy most compassionate help, according to their manifold necessities and wants. Especially do we beseech Thee to show pity upon all widows and orphans; upon all prisoners and captives; upon all sick and dying persons; upon those who are desolate or sore afflicted in any way; and upon all such as are persecuted for righteousness' sake. Enable them to look unto Thee, O most merciful Father, and to call upon Thy name, that they may find Thee a present Saviour in their affliction and distress. And let it please Thee to deliver them, and raise them up in due time, giving them patience under all their sufferings, the rich comfort of Thy grace here below, and eternal rest with Thee in heaven, through our Lord Jesus Christ. *Amen.*

Here may be introduced any special *Collect* or *Collects* suitable to the occasion.

ALMIGHTY God, who hast given us grace at this time with one accord to make our common supplications unto Thee, and dost promise that where two or three are gathered together in Thy name, Thou wilt grant their requests; fulfil now, O Lord, the desires and petitions of Thy servants, as may be most expedient for them, granting us in this world knowledge of Thy truth, and in the world to come, life everlasting. *Amen.*

A suitable *Psalm* or *Hymn* shall now be sung.

Then the Minister, having taken his place in the pulpit, shall proceed to deliver the *Sermon.* This should be in harmony with the general order of the Church Year.

After the Sermon, the service shall be continued as follows:

M. Let us pray.

ALMIGHTY God, Fountain of all goodness and truth, receive our thanks for the lively oracles of Thy grace, which are able to make us wise unto everlasting life; and mercifully grant, we beseech Thee, that the words, which we have heard this day with our outward ears, may through Thy blessing be so grafted inwardly in our hearts, that they may bring forth in us the fruit of good living; to the honor and praise of Thy name, through Jesus Christ our Lord. *Amen.*

O GOD, who art the author of peace and lover of concord, in knowledge of whom standeth our eternal life, whose service is perfect freedom; defend us, Thy humble servants, in all assaults of our enemies; that we, surely trusting in Thy defence, may not fear the power of any adversaries, through the might of our glorious Lord and Saviour Jesus Christ. *Amen.*

Here let the People join aloud in the *Lord's Prayer.*

OUR Father who art in heaven, Hallowed be Thy name. Thy kingdom come. Thy will be done in earth, as it is in heaven. Give us this day our daily bread. And forgive us our debts, as we forgive our debtors. And lead us not into temptation. But deliver us from evil. For Thine is the kingdom, and the power, and the glory, for ever. Amen.

<small>The Deacons shall now collect the *Alms* of the People; and the Minister may make any necessary *Announcements*.</small>

<small>Then a *Psalm* or *Hymn* shall be sung, ending with a *Doxology*.</small>

<small>After which the Minister shall close the whole service with the *Apostolic Benediction*.</small>

The grace of the Lord Jesus Christ, and the love of God, and the communion of the Holy Ghost, be with you all. *Amen.*

THE EVENING SERVICE.

Having taken his place at the altar, the Congregation also standing up, the Minister shall say as follows:

In the name of the Father, and of the Son, and of the Holy Ghost. *Amen.*

Let us pray.

ALMIGHTY GOD, unto whom all hearts are open, all desires known, and from whom no secrets are hid; cleanse the thoughts of our minds, we beseech Thee, by the inspiration of Thy Holy Spirit, that, being delivered from every unholy motion of the flesh and spirit, we may perfectly love Thee, with a pure heart and sanctified lips worship Thee, and worthily magnify Thy holy Name; through Jesus Christ our Lord.

Here, and at the end of every Collect and Prayer, the Congregation shall say:

Amen.

A Psalm or Hymn shall now be sung.

Then shall the Congregation rise, and join with the Minister in repeating the *Apostles' Creed;* immediately after which shall be chanted, or recited, the *Gloria Patri;* all in the following order.

THE EVENING SERVICE.

I BELIEVE in God the Father Almighty, Maker of heaven and earth:
And in Jesus Christ, His only begotten Son our Lord; who was conceived by the Holy Ghost, born of the Virgin Mary; suffered under Pontius Pilate, was crucified, dead, and buried; He descended into hades; the third day He rose from the dead; He ascended into heaven, and sitteth at the right hand of God the Father Almighty; from thence He shall come to judge the quick and the dead.
I believe in the Holy Ghost; the holy catholic Church; the communion of saints; the forgiveness of sins; the resurrection of the body, and the life everlasting. Amen.

Minister. Praise ye the Lord.
Congregation. The Lord's name be praised.

M. Glory be to the Father, and to the Son, and to the Holy Ghost:
C. As it was in the beginning, is now, and ever shall be, world without end. Amen.

Then shall the Minister read the *Evening Lessons*, as indicated in the Table of Scripture Lessons.

After the reading, the service shall proceed thus, the Congregation rising:

M. The Lord be with you.
C. And with thy spirit.

M. Let us pray.

M. Create in us a clean heart, O God:
C. And renew a right spirit within us.

M. Cast us not away from Thy presence :
C. And take not Thy Holy Spirit from us.

Then shall be offered the *Collect* for the day, and after this the following *General Prayer.*

O GOD, from whom all holy desires, all good counsels, and all just works do proceed; give unto Thy servants that peace which the world cannot give; that our hearts may be set to obey Thy commandments, and also that we, being defended from the fear of our enemies, may by Thy protection pass our time in peace and quietness; through Jesus Christ our Lord. Amen.

O LORD, our heavenly Father, by whose almighty power we have been preserved this day, and to whom the darkness and the light are both alike; by Thy great mercy defend us from all perils and dangers of this night; and so refresh our weary nature with the help which our weakness needs, that we may behold the dawn and the day with joyfulness, and be devoted to Thee both in body and soul, for the love of Thine only Son, our Saviour Jesus Christ. *Amen.*

IN goodness art Thou exalted, O Lord, our Father, for ever and ever. We magnify Thee, we praise Thee, we worship Thee, we give thanks unto Thee for Thy bountiful providence, for all the blessings of the present life, and all the hopes of a better life to come; let the memory of Thy goodness, we beseech Thee, fill our hearts with joy and thankfulness unto our life's end; and let no unworthiness of ours provoke Thee to withhold from us any needed good, seeing that all Thy blessings come not by our desert, but only through the merit and mediation of Jesus Christ our Lord. *Amen.*

ALMIGHTY and everlasting God, who hast promised to reveal Thy glory by Jesus Christ among all nations; remember, we beseech Thee, Thy holy Church throughout all the world; unite all who profess and call themselves Christians in the bond of a holy faith as one body, and so replenish them and us with the grace of Thy Holy Spirit, that we may bring forth abundantly the fruits of peace and good works; and that, having persevered in the way of godliness to the end, we may, with prophets, apostles, martyrs, confessors and saints of all ages, come into full communion with Thee and with one another in Thine eternal and glorious kingdom; through the mediation of our Lord and Saviour Jesus Christ. *Amen.*

O MOST powerful Lord God, King of kings, and Lord of lords, who alone ordainest the powers that be; take under Thy most gracious government and guidance, we beseech Thee, Thy servants, the President of the United States, the Governor of this Commonwealth, and all others in authority; and so enrich them with heavenly wisdom and grace, that they may attain Thine everlasting favor, and we lead quiet and peaceable lives, in all godliness and honesty; through Jesus Christ our Lord. *Amen.*

Almighty and most merciful God, who art a seasonable refuge in time of trouble; let the prayers of those who, in tribulation or any sort of extremity, cry unto Thee, reach Thy merciful ears, and grant them relief according to their several necessities, giving them patience under their sufferings, and a happy issue out of all their afflictions; for the sake of the suffering and sorrow of Thy dear Son, our Saviour Jesus Christ. *Amen.*

<small>Here may be introduced any special *Collect* or *Collects* suitable to the occasion.</small>

Almighty God, who hast given us grace at this time with one accord to make our common supplications unto Thee, and dost promise that where two or three are gathered together in Thy name, Thou wilt grant their requests; fulfil now, O Lord, the desires and petitions of Thy servants, as may be most expedient for them, granting us in this world knowledge of Thy truth, and in the world to come, life everlasting. *Amen.*

<small>A suitable *Psalm* or *Hymn* shall now be sung.</small>

<small>Then the Minister, having taken his place in the pulpit, shall proceed to deliver the *Sermon*, or he may expound in course a portion of the *Heidelberg Catechism*.</small>

<small>After the Sermon, the service shall be continued as follows:</small>

M. Let us pray.

O God, who didst teach the hearts of Thy faithful people by sending to them the light of Thy Holy Spirit; grant unto us by the same Spirit to have a right understanding of Thy saving truth. Visit, we pray Thee, this congregation with Thy love and favor; enlighten their minds more and more with the light of the everlasting gospel; graft in their hearts a love of the truth; increase in them true religion; nourish them with all goodness; and of Thy great mercy keep them in the same; through Jesus Christ our Lord. *Amen.*

<small>Here let the People join aloud in the *Lord's Prayer.*</small>

OUR Father who art in heaven, Hallowed be Thy name. Thy kingdom come. Thy will be done in earth, as it is in heaven. Give us this day our daily bread. And forgive us our debts, as we forgive our debtors. And lead us not into temptation. But deliver us from evil. For Thine is the kingdom, and the power, and the glory, for ever. Amen.

<small>The Deacons shall now collect the *Alms* of the people; and the Minister may make any necessary *Announcements.*</small>

<small>Then a *Psalm* or *Hymn* shall be sung, ending with a *Doxology.*</small>

<small>After which the Minister shall close the whole service with the *Apostolic Benediction.*</small>

The grace of the Lord Jesus Christ, and the love of God, and the communion of the Holy Ghost, be with you all. *Amen.*

THE LITANY.

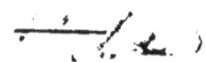

Minister. O God the Father in heaven; have mercy upon us.
Congregation. Have mercy upon us.

M. O God the Son, Redeemer of the world; have mercy upon us.
C. Have mercy upon us.

M. O God the Holy Ghost, proceeding from the Father and the Son; have mercy upon us.
C. Have mercy upon us.

M. O holy, blessed, and glorious Trinity, three persons and one God; have mercy upon us.
C. Have mercy upon us.

M. Remember not, Lord, our offences, nor the offences of our forefathers; neither take Thou vengeance of our sins: spare us, good Lord, spare Thy people, whom Thou hast redeemed with Thy most precious blood, and be not angry with us for ever.
C. Spare us, good Lord.

M. From all evil and harm; from the power of sin, and the snares of the devil; from Thy wrath, and from everlasting damnation;
C. Good Lord, deliver us.

M. From all blindness of heart; from pride, vainglory, and hypocrisy; from envy, hatred, and malice, and all uncharitableness;
C. Good Lord, deliver us.

M. From all impure lusts and desires; and from all the deceits of the world, the flesh, and the devil;
C. Good Lord, deliver us.

M. From lightning, tempest, and earthquake; from plague, pestilence, and famine; from all disasters by land and by water; from battle and murder, and from sudden death;
C. Good Lord, deliver us.

M. From tumult and riot; from sedition and rebellion; from heresy and schism; from hardness of heart, and contempt of Thy word and authority;
C. Good Lord, deliver us.

M. By the mystery of Thy holy incarnation; by Thy holy nativity and circumcision; by Thy baptism, fasting, and temptation;
C. Good Lord, deliver us.

M. By Thine agony and bloody sweat; by Thy cross and passion; by Thy precious death and burial; by Thy glorious resurrection and ascension; and by the coming of the Holy Ghost;
C. Good Lord, deliver us.

M. In all time of our tribulation; in all time of our wealth; in the hour of death, and in the day of judgment;
C. Good Lord, deliver us.

M. We sinners do beseech Thee to hear us, O Lord.
C. Son of God, we beseech Thee to hear us.

M. That it may please Thee to keep us in all time of temptation and heaviness; to comfort and help all the weak-hearted; to raise up them that fall, and finally to beat down Satan under our feet;
C. We beseech Thee to hear us, O Lord.

M. That it may please Thee to succor, help, and comfort all that are in danger, necessity and tribulation;
C. We beseech Thee to hear us, O Lord.

M. That it may please Thee to preserve all travellers and strangers, all women in the perils of childbirth, all sick persons, and young children, and to show Thy pity upon all prisoners and captives;
C. We beseech Thee to hear us, O Lord.

M. That it may please Thee to defend and provide for the fatherless children, and widows, and all that are desolate and oppressed;
C. We·beseech Thee to hear us, O Lord.

M. That it may please Thee to have mercy upon all men;
C. We beseech Thee to hear us, O Lord.

M. O Son of God, Redeemer of the world;
C. Have mercy upon us.

M. O Lamb of God that takest away the sin of the world;
C. Have mercy upon us.

M. O Lamb of God that takest away the sin of the world;
C. Grant us Thy peace.

O GOD, merciful Father, who despisest not the sighing of the contrite, nor rejectest the desire of the sorrowful: be favorable to our prayers which in our afflictions that continually oppress us, we pour out before Thee; and graciously hear them, that those things which the craft of the devil or man worketh against us, may be brought to nought, and by the counsel of Thy goodness be dispersed; so that being hurt by no persecutions, we may evermore give thanks unto Thee in Thy holy Church, through Jesus Christ our Lord. *Amen.*

O GOD, from whom all holy desires, all good counsels, and all just works do proceed; give unto Thy servants that peace which the world cannot give; that our hearts may be set to obey Thy commandments, and also that we, being defended from the fear of our enemies, may by Thy protection pass our time in peace and quietness, through Jesus Christ our Lord. *Amen.*

PRAYERS AND THANKSGIVINGS

FOR

SPECIAL OCCASIONS.

PRAYERS.

For the Opening of a Synod or Classis.

ALMIGHTY and everlasting God, who by Thy Holy Spirit didst preside in the first Synod of the Apostles and Elders at Jerusalem, and hast promised to be with Thy Church alway even unto the end of the world; vouchsafe, we pray Thee, unto us Thy servants, here assembled, Thy gracious presence and benediction. Deliver us from all error, pride and prejudice. Enlighten us with wisdom from above. Fill our hearts with the spirit of unity and peace; and so order and govern us in all our doings, that the kingdom of Satan may be broken down, Thy people comforted and established in their most holy faith, and the pure Gospel truly preached and truly followed; until at length all Thy dispersed sheep shall be gathered into the one fold of the Great Shepherd, Jesus Christ our Lord: to whom be glory forever. *Amen*

For the Catechumens.

ALMIGHTY God, our heavenly Father, who dost, for the sake of Jesus Christ our Lord, accept the intercessions of Thy people; remember in Thy great mercy, we beseech Thee, the Catechumens in this congregation and throughout Thy whole Church. By Thy Holy Spirit inwardly enlighten and instruct them in the knowledge of Thee and divine things; open the ears of their hearts to be occupied with Thy law day and night; strengthen and confirm them in religion; unite them more closely with Thyself and Thy flock; deliver them from all iniquity, and give no place to the Adversary to get advantage against them. Cleanse them from all pollution of flesh and spirit, and let the indwelling of Thy grace be evermore their strength and safety. Prepare them for the full communion of Thy Church here, and for Thy presence and glory in heaven; through Jesus Christ our Lord. *Amen.*

For the Opening of the Year.

ALMIGHTY and eternal God, with whom one day is as a thousand years, and a thousand years as one day; we bring Thee thanks and praise for Thy blessings, more than we can number, with which Thou hast crowned our lives during the year now past; and since Thy mercies are ever new, let the year which has now begun, be to us a year of grace and salvation. Have pity upon us in our misery, whose days are as the grass. Deliver us from the vanity of our old fallen nature; and establish us in the fellowship of that life which is the same yesterday and to-day and forever. Graciously protect and conduct us through the uncertainties of this new year of our earthly pilgrimage. Prepare us for its duties and trials, its joys and sorrows. Help us to watch and pray, and to be always ready like men that wait for their Lord; and grant that every change, whether it be of prosperity or adversity, of life or of death, may bring us nearer to Thee and to that great eternal year of joy and rest, which, after the years of this vain earthly life, awaits the faithful in Thy blissful presence; where we shall unite, from everlasting to everlasting, with angels and saints, in ascribing blessing, and honor, and glory, and power, unto Him who sitteth upon the throne, and unto the Lamb, for ever and ever. *Amen.*

In Time of Dearth.

O GOD, heavenly Father, whose gift it is that the rain doth fall, and the earth bring forth her increase; behold, we beseech Thee, the afflictions of Thy people. Visit the earth with Thy heavenly benediction; and grant that the scarcity and dearth, which we now most justly suffer for our sins, may, through Thy goodness, be mercifully turned into plenty; that we, receiving thy bountiful liberality, may use the same to Thy glory, the relief of those that are needy, and our own comfort: for the love of Jesus Christ our Lord, to whom, with Thee and the Holy Ghost, be all honor and glory, now and forever. *Amen.*

In Time of Pestilence.

HOLY Lord God Almighty, who of old didst stay the angel of pestilence at the cry of Thy repenting children, and bring back health to a dying people; hear us, Thy suppliants, returning unto Thee, as in sackcloth, dust, and ashes, and mercifully lift from us the heavy hand of Thy righteous visitation; that the people may live before Thee, and not die in their sins, and that the land may no longer mourn by reason of Thy judgments, O Lord, who for our iniquities art justly displeased. We humbly ask it for Christ's sake. *Amen.*

In Time of War.

O ALMIGHTY God, Supreme Ruler, and Governor of all things, who art a strong tower of defence to them that fear Thee, and whose power no creature is able to resist; unto Thee do we make our humble cry in this the hour of our country's need. To Thee it belongeth justly to punish sinners and to be merciful to those who repent. Save and deliver us, we humbly beseech Thee, from the hands of our enemies; abate their pride, assuage their malice, and confound their devices; that we, being armed with Thy defence, may be preserved evermore from all perils, to glorify Thee, who art the only Giver of all victory; through the merits of Thy Son, Jesus Christ our Lord. *Amen.*

For the Conversion of the Jews.

ALMIGHTY God, the God of Abraham, of Isaac, and of Jacob, who didst first send Thy Son to the lost sheep of the house of Israel, and hast not shut out from Thy mercy even the most hardened offenders; hear our prayers for Thine ancient people in their dispersion and blindness, that, the veil being taken from their hearts, they may know, through Thy Holy Spirit, both Thee and Him whom Thou hast sent, the only Messiah and Saviour; and so, according to Thy most gracious promise, be gathered again into the true fold, under one Shepherd, Jesus Christ our Lord. *Amen.*

For a Sick Person.

ALMIGHTY GOD, our heavenly Father, of Thine infinite goodness grant unto the soul of thy servant the anointing of the Holy Ghost, who is the Spirit of all strength, comfort, relief and gladness. Vouchsafe for Thy great mercy, if it be Thy blessed will, to restore unto *him* bodily health and strength to serve Thee; and send *him* release of all *his* pains, troubles, and diseases, both in body and mind. And howsoever Thy goodness, by Thy divine and unsearchable Providence, may dispose of *him*, we, Thine unworthy servants, humbly beseech Thy eternal Majesty to do with *him* according to the multitude of Thine innumerable mercies, and to pardon all *his* sins and offences committed by *his* bodily senses, passions and carnal affections. Vouchsafe also mercifully to grant unto *him* ghostly strength, by Thy Holy Spirit, to withstand and overcome all temptations and assaults of the Adversary, that in no wise he prevail against *him*, but that *he* may have perfect victory and triumph against the devil, sin and death: through Christ our Lord, who by His death hath overcome the prince of death, and, with the Father and the Holy Ghost, evermore liveth and reigneth God, world without end. *Amen.*

Or this.

Holy Father, Healer of souls and bodies, who didst send Thine only begotten Son, our Lord Jesus Christ, healing every disease and redeeming from death; heal Thy servant also of the sickness of soul and body which encompasses *him*, and quicken *him* through the grace of Thy Christ; for Thou, O Christ our God, art the Fountain of healing, and to Thee, with the Father and the Holy Ghost, we ascribe all honor and praise. Amen.

THANKSGIVINGS.

A General Thanksgiving.

O GOD, Giver of all good and Fountain of all mercies, in whom are the springs of our life: all glory, thanks and praise be unto Thee for Thine ever-flowing goodness; for Thy faithfulness which is from one generation to another; for Thy mercies which are new every morning, fresh every moment, and more than we can number; for seed-time and harvest, and summer and winter, and nights and days throughout the year; for food and raiment and shelter; for health and reason; for childhood and age, and youth and manhood; for Thy fatherly hand ever upon us in sickness and in health, in joy and in sorrow, in life and in death; for friends and kindred and kind benefactors; for home and country; for Thy Church and for Thy gospel; yea, Lord, for that there is nothing for which we may not bless and thank Thee. And therefore do we take the cup of salvation, and call upon Thy name, and pay our vows now in the presence of all Thy people; humbly beseeching Thee to accept this our becoming service and bounden duty, even as we offer it, in the name and through the infinite merits of Thy Son Jesus Christ our Lord. *Amen.*

Thanksgiving for Harvest.

ALMIGHTY and everlasting God, we yield Thee hearty thanks for all Thy goodness, and especially for this Thy bounty again bestowed upon us, who, through Thy providence and tender mercy, have now reaped the fruits of the earth in due season, and gathered them into our garners. Give us power to use the same to Thy glory, to the relief of those that are needy, and to our own comfort. Continue, we beseech Thee, Thy loving-kindness toward us, that year by year our land may yield her increase, filling our hearts with joy and gladness; and so dispose us by Thy special grace that we, Thy servants, may never sow only to the flesh, lest of the flesh we reap corruption, but may sow spiritually to life everlasting, and reap the same in Thy heavenly kingdom; through Jesus Christ our Lord. *Amen.*

For Deliverance from Dearth.

WE YIELD Thee abounding thanks, O most bountiful God and Father, who hast had compassion upon the multitudes that were ready to perish with hunger; and even as Thou didst make the few loaves and fishes enough for thousands, art now crowning the seed-time with harvest and filling the land with plenty. And we beseech Thee, that unto this Thy miracle of earthly providence, Thou wilt add Thy richer miracle of heavenly grace, and evermore give us that bread which cometh down from heaven, whereof they that eat shall be nourished unto life eternal; through Jesus Christ our Lord. *Amen.*

For Deliverance from Pestilence.

O LORD God of our salvation, who turnest man to destruction and sayest, Return, ye children of men; we yield Thee hearty thanks for that Thou didst not shut the ears of Thy mercy when we cried unto Thee, in the day of Thy terrible visitation, as out of the valley and shadow of death; but hast mercifully driven from our borders the wasting pestilence, and restored the voice of joy and health into our dwellings. Of Thy mercy it is, O Lord, that we were not utterly consumed and wasted away; and, therefore, as the living from the dead, we return to bless and praise and magnify Thee; through Jesus Christ our Lord. *Amen.*

For Deliverance from War, or other Public Calamity.

O ALMIGHTY God, who hast in all ages showed forth Thy power and mercy in all the miraculous deliverances of Thy Church, and in the protection of righteous states and nations, maintaining Thy holy and eternal truth; we adore the wisdom and goodness of Thy providence, which hath so timely interposed in our extreme danger, and again filled our hearts with joy and gladness, after that Thou hadst afflicted us. We beseech Thee, give us such a lively and lasting sense of this Thy great mercy towards us, that we may not grow secure and careless in our obedience by presuming upon Thy goodness, but that it may lead us to repentance, and move us to be the more zealous in all the duties of our religion, as well to Thee as to one another. Let truth and justice, liberty and order, holiness and piety, concord and unity, with all other virtues, so flourish among us, that they may be the stability of our times, and make this nation a bulwark of Thy Church, and a joy and praise in the earth. So will we, Thy people, and the sheep of Thy pasture, give Thee thanks for ever, and always be showing forth Thy praise from generation to generation: through Jesus Christ our only Saviour and Redeemer, to whom, with Thee, O Father, and the Holy Ghost, be glory in the Church throughout all ages, world without end. *Amen*.

THE

GOSPELS, EPISTLES, AND COLLECTS

FOR

THE CHURCH YEAR.

First Sunday in Advent.

The Gospel, St. Matt. xxi. 8–11. (*St. John* i. 1–18.)

And a very great multitude spread their garments in the way; others cut down branches from the trees, and strewed them in the way. And the multitudes that went before, and that followed, cried, saying, Hosanna to the Son of David: Blessed is he that cometh in the name of the Lord; Hosanna in the highest. And when he was come into Jerusalem, all the city was moved, saying, Who is this? And the multitude said, This is Jesus the prophet of Nazareth of Galilee.

The Epistle, Rom. xiii. 11–14. (1 *John* i. 1–ii. 2.)

And that, knowing the time, that now it is high time to awake out of sleep: for now is our salvation nearer than when we believed. The night is far spent, the day is at hand: let us therefore cast off the works of darkness, and let us put on the armor of light. Let us walk honestly, as in the day; not in rioting and drunkenness, not in chambering and wantonness, not in strife and envying: but put ye on the Lord Jesus Christ, and make not provision for the flesh, to fulfil the lusts thereof.

The Collect.

ALMIGHTY GOD, give us grace that we may cast away the works of darkness, and put upon us the armor of light, now in the time of this mortal life, in which Thy Son Jesus Christ came to visit us in great humility; that in the last day, when He shall come again in His glorious majesty, to judge both the quick and the dead, we may rise to the life immortal, through Him who liveth and reigneth with Thee and the Holy Ghost, now and forever. *Amen.*

The Festival Prayer.

ALMIGHTY GOD, Father of all mercies, we Thine unworthy servants do render Thee unfeigned thanks, that after man, created in Thine own image, had, through the fraud and malice of Satan, fallen under the power of the curse, Thou didst not leave him to perish in helpless misery, but didst provide a Deliverer and proclaim to the fathers, by the mouths of the prophets and holy men of old, the Advent of Thy Son, the Hope of Israel, the Desire of all nations, the Redeemer of the world: to whom be glory forever and ever. *Amen.*

GOD of all grace and comfort, who hast not appointed us unto wrath, but to obtain salvation by our Lord Jesus Christ, aid us, we beseech Thee, at this time, to repent heartily and truly of all our sins, and so to humble ourselves, that, when He cometh, we may be prepared to receive Him with childlike faith, and join in the glad cry: Hosanna to the Son of David! Blessed is He that cometh in the name of the Lord. *Amen.*

Second Sunday in Advent.

The Gospel, St. Luke xxi. 25–33. (*St. Matt.* xxv. 1–13.)

And there shall be signs in the sun, and in the moon, and in the stars; and upon the earth distress of nations, with perplexity; the sea and the waves roaring; men's hearts failing them for fear, and for looking after those things which are coming on the earth: for the powers of heaven shall be shaken. And then shall they see the Son of man coming in a cloud with power and great glory. And when these things begin to come to pass, then look up, and lift up your heads; for your redemption draweth nigh. And He spake to them a parable: Behold the fig tree, and all the trees; when they now shoot forth, ye see and know of your own selves that summer is now nigh at hand. So likewise ye, when ye see these things come to pass, know ye that the kingdom of God is nigh at hand. Verily I say unto you, This generation shall not pass away, till all be fulfilled. Heaven and earth shall pass away; but my words shall not pass away.

The Epistle, Rom. xv. 4–13. (*Heb.* x. 1–9.)

For whatsoever things were written aforetime were written for our learning, that we through patience and comfort of the Scriptures might have hope. Now the God of patience and consolation grant you to be like-minded one toward another according to Christ Jesus; that ye may with one mind and one mouth glorify God, even the Father of our Lord Jesus Christ. Wherefore receive ye one another, as Christ also received us, to the glory of God. Now I say that Jesus Christ was a minister of the circumcision for the truth of God, to confirm the promises made unto the fathers: and that the Gentiles might glorify God for His mercy; as it is written, For this cause I will confess to Thee among the Gentiles, and sing unto Thy name. And again He saith, Rejoice, ye Gentiles, with His people. And again, Praise the Lord, all ye Gentiles; and laud Him, all ye people. And again, Esaias saith, There shall be a root of Jesse, and He that shall rise to reign over the Gentiles; in Him shall the Gentiles trust. Now the God of hope fill you with all joy and peace in believing, that ye may abound in hope, through the power of the Holy Ghost.

The Collect.

CLEANSE our conscience, we beseech Thee, Almighty God, by the daily visitation of Thy grace; that when Thy Son, our Lord Jesus Christ, shall come, He may find us fit for His appearing, and ready to meet Him without spot, in the company of all His saints: who liveth and reigneth with Thee and the Holy Ghost, ever one God, world without end. *Amen.*

Third Sunday in Advent.

The Gospel, St. Matt. xi. 2–10. (*St. Luke* xvii. 20–37.)

Now when John had heard in the prison the works of Christ, he sent two of his disciples, and said unto him, Art thou he that should come, or do we look for another? Jesus answered and said unto them, Go and shew John again those things which ye do hear and see: The blind receive their sight, and the lame walk, the lepers are cleansed, and the deaf hear, the dead are raised up, and the poor have the gospel preached to them. And blessed is he, whosoever shall not be offended in me. And as they departed, Jesus began to say unto the multitudes concerning John, What went ye out into the wilderness to see? A reed shaken with the wind? But what went ye out for to see? A man clothed in soft raiment? behold, they that wear soft clothing are in kings' houses. But what went ye out for to see? A prophet? Yea, I say unto you, and more than a prophet. For this is he, of whom it is written, Behold, I send my messenger before thy face, which shall prepare thy way before thee.

The Epistle, 1 Cor. iv. 1–5. (1 Thess. v. 1–8.)

Let a man so account of us, as of the ministers of Christ, and stewards of the mysteries of God. Moreover it is required in stewards, that a man be found faithful. But with me it is a very small thing that I should be judged of you, or of man's judgment: yea, I judge not mine own self. For I know nothing by myself; yet am I not hereby justified: but he that judgeth me is the Lord. Therefore judge nothing before the time, until the Lord come, who both will bring to light the hidden things of darkness, and will make manifest the counsels of the hearts: and then shall every man have praise of God.

The Collect.

INCLINE, O Lord, we beseech Thee, Thine ear to our prayers, and visit the darkness of our mind with the dayspring from on high; that at the second coming of Thy Son to judge the world, we may hasten with joy to meet Him, who liveth and reigneth with Thee and the Holy Ghost, ever one God, world without end. *Amen.*

Fourth Sunday in Advent.

The Gospel, St. John i. 19–34. (St. John iii. 22–36.)

And this is the record of John, when the Jews sent priests and Levites from Jerusalem to ask him, Who art thou? And he confessed, and denied not; but confessed, I am not the Christ. And they asked him, What then? Art thou Elias? And he saith, I am not. Art thou that prophet? And he answered, No. Then said they unto him, Who art thou? that we may give an answer to them that sent us. What sayest thou of thyself? He said, I am the voice of one crying in the wilderness, Make straight the way of the Lord, as said the prophet Esaias. And they which were sent were of the Pharisees. And they asked him, and said unto him, Why baptizest thou then, if thou be not that Christ, nor Elias, neither that prophet? John answered them, saying, I baptize with water: but there standeth one among you, whom ye know not; he it is, who, coming after me, is preferred before me, whose shoe's latchet I am not worthy to unloose. These things were done in Bethabara, beyond Jordan, where John was baptizing. The next day John seeth Jesus coming unto him, and saith, Behold the Lamb of God, which taketh away the sin of the world! This is he of whom I said, After me cometh a man which is preferred before me: for he was before me. And I knew him not: but that he should be made manifest to Israel, therefore am I come baptizing with water. And John bare record, saying, I saw the Spirit descending from heaven like a dove, and it abode upon him. And I knew him not: but he that sent me to baptize with water, the same said unto me, Upon whom thou shalt see the Spirit descending, and remaining on him, the same is he which baptizeth with the Holy Ghost. And I saw, and bare record that this is the Son of God.

The Epistle, Phil. iv. 4–7. (*Gal.* iii. 21–29.)

Rejoice in the Lord alway: and again I say, Rejoice. Let your moderation be known unto all men. The Lord is at hand. Be careful for nothing; but in every thing by prayer and supplication with thanksgiving let your requests be made known unto God. And the peace of God, which passeth al. understanding, shall keep your hearts and minds, through Christ Jesus.

The Collect. ✓

ARISE, O Lord, we beseech Thee, and show unto us speedily the power of Thy glorious salvation; that we, being redeemed from our sins, and delivered out of the hands of our enemies, may be enabled to serve Thee without fear, in holiness and righteousness before Thee, all the days of our life; through the mediation of Thy Son, our Lord and Saviour Jesus Christ, to whom, with Thee and the Holy Ghost, be honor and glory, world without end. *Amen.*

Christmas Day—Nativity of our Lord.

The *Gospel*, St. John i. 1-14. (*St. Luke* ii. 1-20.)

In the beginning was the Word, and the Word was with God, and the Word was God. The same was in the beginning with God. All things were made by him; and without him was not any thing made that was made. In him was life; and the life was the light of men. And the light shineth in darkness; and the darkness comprehended it not. There was a man sent from God, whose name was John. The same came for a witness, to bear witness of the Light, that all men through him might believe. He was not that Light, but was sent to bear witness of that Light. That was the true Light, which lighteth every man that cometh into the world. He was in the world, and the world was made by him, and the world knew him not. He came unto his own, and his own received him not. But as many as received him, to them gave he power to become the sons of God, even to them that believe on his name: which were born, not of blood, nor of the will of the flesh, nor of the will of man, but of God. And the Word was made flesh, and dwelt among us, and we beheld his glory, the glory as of the only begotten of the Father, full of grace and truth.

The Epistle, Heb. i. 1–12. (*Phil.* ii. 5–11.)

God, who at sundry times and in divers manners spake in time past unto the fathers by the prophets, hath in these last days spoken unto us by his Son, whom he hath appointed heir of all things, by whom also he made the worlds; who, being the brightness of his glory, and the express image of his person, and upholding all things by the word of his power, when he had by himself purged our sins, sat down on the right hand of the Majesty on high; being made so much better than the angels, as he hath by inheritance obtained a more excellent name than they. For unto which of the angels said he at any time, Thou art my Son, this day have I begotten thee? And again, I will be to him a Father, and he shall be to me a Son? And again, when he bringeth in the first-begotten into the world, he saith, And let all the angels of God worship him. And of the angels he saith, Who maketh his angels spirits, and his ministers a flame of fire. But unto the Son he saith, Thy throne, O God, is for ever and ever: a sceptre of righteousness is the sceptre of thy kingdom. Thou hast loved righteousness, and hated iniquity; therefore God, even thy God, hath anointed thee with the oil of gladness above thy fellows. And, Thou, Lord, in the beginning hast laid the foundation of the earth; and the heavens are the works of thine hands. They shall perish; but thou remainest: and they all shall wax old as doth a garment; and as a vesture shalt thou fold them up, and they shall be changed: but thou art the same, and thy years shall not fail.

The Collect.

ALMIGHTY and everlasting God, who hast given us

Thy only begotten Son to take our nature upon Him, and as at this time to be born of a pure virgin; grant that we, being regenerate and made Thy children by adoption and grace, may daily be renewed by Thy Holy Spirit after the image of this same blessed and glorious Christ: who liveth and reigneth with Thee and the Holy Ghost, ever one God, world without end. *Amen.*

The Festival Prayer.

O THOU only begotten Son of God, who in the fulness of time coming forth from the bosom of the Father, wast made flesh and didst dwell among us, full of grace and truth, we bless Thee for Thy conception by the Holy Ghost and for Thy birth of the blessed Virgin, whereby Thou hast become the true seed of Abraham and didst take upon Thyself all our sins and infirmities, that we might have salvation' from sin and eternal life in Thee. With the multitude of angels who proclaimed Thy joyous Advent, and with Thy people among all nations we unite in saying, Glory to God in the highest, and on earth peace, good-will toward men. *Amen.*

O GOD, merciful Father, vouchsafe unto us, we humbly beseech Thee, the continual help of Thy grace, that we may acknowledge and confess Thine incarnate Son as our true and only Lord and Saviour, and that receiving Him with childlike faith we may ever feed on His precious body and blood as the true meat and drink of our souls unto everlasting life. *Amen.*

St. Stephen's Day.

[The Festival of St. Stephen, the first martyr, is celebrated on the first day after Christmas, to symbolize the idea that the terrestrial birth of our Saviour is immediately followed by the death, that is, the celestial birth, of His martyrs.]

The Gospel, St. Matt. xxiii. 34-39.

Wherefore, behold, I send unto you prophets, and wise men, and scribes: and some of them ye shall kill and crucify; and some of them shall ye scourge in your synagogues, and persecute them from city to city: that upon you may come all the righteous blood shed upon the earth, from the blood of righteous Abel unto the blood of Zacharias son of Barachias, whom ye slew between the temple and the altar. Verily I say unto you, All these things shall come upon this generation. O Jerusalem, Jerusalem, thou that killest the prophets, and stonest them which are sent unto thee, how often would I have gathered thy children together, even as a hen gathereth her chickens under her wings, and ye would not! Behold, your house is left unto you desolate. For I say unto you, Ye shall not see me henceforth, till ye shall say, Blessed is he that cometh in the name of the Lord.

The Epistle, Acts vi. 8; vii. 60.

And Stephen, full of faith and power, did great wonders and miracles among the people. And he kneeled down, and cried with a loud voice, Lord, lay not this sin to their charge. And when he had said this, he fell asleep.

The Collect.

AS WE honor on this day, O Lord God, the memory of Thy blessed martyr, St. Stephen, grant unto us grace, we beseech Thee, to follow his faith and charity; that however sorely tried by the contradiction of sinners, we may be able, like him, to look steadfastly up into heaven, and to commend even our enemies to the pardoning mercy of our only Mediator and Advocate, Jesus Christ: to whom with Thee and the Holy Ghost, be honor and glory, world without end. *Amen.*

St. John the Evangelist's Day.

[The Festival of St. John is celebrated on the second day after Christmas, because he was the bosom friend of Jesus, and has most fully unfolded the mystery of the Word made flesh for our salvation.]

The Gospel, St. John xxi. 19–24.

This spake he, signifying by what death he should glorify God. And when he had spoken this, he saith unto him, Follow me. Then Peter, turning about, seeth the disciple whom Jesus loved following; which also leaned on his breast at supper and said, Lord, which is he that betrayeth thee? Peter seeing him saith to Jesus, Lord, and what shall this man do? Jesus saith unto him, If I will that he tarry till I come, what is that to thee? follow thou me. Then went this saying abroad among the brethren, that that disciple should not die: yet Jesus said not unto him, He shall not die; but, If I will that he tarry till I come, what is that to thee? This is the disciple which testifieth of these things, and wrote these things: and we know that his testimony is true.

The Epistle, 1 *John* i. 1–10.

That which was from the beginning, which we have heard, which we have seen with our eyes, which we have looked upon, and our hands have handled, of the Word of life; (for the life was manifested, and we have seen it, and bear witness, and show unto you that eternal life, which was with the Father, and was manifested unto us;) that which we have seen and heard declare we unto you, that ye also may have fellowship with us: and truly our fellowship is with the Father, and with his Son Jesus Christ. And these things write we unto you, that your joy may be full. This then is the message which we have heard of him, and declare unto you, that God is light, and in him is no darkness at all. If we say that we have fellowship with him, and walk in darkness, we lie, and do not the truth: but if we walk in the light, as he is in the light, we have fellowship one with another, and the blood of Jesus Christ his son cleanseth us from all sin. If we say that we have no sin, we deceive ourselves, and the truth is not in us. If we confess our sins, he is faithful and just to forgive us our sins, and to cleanse us from all unrighteousness. If we say that we have not sinned, we make him a liar, and his word is not in us.

The Collect.

SHINE graciously upon Thy Church, we beseech Thee, O Lord; that being enlightened by the doctrine and filled with the mind of Thy blessed Apostle and Evangelist, Saint John, whom Jesus loved, it may come at last into Thy beatific presence and enjoy the rewards of everlasting life; through Jesus Christ our Lord, who liveth and reigneth with Thee and the Holy Ghost, ever one God, world without end. *Amen.*

The Innocents' Day.

[This Festival, in memory of the slaughtered infants, is celebrated on the third day after Christmas. Martyrdom was regarded by the ancient Church as a heavenly birth. Hence, the day of St. Stephen, martyr both in will and in fact, of St. John, martyr in will though not in fact, and of the Holy Innocents, martyrs in fact though not in will, follow immediately after Christmas.]

The Gospel, St. Matt. ii. 13–18.

And when they were departed, behold, the angel of the Lord appeareth to Joseph in a dream, saying, Arise, and

THE INNOCENTS' DAY.

take the young child and his mother, and flee into Egypt, and be thou there until I bring thee word: for Herod will seek the young child to destroy him. When he arose, he took the young child and his mother by night, and departed into Egypt: and was there until the death of Herod: that it might be fulfilled which was spoken of the Lord by the prophet, saying, Out of Egypt have I called my son. Then Herod, when he saw that he was mocked of the wise men, was exceeding wroth, and sent forth, and slew all the children that were in Bethlehem, and in all the coasts thereof, from two years old and under, according to the time which he had diligently inquired of the wise men. Then was fulfilled that which was spoken by Jeremy the prophet, saying, In Rama was there a voice heard, lamentation, and weeping, and great mourning, Rachel weeping for her children, and would not be comforted, because they are not.

The Epistle, Rev. xiv. 1–5.

And I looked, and, lo, a Lamb stood on the mount Sion, and with him an hundred forty and four thousand, having his Father's name written in their foreheads. And I heard a voice from heaven, as the voice of many waters, and as the voice of a great thunder: and I heard the voice of harpers harping with their harps: and they sung as it were a new song before the throne, and before the four beasts, and the elders: and no man could learn that song but the hundred and forty and four thousand, which were redeemed from the earth. These are they which were not defiled with women; for they are virgins. These are they which follow the Lamb whithersoever he goeth. These were redeemed from among men, being the first fruits unto God and to the Lamb. And in their mouth was found no guile: for they are without fault before the throne of God.

The Collect.

O GOD, who out of the mouths of babes and sucklings hast ordained strength, and whose praise the slaughtered infants of Bethlehem proclaimed, not by speaking, but by dying; mortify and kill in us, we beseech Thee, all evil propensities and wrong des.res, and so strengthen us by Thy grace, that the same holy faith, which we own with our tongues, we may confess also by the innocency of our lives: to the glory of Thy great name, through Jesus Christ our Lord. *Amen.*

First Sunday after Christmas.

The Gospel, St. *Matt.* i. 18–25. (*St. Luke* ii. 23–35.)

Now the birth of Jesus Christ was on this wise: When as his mother Mary was espoused to Joseph, before they came together, she was found with child of the Holy Ghost. Then Joseph her husband, being a just man, and not willing to make her a public example, was minded to put her away privily. But while he thought on these things, behold, the angel of the Lord appeared unto him in a dream, saying, Joseph, thou son of David, fear not to take unto thee Mary thy wife: for that which is conceived in her is of the Holy Ghost. And she shall bring forth a son, and thou shalt call his name JESUS: for he shall save his people from their sins. Now all this was done, that it might be fulfilled which was spoken of the Lord by the prophet, saying, Behold, a virgin shall be with child, and shall bring forth a son, and they shall call his name Emmanuel, which being interpreted, is, God with us. Then Joseph, being raised from sleep, did as the angel of the Lord had bidden him, and took unto him his wife: and knew her not till she had brought forth her first-born son: and he called his name JESUS.

THE CIRCUMCISION OF CHRIST—NEW YEAR'S DAY. 51

The Epistle, Gal. iv. 1-7. (1 *John* iv. 1-10.)

Now I say, That the heir, as long as he is a child, differeth nothing from a servant, though he be lord of all; but is under tutors and governors until the time appointed of the father. Even so we, when we were children, were in bondage under the elements of the world: but when the fulness of the time was come, God sent forth his Son, made of a woman, male under the law, to redeem them that were under the law, that we might receive the adoption of sons. And because ye are sons, God hath sent forth the Spirit of his Son into your hearts, crying, Abba, Father. Wherefore thou art no more a servant, but a son; and if a son, then an heir of God through Christ.

The Collect.

MOST merciful God, who hast so loved the world as to give Thine only begotten Son, that whosoever believeth in Him should not perish, but have everlasting life; vouchsafe unto us, we humbly pray Thee, the precious gift of faith, whereby we may know that the Son of God is come, and being always rooted and grounded in the mystery of the Word made flesh, may have power to overcome the world, and gain the blessed immortality of heaven: through the merits of this same incarnate Christ, who liveth and reigneth with Thee, in the unity of the Holy Ghost, ever one God, world without end. *Amen.*

The Circumcision of Christ—New Year's Day.

The Gospel, St. Luke ii. 15-21. (*Psalm* xc.)

And it came to pass, as the angels were gone away from them into heaven, the shepherds said one to another, Let us now go even unto Bethlehem, and see this thing which is come to pass, which the Lord hath made known unto us. And they came with haste, and found Mary and Joseph, and the babe lying in a manger. And when they had seen it, they made known abroad the saying which was told them concerning this child. And all they that heard it wondered at those things which were told them by the shepherds. But Mary kept all these things, and pondered them in her heart. And the shepherds returned, glorifying and praising God for all the things that they had heard and seen, as it was told unto them. And when eight days were accomplished for the circumcising of the child, his name was called JESUS, which was so named of the angel before he was conceived in the womb.

The Epistle, Col. ii. 8–17. (*Heb.* xi. 8–16.)

Beware lest any man spoil you through philosophy and vain deceit, after the tradition of men, after the rudiments of the world, and not after Christ. For in him dwelleth all the fulness of the Godhead bodily. And ye are complete in him, which is the head of all principality and power: in whom also ye are circumcised with the circumcision made without hands, in putting off the body of the sins of the flesh by the circumcision of Christ: buried with him in baptism, wherein also ye are risen with him through the faith of the operation of God, who hath raised him from the dead. And you, being dead in your sins and the uncircumcision of your flesh, hath he quickened together with him, having forgiven you all trespasses; blotting out the handwriting of ordinances that was against us, which was contrary to us, and took it out of the way, nailing it to his cross; and having spoiled principalities and powers, he made a shew of them openly, triumphing over them in it. Let no man therefore judge you in meat, or in drink, or in respect of an holy day, or of the new moon, or of the sabbath days: which are a shadow of things to come; but the body is of Christ.

The Collect.

ALMIGHTY and most merciful God, by whose will Thy well-beloved Son, the Saviour of the world, was circumcised in His spotless flesh, to put honor on the law which He had come to fulfil; grant unto us, we beseech Thee, the true circumcision of the spirit, whereby being inwardly purged from all worldly and carnal lusts, we may offer ourselves unto Thee a living sacrifice, holy and acceptable through Jesus Christ: to whom, with Thee and the Holy Ghost, be honor and glory, world without end. *Amen.*

Second Sunday after Christmas.

The Gospel, St. Luke ii. 33–40.

And Joseph and his mother marvelled at those things which were spoken of him. And Simeon blessed them, and said unto Mary his mother, Behold, this child is set for the fall and rising again of many in Israel; and for a sign which shall be spoken against; (yea, a sword shall pierce through thy own soul also,) that the thoughts of many hearts may be revealed. And there was one Anna, a prophetess, the daughter of Phanuel, of the tribe of Aser: she was of a great age, and had lived with an husband seven years from her virginity; and she was a widow of about fourscore and four years, which departed not from the temple, but served God with fastings and prayers night and day. And she coming in that instant gave thanks likewise unto the Lord, and spake of him to all them that looked for redemption in Jerusalem. And when they had performed all things according to the law of the Lord, they returned into Galilee, to their own city, Nazareth. And the child grew, and waxed strong in spirit, filled with wisdom: and the grace of God was upon him.

The Epistle, Rom. vi. 12-18.

Let not sin therefore reign in your mortal body, that ye should obey it in the lusts thereof. Neither yield ye your members as instruments of unrighteousness unto sin: but yield yourselves unto God, as those that are alive from the dead, and your members as instruments of righteousness unto God. For sin shall not have dominion over you: for ye are not under the law, but under grace. What then? Shall we sin, because we are not under the law, but under grace? God forbid. Know ye not, that to whom ye yield yourselves servants to obey, his servants ye are to whom ye obey; whether of sin unto death, or of obedience unto righteousness? But God be thanked, that ye were the servants of sin, but ye have obeyed from the heart that form of doctrine which was delivered you. Being then made free from sin, ye became the servants of righteousness.

The Collect.

ALMIGHTY and everlasting God, who by Thine only begotten Son hast made us to be a new creation for Thyself, and hast bathed us in the new light of Thine Incarnate Word; preserve in us, we beseech Thee, the works of Thy mercy, and cleanse us from all our ancient stains; that by the assistance of Thy grace we may be found in His form, in whom our substance dwells with Thee; through Jesus Christ our Lord. *Amen.*

The Epiphany.

[The Epiphany, or Manifestation of Christ to the Gentiles, is celebrated on the sixth day of January.]

The Gospel, St. Matt. ii. 1-12. (*Is.* lx. 1-15.)

Now when Jesus was born in Bethlehem of Judea in the

days of Herod the king, behold, there came wise men from
the east to Jerusalem, saying, Where is he that is born King
of the Jews? for we have seen his star in the east, and are
come to worship him. When Herod the king had heard
these things, he was troubled, and all Jerusalem with him.
And when he had gathered all the chief priests and scribes
of the people together, he demanded of them where Christ
should be born. And they said unto him, In Bethlehem of
Judea: for thus it is written by the prophet, And thou
Bethlehem, in the land of Juda, are not the least among the
princes of Juda: for out of thee shall come a Governor, that
shall rule my people Israel. Then Herod, when he had
privily called the wise men, inquired of them diligently what
time the star appeared. And he sent them to Bethlehem,
and said, Go and search diligently for the young child; and
when ye have found him, bring me word again, that I may
come and worship him also. When they had heard the king,
they departed; and, lo, the star, which they saw in the east,
went before them, till it came and stood over where the
young child was. When they saw the star, they rejoiced
with exceeding great joy. And when they were come into
the house, they saw the young child with Mary his mother,
and fell down, and worshipped him: and when they had
opened their treasures, they presented unto him gifts; gold,
and frankincense, and myrrh. And being warned of God in
a dream that they should not return to Herod, they departed
into their own country another way.

The Epistle, Eph. iii. 1–12. (*Rom.* xv. 8–12.)

For this cause, I Paul, the prisoner of Jesus Christ for you
Gentiles, if ye have heard of the dispensation of the grace of
God which is given me to you-ward: how that by revelation
he made known unto me the mystery, as I wrote afore in few
words; whereby, when ye read, ye may understand my
knowledge in the mystery of Christ, which in other ages was
not made known unto the sons of men, as it is now revealed

unto his holy apostles and prophets by the Spirit; that the Gentiles should be fellow heirs, and of the same body, and partakers of his promise in Christ by the gospel: whereof I was made a minister, according to the gift of the grace of God given unto me by the effectual working of his power. Unto me, who am less than the least of all saints, is this grace given, that I should preach among the Gentiles the unsearchable riches of Christ; and to make all men see what is the fellowship of the mystery, which from the beginning of the world hath been hid in God, who created all things by Jesus Christ: to the intent that now unto the principalities and powers in heavenly places might be known, by the church, the manifold wisdom of God, according to the eternal purpose which he purposed in Christ Jesus our Lord: in whom we have boldness and access with confidence by the faith of him.

The Collect.

O GOD, who by the leading of a star didst manifest Thy only-begotten Son to the Gentiles; mercifully grant that we, who have now come to know Thee here by faith, may be conducted to the full vision of Thy glory hereafter in heaven; through Jesus Christ our Lord, who liveth and reigneth with Thee and the Holy Ghost, ever one God, world without end. *Amen.*

First Sunday after the Epiphany.

The Gospel, St. Luke ii. 41–52. (*St. Matt.* iii. 13–17.)

Now his parents went to Jerusalem every year at the feast of the passover. And when he was twelve years old, they went up to Jerusalem after the custom of the feast. And when they had fulfilled the days, as they returned, the child Jesus tarried behind in Jerusalem; and Joseph and his mother knew not of it. But they, supposing him to have been in the company, went a day's journey; and they sought him among their kinsfolk and acquaintance. And when they found him not, they turned back again to Jerusalem, seeking him. And it came to pass, that after three days they found him in the temple, sitting in the midst of the doctors, both hearing them, and asking them questions. And all that heard him were astonished at his understanding and answers. And when they saw him, they were amazed: and his mother said unto him, Son, why hast thôu thus dealt with us? behold, thy father and I have sought thee sorrowing. And he said unto them, How is it that ye sought me? wist ye not that I must be about my Father's business? And they understood not the saying which he spake unto them. And he went down with them, and came to Nazareth, and was subject unto them: but his mother kept all these sayings in her heart. And Jesus increased in wisdom and stature, and in favor with God and man.

The Epistle, Rom. xii. 1-5. (*Rom.* vi. 3-11.)

I beseech you therefore, brethren, by the mercies of God, that ye present your bodies a living sacrifice, holy, acceptable unto God, which is your reasonable service. And be not conformed to this world: but be ye transformed by the renewing of your mind, that ye may prove what is that good, and acceptable, and perfect will of God. For I say, through the grace given unto me, to every man that is among you, not to think of himself more highly than he ought to think; but to think soberly, according as God hath dealt to every man the measure of faith. For as we have many members in one body, and all members have not the same office: so we, being many, are one body in Christ, and every one members one of another.

The Collect.

RECEIVE, O Lord, with compassionate kindness, the prayers of Thy suppliant people, and bestow upon them plenteously the aids of Thy heavenly grace; that they may both know what things they ought to do, and be strong also to do what they know; through Jesus Christ our Lord, who liveth and reigneth with Thee and the Holy Ghost, ever one God, world without end. *Amen.*

Second Sunday after the Epiphany.

The Gospel, St. John ii. 1–11. (*St. Luke* iv. 1–13.)

And the third day there was a marriage in Cana of Galilee; and the mother of Jesus was there: and both Jesus was called, and his disciples, to the marriage. And when they wanted wine, the mother of Jesus saith unto him, They have no wine. Jesus saith unto her, Woman, what have I to do with thee? mine hour is not yet come. His mother saith unto the servants, Whatsoever he saith unto you, do it. And there were set there six waterpots of stone, after the manner of the purifying of the Jews, containing two or three firkins apiece. Jesus saith unto them, Fill the waterpots with water. And they filled them up to the brim. And he saith unto them, Draw out now, and bear unto the governor of the feast. And they bare it. When the ruler of the feast had tasted the water that was made wine, and knew not whence it was: (but the servants which drew the water knew:) the governor of the feast called the bridegroom, and saith unto him, Every man at the beginning doth set forth good wine; and when men have well drunk, then that which is worse: but thou hast kept the good wine until now. This beginning of miracles did Jesus in Cana of Galilee, and manifested forth his glory; and his disciples believed on him.

THIRD SUNDAY AFTER THE EPIPHANY.

The Epistle, Rom. xii. 6–16. (*Heb.* ii. 14–18.)

Having then gifts differing according to the grace that is given to us, whether prophecy, let us prophesy according to the proportion of faith; or ministry, let us wait on our ministering: or he that teacheth, on teaching; or he that exhorteth, on exhortation: he that giveth, let him do it with simplicity: he that ruleth, with diligence; he that showeth mercy, with cheerfulness. Let love be without dissimulation. Abhor that which is evil; cleave to that which is good. Be kindly affectioned one to another with brotherly love; in honor preferring one another; not slothful in business; fervent in spirit; serving the Lord; rejoicing in hope; patient in tribulation; continuing instant in prayer; distributing to the necessity of saints; given to hospitality. Bless them which persecute you: bless, and curse not. Rejoice with them that do rejoice, and weep with them that weep. Be of the same mind one toward another. Mind not high things, but condescend to men of low estate. Be not wise in your own conceits.

The Collect.

O GOD, the Fountain of all truth and grace, who hast called us out of darkness into marvellous light by the glorious gospel of Thy Son; grant unto us power, we beseech Thee, to walk worthy of this vocation, with all lowliness and meekness, endeavoring to keep the unity of the spirit in the bond of peace; that we may have our fruit unto holiness, and the end everlasting life; through Jesus Christ our Lord. *Amen.*

Third Sunday after the Epiphany.

The Gospel, St. Matt. viii. 1–13. (*St. Mark* i. 14–22.)

When he was come down from the mountain, great multitudes followed him. And, behold, there came a leper and worshipped him, saying, Lord, if thou wilt, thou canst make me clean. And Jesus put forth his hand, and touched him, saying, I will; be thou clean. And immediately his leprosy was cleansed. And Jesus saith unto him, See thou tell no man; but go thy way, show thyself to the priest, and offer the gift that Moses commanded, for a testimony unto them. And when Jesus was entered into Capernaum, there came unto him a centurion, beseeching him, and saying, Lord, my servant lieth at home sick of the palsy, grievously tormented. And Jesus saith unto him, I will come and heal him. The centurion answered and said, Lord, I am not worthy that thou shouldest come under my roof: but speak the word only, and my servant shall be healed. For I am a man under authority, having soldiers under me: and I say to this man, Go, and he goeth; and to another, Come, and he cometh; and to my servant, Do this, and he doeth it. When Jesus heard it, he marvelled, and said to them that followed, Verily I say unto you, I have not found so great faith, no, not in Israel. And I say unto you, That many shall come from the east and west, and shall sit down with Abraham, and Isaac, and Jacob, in the kingdom of heaven. But the children of the kingdom shall be cast out into outer darkness: there shall be weeping and gnashing of teeth. And Jesus said unto the centurion, Go thy way; and as thou hast believed, so be it done unto thee. And his servant was healed in the selfsame hour.

The Epistle, Rom. xii. 17–21. (1 *Cor.* i. 17–25.)

Recompense to no man evil for evil. Provide things honest in the sight of all men. If it be possible, as much as lieth in you, live peaceably with all men. Dearly beloved, avenge not yourselves, but rather give place unto wrath: for it is written, Vengeance is mine; I will repay, saith the Lord. Therefore if thine enemy hunger, feed him; if he thirst, give him drink: for in so doing thou shalt heap coals of fire on his head. Be not overcome of evil, but overcome evil with good.

FOURTH SUNDAY AFTER THE EPIPHANY. 61

The Collect.
ALMIGHTY and everlasting God, look mercifully, we beseech Thee, upon our great weakness; and in the midst of the manifold trials and dangers which beset us on all sides, stretch forth the right hand of Thy majesty for our protection and help; through Jesus Christ our Saviour, who liveth and reigneth with Thee and the Holy Ghost, ever one God, world without end. *Amen.*

Fourth Sunday after the Epiphany.

The Gospel, St. *Matt.* viii. 23-27. (*St. Luke* iv. 14-21.)

And when he was entered into a ship, his disciples followed him. And, behold, there arose a great tempest in the sea, insomuch that the ship was covered with the waves: but he was asleep. And his disciples came to him, and awoke him, saying, Lord, save us: we perish. And he saith unto them, Why are ye fearful, O ye of little faith? Then he arose, and rebuked the winds and the sea; and there was a great calm. But the men marvelled, saying, What manner of man is this, that even the winds and the sea obey him!

The Epistle, Rom. xiii. 1-7. (2 *Cor.* iv. 1-6.)

Let every soul be subject unto the higher powers. For there is no power but of God: the powers that be are ordained of God. Whosoever therefore resisteth the power, resisteth the ordinance of God: and they that resist shall receive to themselves damnation. For rulers are not a terror to good works, but to the evil. Wilt thou then not be afraid of the power? do that which is good, and thou shalt have praise of the same: for he is the minister of God to thee for good. But if thou do that which is evil, be afraid; for he beareth not the sword in vain: for he is the minister of God, a revenger to execute wrath upon him that doeth evil. Wherefore ye must needs be subject, not only for wrath, but also for conscience sake. For, for this cause pay ye tribute also: for they are God's ministers, attending continually upon this very thing. Render therefore to all their dues: tribute to whom tribute is due; custom to whom custom; fear to whom fear; honor to whom honor.

The Collect.

O GOD, who hast founded the earth upon the seas, and established it upon the floods, and whose word is forever settled in heaven; grant unto us grace, we beseech Thee, to look beyond the things which are seen and temporal to the things which are not seen and eternal; that walking by faith more than by sight, we may not be unduly moved by any occasions in this world, but be able to endure unto the end in the way of life; through Jesus Christ our Lord, who is the same yesterday, and to-day, and forever. *Amen.*

Fifth Sunday after the Epiphany.

[The number of Sundays after the Epiphany depends upon the date of Easter, which is a movable Feast, and varies from one to six.]

The Gospel, St. Matt. xiii. 24–30. (*St. Matt.* xiii. 1–9.)

Another parable put he forth unto them, saying, The kingdom of heaven is likened unto a man which sowed good seed in his field: but while men slept, his enemy came and sowed tares among the wheat, and went his way. But when the blade was sprung up, and brought forth fruit, then appeared the tares also. So the servants of the householder came and said unto him, Sir, didst not thou sow good seed in thy field? from whence then hath it tares? He said unto them, An enemy hath done this. The servants said unto him, Wilt thou then that we go and gather them up? But he said, Nay; lest while ye gather up the tares, ye root up also the wheat with them. Let both grow together until the harvest: and in the time of harvest I will say to the reapers, Gather ye together first the tares, and bind them in bundles to burn them: but gather the wheat into my barn.

The Epistle, Col. iii. 12–17. (1 Pet. i. 22–25.)

Put on therefore, as the elect of God, holy and beloved, bowels of mercies, kindness, humbleness of mind, meekness, long-suffering; forbearing one another, and forgiving one another, if any man have a quarrel against any: even as Christ forgave you, so also do ye. And above all these things put on charity, which is the bond of perfectness. And let the peace of God rule in your hearts, to the which also ye are called in one body; and be ye thankful. Let the word of Christ dwell in you richly in all wisdom; teaching and admonishing one another in psalms and hymns and spiritual songs, singing with grace in your hearts to the Lord. And whatsoever ye do in word or deed, do all in the name of the Lord Jesus, giving thanks to God and the Father by him.

The Collect. ✓

O LORD, we beseech Thee to keep Thy Church and household continually in Thy true religion; that they who do lean only upon the hope of Thy heavenly grace, may evermore be defended by Thy mighty power; through Jesus Christ our Lord, who liveth and reigneth with Thee and the Holy Ghost, ever one God, world without end. *Amen.*

Sixth Sunday after the Epiphany.

The Gospel, St. Matt. xvii. 1–9. (St. Matt. xiii. 44–52.)

And after six days, Jesus taketh Peter, James, and John his brother, and bringeth them up into an high mountain apart, and was transfigured before them: and his face did shine as the sun, and his raiment was white as the light. And, behold, there appeared unto them Moses and Elias, talking with him. Then answered Peter, and said unto Jesus, Lord, it is good for us to be here: if thou wilt, let us make here three tabernacles; one for thee, and one for Moses, and one for Elias. While he yet spake, behold, a bright cloud overshadowed them: and behold a voice out of the cloud, which said, This is my beloved Son, in whom I am well pleased; hear ye him. And when the disciples heard it, they fell on their face, and were sore afraid. And Jesus came and touched them, and said, Arise, and be not afraid. And when they had lifted up their eyes, they saw no man, save Jesus only. And as they came down from the mountain, Jesus charged them, saying, Tell the vision to no man, until the Son of man be risen again from the dead.

The Epistle, 1 *John* iii. 1-10. (1 *Pet.* ii. 1-10.)

Behold, what manner of love the Father hath bestowed upon us, that we should be called the sons of God: therefore the world knoweth us not, because it knew him not. Beloved, now are we the sons of God, and it doth not yet appear what we shall be: but we know that, when he shall appear, we shall be like him; for we shall see him as he is. And every man that hath this hope in him, purifieth himself, even as he is pure. Whosoever committeth sin transgresseth also the law: for sin is the transgression of the law. And ye know that he was manifested to take away our sins; and in him is no sin. Whosoever abideth in him sinneth not: whosoever sinneth hath not seen him, neither known him. Little children, let no man deceive you: he that doeth righteousness is righteous, even as he is righteous. He that committeth sin is of the devil; for the devil sinneth from the beginning. For this purpose the Son of God was manifested, that he might destroy the works of the devil. Whosoever is born of God doth not commit sin; for his seed remaineth in him: and he cannot sin, because he is born of God. In this the children of God are manifest, and the children of the devil: whosoever doeth not righteousness is not of God, neither he that loveth not his brother.

The Collect. ✓

O GOD, whose blessed Son was manifested that He might destroy the works of the devil, and make us the sons of God, and heirs of eternal life; enable us, we beseech Thee, having this hope, to purify ourselves, even as He is pure; that when He shall appear again with power and great glory, we may be made like unto Him in His eternal and glorious kingdom: where He liveth and reigneth with Thee and the Holy Ghost, ever one God, world without end. *Amen.*

Third Sunday before Lent—Septuagesima.

The Gospel, St. Matt. xx. 1–16. (*St. Matt.* xiv. 22–33.)

For the kingdom of heaven is like unto a man that is an householder, which went out early in the morning to hire laborers into his vineyard. And when he had agreed with the laborers for a penny a day, he sent them into his vineyard. And he went out about the third hour, and saw others standing idle in the market-place, and said unto them, Go ye also into the vineyard, and whatsoever is right, I will give you. And they went their way. Again he went out about the sixth and ninth hour, and did likewise. And about the eleventh hour he went out, and found others standing idle, and saith unto them, Why stand ye here all the day idle? They say unto him, Because no man hath hired us. He saith unto them, Go ye also into the vineyard; and whatsoever is right, that shall ye receive. So when even was come, the lord of the vineyard saith unto his steward, Call the laborers, and give them their hire, beginning from the last unto the first. And when they came that were hired about the eleventh hour, they received every man a penny. But when the first came, they supposed that they should have received more; and they likewise received every man a penny. And when they had received it, they murmured against the good man of the house, saying, These last have wrought but one hour, and thou hast made them equal unto us, which have borne the burden and heat of the day. But he answered one of them, and said, Friend, I do thee no wrong: didst not thou agree with me for a penny? Take that thine is, and go thy way: I will give unto this last even as unto thee. Is it not lawful for me to do what I will with mine own? Is thine eye evil because I am good? So the last shall be first, and the first last: for many be called, but few chosen.

The Epistle, 1 Cor. ix. 24-27.—x. 1-5. (*Rom.* viii. 31-39.)

Know ye not, that they which run in a race, run all, but one receiveth the prize? So run, that ye may obtain. And every man that striveth for the mastery is temperate in all things. Now they do it to obtain a corruptible crown; but we an incorruptible. I therefore so run, not as uncertainly; so fight I, not as one that beateth the air: but I keep under my body, and bring it into subjection; lest that by any means when I have preached to others, I myself should be a castaway.—Moreover, brethren, I would not that ye should be ignorant, how that all our fathers were under the cloud, and all passed through the sea; and were all baptized unto Moses in the cloud and in the sea; and did all eat the same spiritual meat; and did all drink the same spiritual drink: for they drank of that spiritual Rock that followed them: and that Rock was Christ. But with many of them God was not well pleased: for they were overthrown in the wilderness.

SECOND SUNDAY BEFORE LENT.

The Collect.

O LORD, we beseech Thee favorably to hear the prayers of Thy people; that we who are justly punished for our offences, may be mercifully delivered by Thy goodness, for the glory of Thy name; through Jesus Christ our Saviour, who liveth and reigneth with Thee and the Holy Ghost, ever one God, world without end. *Amen.*

Second Sunday before Lent—Sexagesima.

The Gospel, St. *Luke* viii. 4–15. (*St. John* x. 1–18.)

And when much people were gathered together, and were come to him out of every city, he spake by a parable: A sower went out to sow his seed: and as he sowed, some fell by the wayside; and it was trodden down, and the fowls of the air devoured it. And some fell upon a rock; and as soon as it was sprung up, it withered away, because it lacked moisture. And some fell among thorns; and the thorns sprang up with it, and choked it. And other fell on good ground, and sprang up, and bare fruit an hundredfold. And when he had said these things, he cried, He that hath ears to hear, let him hear. And his disciples asked him, saying, What might this parable be? And he said, Unto you it is given to know the mysteries of the kingdom of God: but to others in parables; that seeing they might not see, and hearing they might not understand. Now the parable is this: The seed is the word of God. Those by the wayside are they that hear; then cometh the devil, and taketh away the word out of their hearts, lest they should believe and be saved. They on the rock are they, which, when they hear, receive the word with joy; and these have no root, which for awhile believe, and in time of temptation fall away. And that which fell among thorns are they, which, when they have heard, go forth, and are choked with cares and riches and pleasures of this life, and bring no fruit to perfection. But that on the good ground are they, which in an honest and good heart, having heard the word, keep it, and bring forth fruit with patience.

The Epistle, 2 *Cor.* xi. 19-33.—xii. 1-9. (1 *Pet.* ii. 17-25.)

For ye suffer fools gladly, seeing ye yourselves are wise. For ye suffer, if a man bring you into bondage, if a man devour you, if a man take of you, if a man exalt himself, if a man smite you on the face. I speak as concerning reproach, as though we had been weak. Howbeit, whereinsoever any is bold, (I speak foolishly,) I am bold also. Are they Hebrews? so am I. Are they Israelites? so am I. Are they the seed of Abraham? so am I. Are they ministers of Christ? (I speak as a fool,) I am more; in labors more abundant, in stripes above measure, in prisons more frequent, in deaths oft. Of the Jews five times received I forty stripes save one. Thrice was I beaten with rods, once was I stoned, thrice I suffered shipwreck, a night and a day I have been in the deep; in journeyings often, in perils of waters, in perils of robbers, in perils by mine own countrymen, in perils by the heathen, in perils in the city, in perils in the wilderness, in perils in the sea, in perils among false brethren; in weariness and painfulness, in watchings often, in hunger and thirst, in fastings often, in cold and nakedness. Besides those things that are without, that which cometh upon me daily, the care of all the churches. Who is weak, and I am not weak? who is offended, and I burn not? If I must needs glory, I will glory of the things which concern mine infirmities. The God and Father of our Lord Jesus Christ, which is blessed for evermore, knoweth that I lie not. In Damascus the governor under Aretas the king kept the city of the Damascenes with a garrison, desirous to apprehend me: and through a window in a basket was I let down by the wall, and escaped his hands.— It is not expedient for me doubtless to glory. I will come to visions and revelations of the Lord. I knew a man in Christ above fourteen years ago, (whether in the body, I cannot tell; or whether out of the body, I cannot tell: God knoweth;) such an one caught up to the third heaven. And I knew such a man, (whether in the body, or out of the body, I cannot tell: God knoweth;) how that he was caught up into paradise, and heard unspeakable words, which it is not lawful for a man to utter. Of such an one will I glory: yet of myself I will not glory, but in mine infirmities. For though I would desire to glory, I shall not be a fool; for I will say the truth: but now I forbear, lest any man should think of me above that which he seeth me to be, or that he heareth of me. And lest I should be exalted above measure through the abundance of the revelations, there was given to me a thorn in the flesh, the messenger of Satan to buffet me, lest I should be exalted above measure. For this thing I besought the Lord thrice, that it might depart from me. And he said unto me, My grace is sufficient for thee: for my strength is made perfect in weakness. Most gladly therefore will I rather glory in my infirmities, that the power of Christ may rest upon me.

The Collect.

ALMIGHTY and everlasting God, the Creator of the ends of the earth, who givest power to the faint, and strength to them that have no might; look mercifully, we beseech Thee, on our low estate, and cause Thy grace to triumph in our weakness; that we may arise and follow in the way of righteousness those who by their faith and patience already inherit the promises; through Jesus Christ our Lord. *Amen.*

Sunday before Lent—Quinquagesima, or Estomihi.
The Gospel, St. Luke xviii. 31–43. (*St. Matt.* xvi. 21–23.)
Then he took unto him the twelve, and said unto them, Be-

hold, we go up to Jerusalem, and all things that are written by the prophets concerning the Son of man shall be accomplished. For he shall be delivered unto the Gentiles, and shall be mocked, and spitefully entreated, and spitted on: and they shall scourge him, and put him to death: and the third day he shall rise again. And they understood none of these things: and this saying was hid from them, neither knew they the things which were spoken. And it came to pass, that as he was come nigh unto Jericho, a certain blind man sat by the wayside, begging: and hearing the multitude pass by, he asked what it meant. And they told him, that Jesus of Nazareth passeth by. And he cried, saying, Jesus, thou Son of David, have mercy on me. And they which went before, rebuked him, that he should hold his peace: but he cried so much the more, Thou Son of David, have mercy on me. And Jesus stood, and commanded him to be brought unto him: and when he was come near, he asked him, saying, What wilt thou that I should do unto thee? And he said, Lord, that I may receive my sight. And Jesus said unto him, Receive thy sight: thy faith hath saved thee. And immediately he received his sight, and followed him, glorifying God: and all the people, when they saw it, gave praise unto God.

The Epistle, 1 *Cor.* xiii. 1–13. (1 *Pet.* iv. 12–19.)

Though I speak with the tongues of men and of angels, and have not charity, I am become as sounding brass, or a tinkling cymbal. And though I have the gift of prophecy, and understand all mysteries, and all knowledge; and though I have all faith, so that I could remove mountains, and have not charity, I am nothing. And though I bestow all my goods to feed the poor, and though I give my body to be burned, and have not charity, it profiteth me nothing. Charity suffereth long, and is kind; charity envieth not; charity vaunteth not itself, is not puffed up, doth not behave itself unseemly, seeketh not her own, is not easily provoked, thinketh no evil; rejoiceth not in iniquity, but rejoiceth in the truth; beareth all things, believeth all things, hopeth all things, endureth all things. Charity never faileth: but whether there be prophecies, they shall fail; whether there be tongues, they shall cease; whether there be knowledge, it shall vanish away. For we know in part, and we prophesy in part. But when that which is perfect is come, then that which is in part shall be done away. When I was a child, I spake as a child, I understood as a child, I thought as a child: but when I became a man, I put away childish things. For now we see through a glass, darkly; but then face to face: now I know in part; but then shall I know even as also I am known. And now abideth faith, hope, charity, these three; but the greatest of these is charity.

The Collect.

O LORD, who hast taught us that all our doings without charity are nothing worth; send Thy Holy Ghost, and pour into our hearts that most excellent gift of charity, the very bond of perfectness, and of all virtues; without which, whosoever liveth is counted dead before Thee. Grant this for Thine only Son Jesus Christ's sake. *Amen.*

First Day in Lent—Ash-Wednesday.

The Gospel, St. Matt. vi. 16–21. (*Psalm* li.)

Moreover when ye fast, be not, as the hypocrites, of a sad countenance: for they disfigure their faces, that they may appear unto men to fast. Verily I say unto you, they have their reward. But thou, when thou fastest, anoint thine head, and wash thy face; that thou appear not unto men to fast, but unto thy Father which is in secret: and thy Father which seeth in secret shall reward thee openly. Lay not up for yourselves treasures upon earth, where moth and rust doth corrupt, and where thieves break through and steal: but lay up for yourselves treasures in heaven, where neither moth nor rust doth corrupt, and where thieves do not break through nor steal. For where your treasure is, there will your heart be also.

The Epistle, Joel. ii. 12–18. (*Rev.* iii. 14–22.)

Therefore also now, saith the Lord, turn ye even to me with all your heart, and with fasting, and with weeping, and with mourning: and rend your heart, and not your garments, and turn unto the Lord your God: for he is gracious and merciful, slow to anger, and of great kindness, and repenteth him of the evil. Who knoweth if he will return and repent, and leave a blessing behind him; even a meat offering and a drink offering unto the Lord your God? Blow the trumpet in Zion, sanctify a fast, call a solemn assembly: gather the people, sanctify the congregation, assemble the elders, gather the children, and those that suck the breasts: let the bridegroom go forth of his chamber, and the bride out of her closet. Let the priests, the ministers of the Lord, weep between the porch and the altar, and let them say, Spare thy people, O Lord, and give not thine heritage to reproach, that the heathen should rule over them: wherefore should they say among the people, Where is their God? Then will the Lord be jealous for his land, and pity his people.

The Collect.

ALMIGHTY and everlasting God, who hatest nothing that Thou hast made, and dost forgive the sins of all those who are penitent; create and make in us new and contrite hearts, that we, worthily lamenting our sins and acknowledging our wretchedness, may obtain of Thee, the God of all mercy, perfect remission and forgiveness; through Jesus Christ our Lord. *Amen.*

First Sunday in Lent—Invocavit.

The Gospel, St. Matt. iv. 1-11. (*St. Matt* vi. 1-21.)

Then was Jesus led up of the Spirit into the wilderness to be tempted of the devil. And when he had fasted forty days and forty nights, he was afterward an hungered. And when the tempter came to him, he said, If thou be the Son of God, command that these stones be made bread. But he answered and said, It is written, Man shall not live by bread alone, but by every word that proceedeth out of the mouth of God. Then the devil taketh him up into the holy city, and setteth him on a pinnacle of the temple, and saith unto him, If thou be the Son of God, cast thyself down: for it is written, He shall give his angels charge concerning thee: and in their hands they shall bear thee up, lest at any time thou dash thy foot against a stone. Jesus said unto him, It is written again, Thou shalt not tempt the Lord thy God. Again, the devil taketh him up into an exceeding high mountain, and sheweth him all the kingdoms of the world, and the glory of them; and saith unto him, All these things will I give thee, if thou wilt fall down and worship me. Then saith Jesus unto him, Get thee hence, Satan: for it is written, Thou shalt worship the Lord thy God, and him only shalt thou serve. Then the devil leaveth him, and, behold, angels came and ministered unto him.

The Epistle, 2 Cor. vi. 1-10. (*Eph.* vi. 10-20.)

We then, as workers together with him, beseech you also that ye receive not the grace of God in vain. (For he saith, I have heard thee in a time accepted, and in the day of salvation have I succoured thee: behold, now is the accepted time; behold, now is the day of salvation.) Giving no offence in anything, that the ministry be not blamed: but in all things approving ourselves, as the ministers of God, in much patience, in afflictions, in necessities, in distresses, in stripes, in imprisonments, in tumults, in labours, in watchings, in fastings; by pureness, by knowledge, by long-suffering, by kindness, by the Holy Ghost, by love unfeigned, by the word of truth, by the power of God, by the armour of righteousness on the right hand and on the left, by honour and dishonour, by evil report and good report: as deceivers, and yet true; as unknown, and yet well known; as dying, and, behold, we live; as chastened, and not killed; as sorrowful, yet always rejoicing; as poor, yet making many rich; as having nothing, and yet possessing all things.

The Collect.

WE beseech Thee, O Lord, by the mystery of our Saviour's fasting and temptation, to arm us with the same mind that was in Him toward all evil and sin; and give us grace to keep our bodies in such holy discipline, that our minds may be always ready to resist Satan, and obey the motions of Thy Holy Spirit; through Jesus Christ our Lord. *Amen.*

Second Sunday in Lent—Reminiscere.

The Gospel, St. Matt. xv. 21-28. (*St. Luke* xi. 29-36.)

Then Jesus went thence, and departed into the coasts of Tyre and Sidon. And, behold, a woman of Canaan came out of the same coasts, and cried unto him, saying, Have mercy on me, O Lord, thou son of David; my daughter is grievously vexed with a devil. But he answered her not a word. And his disciples came and besought him, saying, Send her away; for she crieth after us. But he answered and said, I am not sent but unto the lost sheep of the house of Israel. Then came she and worshipped him, saying, Lord, help me. But he answered and said, It is not meet to take the children's bread, and to cast it to dogs. And she said, Truth, Lord: yet the dogs eat of the crumbs which fall from their masters' table. Then Jesus answered and said unto her, O woman, great is thy faith: be it unto thee even as thou wilt. And her daughter was made whole from that very hour.

The Epistle, 1 Thess. iv. 1–8. (*Heb.* ii. 1–4.)

Furthermore then we beseech you, brethren, and exhort you by the Lord Jesus, that as ye have received of us how ye ought to walk and to please God, so ye would abound more and more. For ye know what commandments we gave you by the Lord Jesus. For this is the will of God, even your sanctification, that ye should abstain from fornication: that every one of you should know how to possess his vessel in sanctification and honour; not in the lust of concupiscence, even as the Gentiles which know not God: that no man go beyond and defraud his brother in any matter: because that the Lord is the avenger of all such, as we also have forewarned you and testified. For God hath not called us unto uncleanness, but unto holiness. He therefore that despiseth, despiseth not man, but God, who hath also given unto us his Holy Spirit.

The Collect.

ALMIGHTY GOD, who seest the helpless misery of our fallen life; vouchsafe unto us, we humbly beseech Thee, both the outward and inward defence of Thy guardian care; that we may be shielded from the evils which assault the body, and be kept pure from all thoughts that harm and pollute the soul; through Jesus Christ our Lord. *Amen.*

Third Sunday in Lent—Oculi.

The Gospel, St. Luke xi. 14-28. (St. Matt. xii. 22-32.)

And he was casting out a devil, and it was dumb. And it came to pass, when the devil was gone out, the dumb spake; and the people wondered. But some of them said, He casteth out devils through Beelzebub the chief of the devils. And others, tempting him, sought of him a sign from heaven. But he, knowing their thoughts, said unto them, Every kingdom divided against itself is brought to desolation; and a house divided against a house falleth. If Satan also be divided against himself, how shall his kingdom stand? because ye say that I cast out devils through Beelzebub. And if I by Beelzebub cast out devils, by whom do your sons cast them out? therefore shall they be your judges. But if I with the finger of God cast out devils, no doubt the kingdom of God is come upon you. When a strong man armed keepeth his palace, his goods are in peace: but when a stronger than he shall come upon him, and overcome him, he taketh from him all his armour wherein he trusted, and divideth his spoils. He that is not with me is against me: and he that gathereth not with me scattereth. When the unclean spirit is gone out of a man, he walketh through dry places, seeking rest; and finding none, he saith, I will return unto my house whence I came out. And when he cometh, he findeth it swept and garnished. Then goeth he, and taketh to him seven other spirits more wicked than himself; and they enter in, and dwell there: and the last state of that man is worse than the first. And it came to pass, as he spake these things, a certain woman of the company lifted up her voice, and said unto him, Blessed is the womb that bare thee, and the paps which thou hast sucked. But he said, Yea rather, blessed are they that hear the word of God, and keep it.

FOURTH SUNDAY IN LENT.

The Epistle, Eph. v. 1–9. (*Heb.* x. 26–31.)

Be ye therefore followers of God, as dear children; and walk in love, as Christ also hath loved us, and hath given himself for us an offering and a sacrifice to God for a sweet-smelling savour. But fornication, and all uncleanness, or covetousness, let it not be once named among you, as becometh saints; neither filthiness, nor foolish talking, nor jesting, which are not convenient: but rather giving of thanks. For this ye know, that no whoremonger, nor unclean person, nor covetous man, who is an idolater, hath any inheritance in the kingdom of Christ and of God. Let no man deceive you with vain words: for because of these things cometh the wrath of God upon the children of disobedience. Be not ye therefore partakers with them. For ye were sometimes darkness, but now are ye light in the Lord: walk as children of light: for the fruit of the Spirit is in all goodness and righteousness and truth.

The Collect.

ALMIGHTY GOD, who hast been the hope and confidence of Thy people in all ages; mercifully regard, we beseech Thee, the prayer with which we cry unto Thee out of the depths, and stretch forth the right hand of Thy majesty for our salvation and defence; through Jesus Christ our Lord. *Amen.*

Fourth Sunday in Lent.—Laetare

The Gospel, St. John vi. 1–14. (*St. John* vi. 47–59.)

After these things Jesus went over the sea of Galilee, which is the sea of Tiberias. And a great multitude followed him, because they saw his miracles which he did on them that were diseased. And Jesus went up into a mountain, and there he sat with his disciples. And the passover, a feast of the Jews, was nigh. When Jesus then lifted up his eyes, and saw a great company come unto him, he saith unto Philip, Whence shall we buy bread, that these may eat? And this he said to prove him: for he himself knew what he would do. Philip answered him, Two hundred pennyworth of bread is not sufficient for them, that every one of them may take a little. One of his disciples, Andrew, Simon Peter's brother, saith unto him, There is a lad here, which hath five barley loaves, and two small fishes: but what are they among so many? And Jesus said, Make the men sit down. Now there was much grass in the place. So the men sat down, in number about five thousand. And Jesus took the loaves; and when he had given thanks, he distributed to the disciples, and the disciples to them that were set down; and likewise of the fishes as much as they would. When they were filled, he said unto his disciples, Gather up the fragments that remain, that nothing be lost. Therefore they gathered them together, and filled twelve baskets with the fragments of the five barley loaves, which remained over and above unto them that had eaten. Then those men, when they had seen the miracle that Jesus did, said, This is of a truth that Prophet that should come into the world.

The Epistle, Gal. iv. 21-31. (1 *John* v. 11-21.)

Tell me, ye that desire to be under the law, do ye not hear the law? For it is written, that Abraham had two sons, the one by a bondmaid, the other by a free woman. But he who was of the bondwoman was born after the flesh; but he of the free woman was by promise. Which things are an allegory: for these are the two covenants; the one from the mount Sinai, which gendereth to bondage, which is Agar. For this Agar is mount Sinai in Arabia, and answereth to Jerusalem, which now is, and is in bondage with her children. But Jerusalem which is above is free, which is the mother of us all. For it is written, Rejoice, thou barren that bearest not; break forth and cry, thou that travailest not: for the desolate hath many more children than she which hath an husband. Now we, brethren, as Isaac was, are the children of promise. But as then he that was born after the flesh persecuted him that was born after the Spirit, even so it is now. Nevertheless what saith the Scripture? Cast out the bondwoman and her son: for the son of the bondwoman shall not be heir with the son of the free woman. So then, brethren, we are not children of the bondwoman, but of the free.

The Collect.

O LORD GOD, merciful and gracious, long-suffering and abundant in goodness and truth; enter not into judgment with Thy servants, we beseech Thee, but be pleased of Thy great kindness to grant, that we who are now righteously afflicted and bowed down by the sense of our sins, may be refreshed and lifted up with the joy of Thy salvation; through Jesus Christ our Lord. *Amen.*

Fifth Sunday in Lent—Judica.

The Gospel, St. John viii. 46–59. (*St. John* xii. 20–32.)

Which of you convinceth me of sin? And if I say the truth, why do ye not believe me? He that is of God heareth God's words: ye therefore hear them not, because ye are not of God. Then answered the Jews, and said unto him, Say we not well that thou art a Samaritan, and hast a devil? Jesus answered, I have not a devil; but I honour my Father, and ye do dishonour me. And I seek not mine own glory: there is one that seeketh and judgeth. Verily, verily, I say unto you, If a man keep my saying, he shall never see death. Then said the Jews unto him, Now we know that thou hast a devil. Abraham is dead, and the prophets; and thou sayest, If a man keep my saying, he shall never taste of death. Art thou greater than our father Abraham, which is dead? and the prophets are dead: whom makest thou thyself? Jesus answered, If I honour myself, my honour is nothing: it is my Father that honoureth me; of whom ye say that he is your God: yet ye have not known him; but I know him: and if I should say, I know him not, I shall be a liar like unto you: but I know him, and keep his saying. Your father Abraham rejoiced to see my day: and he saw it, and was glad. Then said the Jews unto him, Thou art not yet fifty years old, and hast thou seen Abraham? Jesus said unto them, Verily, verily, I say unto you, Before Abraham was, I am. Then took they up stones to cast at him: but Jesus hid himself, and went out of the temple, going through the midst of them, and so passed by.

The Epistle, Heb. ix. 11-15. (2 Cor. v. 14-21.)

But Christ being come an high priest of good things to come, by a greater and more perfect tabernacle, not made with hands, that is to say, not of this building; neither by the blood of goats and calves, but by his own blood he entered in once into the holy place, having obtained eternal redemption for us. For if the blood of bulls and of goats, and the ashes of an heifer sprinkling the unclean, sanctifieth to the purifying of the flesh: how much more shall the blood of Christ, who through the eternal Spirit offered himself without spot to God, purge your conscience from dead works to serve the living God? And for this cause he is the mediator of the new testament, that by means of death, for the redemption of the transgressions that were under the first testament, they which are called might receive the promise of eternal inheritance.

The Collect. ✓

ALMIGHTY and most merciful God, who hast given Thy Son to die for our sins, and to obtain forgiveness and redemption for us through His own blood; let the merit of this spotless sacrifice, we beseech Thee, purge our consciences from dead works, that we may serve Thee, the living God, and receive the promise of eternal inheritance in Christ Jesus our Lord: to whom, with Thee and the Holy Ghost, be honor and glory, world without end. *Amen.*

Sixth Sunday in Lent—Palm Sunday—Palmarum.

[During the Holy Week, there should be Divine Service every day; in which case, the entire gospel history of Christ's Passion and Death should be read.]

The Gospel, St. John xii. 1-16. (*St. Luke* xix. 28-46.)

Then Jesus six days before the passover came to Bethany, where Lazarus was which had been dead, whom he raised from the dead. There they made him a supper; and Martha served: but Lazarus was one of them that sat at the table with him. Then took Mary a pound of ointment of spikenard, very costly, and anointed the feet of Jesus, and wiped his feet with her hair: and the house was filled with the odour of the ointment. Then saith one of his disciples, Judas Iscariot, Simon's son, which should betray him, Why was not this ointment sold for three hundred pence, and given to the poor? This he said, not that he cared for the poor; but because he was a thief, and had the bag, and bare what was put therein. Then said Jesus, Let her alone: against the day of my burying hath she kept this. For the poor always ye have with you; but me ye have not always. Much people of the Jews therefore knew that he was there: and they came not for Jesus' sake only, but that they might see Lazarus also, whom he had raised from the dead. But the chief priests consulted that they might put Lazarus also to death; because

F

that by reason of him many of the Jews went away, and believed on Jesus. On the next day much people that were come to the feast, when they heard that Jesus was coming to Jerusalem, took branches of palm trees, and went forth to meet him, and cried, Hosanna: Blessed is the King of Israel that cometh in the name of the Lord. And Jesus, when he had found a young ass, sat thereon; as it is written, Fear not, daughter of Zion: behold, thy King cometh, sitting on an ass's colt. These things understood not his disciples at the first: but when Jesus was glorified, then remembered they that these things were written of him, and that they had done these things unto him.

The Epistle, Phil. ii. 5–10. (*Rev.* i. 4–8.)

Let this mind be in you, which was also in Christ Jesus: who, being in the form of God, thought it not robbery to be equal with God: but made himself of no reputation, and took upon him the form of a servant, and was made in the likeness of men: and being found in fashion as a man, he humbled himself, and became obedient unto death, even the death of the cross. Wherefore God also hath highly exalted him, and given him a name which is above every name: that at the name of Jesus every knee should bow, of things in heaven, and things in earth, and things under the earth.

The Collect.

ALMIGHTY and everlasting God, whose Son, our Saviour Jesus Christ, for an example of humility to the world, took upon Him our flesh and endured the passion of the cross; mercifully grant, we beseech Thee, that we may be counted worthy to have part, both in the fellowship of His sufferings and in the glorious power of His resurrection: to whom, with Thee and the Holy Ghost, be honor and glory, world without end. *Amen.*

Good Friday.

The Gospel, St. John xix. 1–37. (*St. Matt.* xxvii. 33–54.)

Then Pilate therefore took Jesus, and scourged him. And the soldiers platted a crown of thorns, and put it on his head, and they put on him a purple robe, and said, Hail, King of the Jews! and they smote him with their hands. Pilate therefore went forth again, and saith unto them, Behold, I bring him forth to you, that ye may know that I find no fault in him. Then came Jesus forth, wearing the crown of thorns, and the purple robe. And Pilate saith unto them, Behold the man! When the chief priests therefore and officers saw him, they cried out, saying, Crucify him, crucify him. Pilate saith unto them, Take ye him, and crucify him: for I find no fault in him. The Jews answered him, We have a law, and by our law he ought to die, because he made himself the Son of God. When Pilate therefore heard that saying, he was the more afraid; and went again into the judgment hall, and saith unto Jesus, Whence art thou? But Jesus gave him no answer. Then saith Pilate unto him, Speakest thou not unto me? knowest thou not that I have power to crucify thee, and have power to release thee? Jesus answered, Thou couldest have no power at all against me, except it were given thee from above: therefore he that delivered me unto thee hath the greater sin. And from thenceforth Pilate sought to release him: but the Jews cried out, saying, If thou let this man go, thou art not Cæsar's friend: whosoever maketh himself a king speaketh against Cæsar. When Pilate therefore heard that saying, he brought Jesus forth, and sat down in the judgment seat in a place that is called the Pavement, but in the Hebrew, Gabbatha. And it was the preparation of the passover, and about the sixth hour: and he saith unto the Jews, Behold your King! But they cried out, Away with him, away with him, crucify him. Pilate saith unto them, Shall I crucify your King? The chief priests answered, We have no king but Cæsar. Then delivered he him therefore unto them to be crucified. And they took Jesus, and led him away. And he bearing his cross went forth into a place called the place of a skull, which is called in the Hebrew Golgotha: where they crucified him, and two other with him, on either side one, and Jesus in the midst. And Pilate wrote a title, and put it on the cross. And the writing was, JESUS OF NAZARETH THE KING OF THE JEWS. This title then read many of the Jews: for the place where Jesus was crucified was nigh to the city: and it was written in Hebrew, and Greek, and Latin. Then said the chief priests of the Jews to Pilate, Write not, the King of the Jews; but that he said, I am King of the Jews. Pilate answered, What I have written I have written. Then the soldiers, when they had crucified Jesus, took his garments, and made four parts, to every soldier a part; and also his coat: now the coat was without seam, woven from the top throughout. They said therefore among themselves, Let us not rend it, but cast lots for it, whose it shall be: that the Scripture might be fulfilled, which saith, They parted my raiment among them, and for my vesture they did cast lots. These things therefore the soldiers did. Now there stood by the cross of Jesus his mother, and his mother's sister, Mary the wife of Cleophas, and Mary Magdalene. When Jesus therefore saw his mother, and the disciple standing by, whom he loved, he saith unto his mother, Woman, behold thy son! Then saith he to the disciple, Behold thy mother! And from that hour that disciple took her unto his own home. After this, Jesus knowing that all things were now accomplished, that the Scripture might be fulfilled, saith, I thirst. Now there was set a vessel full of vinegar: and they filled a sponge with vinegar, and put it upon hyssop, and put it to his mouth. When Jesus therefore had received the vinegar, he said, It is finished: and he bowed his head, and gave up the ghost.

The Jews therefore, because it was the preparation, that the bodies should not remain upon the cross on the sabbath day, (for that sabbath day was an high day,) besought Pilate that their legs might be broken, and that they might be taken away. Then came the soldiers, and brake the legs of the first, and of the other which was crucified with him. But when they came to Jesus, and saw that he was dead already, they brake not his legs: but one of the soldiers with a spear pierced his side, and forthwith came there out blood and water. And he that saw it bare record, and his record is true: and he knoweth that he saith true, that ye might believe. For these things were done, that the scripture should be fulfilled, A bone of him shall not be broken. And again another scripture saith, They shall look on him whom they pierced.

The Epistle, Heb. x. 1-25 (*Isaiah* liii.)

For the law having a shadow of good things to come, and not the very image of the things, can never with those sacrifices, which they offered year by year continually, make the comers thereunto perfect. For then would they not have ceased to be offered? because that the worshippers once purged should have had no more conscience of sins. But in those sacrifices there is a remembrance again made of sins every year. For it is not possible that the blood of bulls and of goats should take away sins. Wherefore when he cometh into the world, he saith, Sacrifice and offering thou wouldest not, but a body hast thou prepared me: in burnt offerings and sacrifices for sin thou hast had no pleasure. Then said I, Lo, I come (in the volume of the book it is written of me,) to do thy will, O God. Above when he said, Sacrifice and offering and burnt offerings and offering for sin thou wouldest not, neither hadst pleasure therein; which are offered by the law; then said he, Lo, I come to do thy will, O God. He taketh away the first, that he may establish the second. By the which will we are sanctified through the offering of the body of Jesus Christ once for all. And every priest standeth daily ministering and offering oftentimes the same sacrifices, which can never take away sins: but this man, after he had offered one sacrifice for sins for ever, sat down on the right hand of God; from henceforth expecting till his enemies be made his footstool. For by one offering he hath perfected for ever them that are sanctified. Whereof the Holy Ghost also is a witness to us: for after that he had said before, This is the covenant that I will make with them after those days, saith the Lord, I will put my laws into their hearts, and in their minds will I write them; and their sins and iniquities will I remember no more. Now where remission of these is, there is no more offering for sin. Having therefore, brethren, boldness to enter into the holiest by the blood of Jesus, by a new and living way, which he hath consecrated for us, through the vail, that is to say, his flesh; and having an high priest over the house of God; let us draw near with a true heart and full assurance of faith, having our hearts sprinkled from an evil conscience, and our bodies washed with pure water. Let us hold fast the profession of our faith without wavering; (for he is faithful that promised;) and let us consider one another to provoke unto love and to good works: not forsaking the assembling of ourselves together, as the manner of some is; but exhorting one another: and so much the more, as ye see the day approaching.

The Collect.

O RIGHTEOUS and holy God, who has manifested toward us Thine unfathomable love, in not sparing Thine own Son, but delivering Him up for us all; by the memory of His bitter death, by the awful mystery of His sorrows in the garden and upon the cross, we humbly beseech Thee to have mercy upon us and upon all men, and to make known Thy saving health among the nations, that He may see the travail of His soul and be satisfied: to whom with Thee and the Holy Ghost, be honor and glory, world without end. *Amen.*

The Festival Prayer.

LORD Jesus Christ! Thou holy and spotless Lamb of God, who didst take upon Thyself the curse of sin which was due to us, with all the heavenly host of the redeemed, we unite in ascribing unto Thee power, and riches, and wisdom, and strength, and honor, and glory, and blessing. We bless Thee for all the burdens Thou hast borne, for all the tears Thou hast wept, for all the pains Thou hast suffered, for every drop of blood Thou hast shed, for every word of comfort Thou hast spoken on the cross, for every conflict with the powers of darkness, and for Thine eternal victory over the terrors of death and the pains of hell. *Amen.*

O MOST merciful Father, who of Thy tender compassion towards us guilty sinners, didst give Thine only-begotten Son to be an offering for our sins, grant us grace, we humbly beseech Thee, that, being engrafted into Him by Thy Spirit and made partakers of His sufferings and His death, we may crucify the corrupt inclinations of the flesh, die daily unto the world, and lead holy and unblamable lives. Cleaving unto His cross in all the temptations of life, may we hold fast the profession of our faith without wavering, and finally attain unto the resurrection of the dead, through the merits of this same once crucified, but now risen and exalted Saviour. *Amen.*

Easter Eve.

The Gospel, St. Matt. xxvii. 57-66.

When the even was come, there came a rich man of Arimathæa, named Joseph, who also himself was Jesus' disciple: he went to Pilate, and begged the body of Jesus. Then Pilate commanded the body to be delivered. And when Joseph had taken the body, he wrapped it in a clean linen cloth, and laid it in his own new tomb, which he had hewn out in the rock: and he rolled a great stone to the door of the sepulchre, and departed. And there was Mary Magdalene, and the other Mary, sitting over against the sepulchre. Now the next day, that followed the day of the preparation, the chief priests and Pharisees came together unto Pilate, saying, Sir, we remember that that deceiver said, while he was yet alive, After three days I will rise again. Command therefore that the sepulchre be made sure until the third day, lest his disciples come by night, and steal him away, and say unto the people, He is risen from the dead: so the last error shall be worse than the first. Pilate said unto them, Ye have a watch: go your way, make it as sure as ye can. So they went, and made the sepulchre sure, sealing the stone, and setting a watch.

The Epistle, 1 Pet. iii. 17-22.

For it is better, if the will of God be so, that ye suffer for well-doing, than for evil-doing. For Christ also hath once suffered for sins, the just for the unjust, that he might bring us to God, being put to death in the flesh, but quickened by the Spirit: by which also he went and preached unto the spirits in prison; which sometime were disobedient, when once the long-suffering of God waited in the days of Noah, while the ark was a preparing, wherein few, that is, eight souls were saved by water. The like figure whereunto even baptism doth also now save us, (not the putting away of the filth of the flesh, but the answer of a good conscience toward God,) by the resurrection of Jesus Christ: who is gone into heaven, and is on the right hand of God; angels and authorities and powers being made subject unto him.

The Collect.

O ALMIGHTY God, who, by the descent of our Saviour Jesus Christ into hades, and His rising again from the dead, hast given assurance that the spirits of those who sleep in Him do abide in joy and felicity; grant unto us, we beseech Thee, such steadfast faith and lively hope, that we may purify ourselves as He is pure; and that we, with Thy whole redeemed Church, may speedily attain unto the resurrection of the dead, when our mortal bodies shall put on immortality and incorruption, and we shall be changed into the likeness of His glorious body: who liveth and reigneth with Thee and the Holy Ghost, one God, world without end. *Amen.*

Easter Day.

The Gospel, St. John xx. 1-10. (*St. Matt.* xxviii. 1-10.)

The first day of the week cometh Mary Magdalene early, when it was yet dark, unto the sepulchre, and seeth the stone taken away from the sepulchre. Then she runneth and cometh to Simon Peter, and to the other disciple, whom Jesus loved, and saith unto them, They have taken away the Lord out of the sepulchre, and we know not where they have laid him. Peter therefore went forth, and that other disciple, and came to the sepulchre. So they ran both together: and the other disciple did outrun Peter, and came first to the sepulchre. And he stooping down, and looking in, saw the linen clothes lying; yet went he not in. Then cometh Simon Peter following him, and went into the sepulchre, and seeth the linen clothes lie, and the napkin, that was about his head, not lying with the linen clothes, but wrapped together in a place by itself. Then went in also that other disciple, which came first to the sepulchre, and he saw, and believed. For as yet they knew not the scripture, that he must rise again from the dead. Then the disciples went away again unto their own home.

The Epistle, Col. iii. 1–11. (1 *Cor.* xv. 1–20.)

If ye then be risen with Christ, seek those things which are above, where Christ sitteth on the right hand of God. Set your affection on things above, not on things on the earth. For ye are dead, and your life is hid with Christ in God. When Christ, who is our life, shall appear, then shall ye also appear with him in glory. Mortify therefore your members which are upon the earth; fornication, uncleanness, inordinate affection, evil concupiscence, and covetousness, which is idolatry: for which things' sake the wrath of God cometh on the children of disobedience: in the which ye also walked sometime when ye lived in them. But now ye also put off all these; anger, wrath, malice, blasphemy, filthy communication out of your mouth. Lie not one to another, seeing that ye have put off the old man with his deeds; and have put on the new man, which is renewed in knowledge after the image of him that created him: where there is neither Greek nor Jew, circumcision nor uncircumcision, Barbarian, Scythian, bond nor free: but Christ is all, and in all.

The Collect.

ALMIGHTY God, who through the resurrection of Thine only begotten Son Jesus Christ, hast overcome death, and opened unto us the gate of everlasting life;

assist and support in us, we beseech Thee, the aspirations of Thy heavenly grace, that dying unto sin always, and living unto righteousness, we may at last triumph over death and the grave, in the full image of our risen Lord: to whom, with Thee and the Holy Ghost, be honor and glory, world without end. *Amen*

The Festival Prayer.

O THOU God and Father of our Lord Jesus Christ, we render Thee most humble and hearty thanks, that, when He had descended into the grave, Thou didst not suffer Thy Holy One to see corruption, nor leave His soul in hades, but didst show unto Him the path of life, and raise Him from the dead, and set Him at Thine own right hand in the heavenly places. Grant us grace, we beseech Thee, to apprehend with true faith the glorious mystery of our Saviour's resurrection, and fill our hearts with joy and a lively hope, that amid all the sorrows, trials and temptations of our mortal state, and in the hour of death, we may derive strength and comfort from this sure pledge, of an inheritance incorruptible and undefiled and that fadeth not away. *Amen.*

O THOU Prince of Life and First-Begotten of the dead, whom not having seen we love, breathe upon us that we may receive the Holy Ghost, to abide with us continually both as the seal of our adoption, and as an earnest of the promised possession. Give us power to walk in the Spirit that we may not fulfill the lusts of the flesh, but mortify our members which are upon the earth and purify ourselves even as Thou art pure, so that at Thy second coming to judge the world in righteousness, we also may appear with Thee, having our vile bodies changed into the fashion of Thine own glorious body, according to the working whereby Thou art able even to subdue all things unto Thyself: who art God over all, blessed forever. *Amen.*

Monday in Easter Week.

The Gospel, St. Luke xxiv. 13-35. (*St. John* xx. 11-18.)

And, behold, two of them went that same day to a village called Emmaus, which was from Jerusalem about threescore furlongs. And they talked together of all these things which had happened. And it came to pass, that, while they communed together and reasoned, Jesus himself drew near, and went with them. But their eyes were holden that they should not know him. And he said unto them, What manner of communications are these that ye have one to another, as ye walk, and are sad? And the one of them, whose name was Cleopas, answering, said unto him, Art thou only a stranger in Jerusalem, and hast not known the things which are come to pass there in these days? And he said unto them, What things? And they said unto him, Concerning Jesus of Nazareth, which was a prophet mighty in deed and word before God and all the people: and how the chief priests and our rulers delivered him to be condemned to death, and have crucified him. But we trusted that it had been he which should have redeemed Israel: and beside all this, to-day is the third day since these things were done. Yea, and certain women also of our company made us astonished, which were early at the sepulchre; and when they found not his body, they came, saying, that they had also seen a vision of angels, which said that he was alive. And certain of them which were with us went to the sepulchre, and found it even so as the women had said: but him they saw not. Then he said unto them, O fools, and slow of heart to believe all that the prophets have spoken: Ought not Christ to have suffered these things, and to enter into his glory? And beginning at Moses and all the prophets, he expounded unto them in all the Scriptures the things concerning himself. And they drew nigh unto the village, whither they went: and he made as though he would have gone further. But they constrained him, saying, Abide with us: for it is toward evening, and the day is far spent. And he went in to tarry with them. And it came to pass, as he sat at meat with them, he took bread and blessed it, and brake, and gave to them. And their eyes were opened, and they knew him; and he vanished out of their sight. And they said one to another, Did not our heart burn within us, while he talked with us by the way, and while he opened to us the Scriptures? And they rose up the same hour, and returned to Jerusalem, and found the eleven gathered together, and them that were with them, saying, The Lord is risen indeed, and hath appeared to Simon. And they told what things were done in the way, and how he was known of them in breaking of bread.

The Epistle, Acts x. 34–43. (1 *Cor.* xv. 51–58.)

Then Peter opened his mouth, and said, Of a truth I perceive that God is no respecter of persons: but in every nation he that feareth him, and worketh righteousness, is accepted with him. The word which God sent unto the children of Israel, preaching peace by Jesus Christ: (he is Lord of all:) that word, I say, ye know, which was published throughout all Judea, and began from Galilee, after the baptism which John preached; how God anointed Jesus of Nazareth with the Holy Ghost and with power: who went about doing good, and healing all that were oppressed of the devil; for God was with him. And we are witnesses of all things which he did both in the land of the Jews, and in Jerusalem; whom they slew and hanged on a tree: him God raised up the third day, and shewed him openly; not to all the people, but unto witnesses chosen before of God, even to us, who did eat and drink with him after he rose from the dead. And he commanded us to preach unto the people, and to testify that it is he which was ordained of God to be the Judge of quick and dead. To him give all the prophets witness, that through his name whosoever believeth in him shall receive remission of sins.

The Collect.

ALMIGHTY God, who from the tomb of our Lord Jesus Christ hast caused the light of Eternal Life to shine upon the world; be pleased, at this season of solemn joy, to shed abroad Thy love in our hearts by the Holy Ghost, and to inflame them with heavenly desires; that we may continually seek the things which are above, where Christ sitteth at Thy right hand, and so, abiding in purity of heart and mind, may at length attain unto Thine everlasting kingdom, there to dwell in the glorious light of Thy presence, world without end; through the same Jesus Christ our Lord. *Amen.*

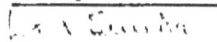

First Sunday after Easter—Quasimodogeniti, or Dominica in Albis.

The Gospel, St. John xx. 19-31. (St. Luke xxiv. 36-47.)

Then the same day at evening, being the first day of the week, when the doors were shut where the disciples were assembled for fear of the Jews, came Jesus and stood in the midst, and saith unto them, Peace be unto you. And when he had so said, he shewed unto them his hands and his side. Then were the disciples glad, when they saw the Lord. Then said Jesus to them again, Peace be unto you: as my Father hath sent me, even so send I you. And when he had said this, he breathed on them, and saith unto them, Receive ye the Holy Ghost: whosesoever sins ye remit, they are remitted unto them; and whosesoever sins ye retain, they are retained. But Thomas, one of the twelve, called Didymus, was not with them when Jesus came. The other disciples therefore said unto him, We have seen the Lord. But he said unto them, Except I shall see in his hands the print of the nails, and put my finger into the print of the nails, and thrust my hand into his side, I will not believe. And after eight days again his disciples were within, and Thomas with them: then came Jesus, the doors being shut, and stood in the midst, and said, Peace be unto you. Then saith he to Thomas, Reach hither thy fingers, and behold my hands; and reach hither thy hand, and thrust it into my side: and be not faithless, but believing. And Thomas answered and said unto him, My Lord and my God. Jesus saith unto him, Thomas, because thou hast seen me, thou hast believed: blessed are they that have not seen, and yet have believed. And many other signs truly did Jesus in the presence of his disciples, which are not written in this book: but these are written, that ye might believe that Jesus is the Christ, the Son of God; and that believing ye might have life through his name.

The Epistle, 1 *John* v. 4–12. (2 *Tim.* ii. 7–13.)

For whatsoever is born of God overcometh the world: and this is the victory that overcometh the world, even our faith. Who is he that overcometh the world, but he that believeth that Jesus is the Son of God? This is he that came by water and blood, even Jesus Christ; not by water only, but by water and blood. And it is the Spirit that beareth witness, because the Spirit is truth. For there are three that bear record in heaven, the Father, the Word, and the Holy Ghost: and these three are one. And there are three that bear witness in earth, the Spirit, and the water, and the blood: and these three agree in one. If we receive the witness of men, the witness of God is greater: for this is the witness of God which he hath testified of his Son. He that believeth on the Son of God hath the witness in himself: he that believeth not God hath made him a liar; because he believeth not the record that God gave of his Son. And this is the record, that God hath given to us eternal life, and this life is in his Son. He that hath the Son hath life; and he that hath not the Son of God hath not life.

The Collect.

ALMIGHTY God, who hast brought again from the dead our Lord Jesus, the glorious Prince of salvation, with everlasting victory over hell and the grave; grant unto us power, we beseech Thee, to rise with Him to newness of life, that we may overcome the world with the victory of faith, and have part at last in the resurrection of the just; through the merits of this same risen Saviour, who liveth and reigneth with Thee and the Holy Ghost, ever one God, world without end. *Amen.*

Second Sunday after Easter—Misericordias Domini.

The Gospel, St. John x. 11–16. (St. John xxi. 15–19.)

I am the good shepherd: the good shepherd giveth his life for the sheep. But he that is an hireling, and not the shepherd, whose own the sheep are not, seeth the wolf coming, and leaveth the sheep, and fleeth: and the wolf catcheth them, and scattereth the sheep. The hireling fleeth, because he is an hireling, and careth not for the sheep. I am the good shepherd, and know my sheep, and am known of mine. As the Father knoweth me, even so know I the Father: and I lay down my life for the sheep. And other sheep I have, which are not of this fold: them also I must bring, and they shall hear my voice; and there shall be one fold, and one shepherd.

The Epistle, 1 *Pet.* ii. 20–25. (*Rev.* vii. 13–17.)

For what glory is it, if, when ye be buffeted for your faults, ye shall take it patiently? but if, when ye do well, and suffer for it, ye take it patiently, this is acceptable with God. For even hereunto were ye called: because Christ also suffered for us, leaving us an example, that ye should follow his steps: who did no sin, neither was guile found in his mouth: who, when he was reviled, reviled not again; when he suffered, he threatened not; but committed himself to him that judgeth righteously: who his own self bare our sins in his own body on the tree, that we, being dead to sins, should live unto righteousness: by whose stripes ye were healed. For ye were as sheep going astray; but are now returned unto the Shepherd and Bishop of your souls.

The Collect.

O God, who, of Thine abundant mercy, hast begotten us again unto a lively hope, by the resurrection of Jesus Christ from the dead; let Thy great love constrain us, we beseech Thee, to rise up, forsake all, and follow Him; that as we have been redeemed by His blood, so we may walk also in the light of His holy example, and be joined to Him evermore as the Shepherd and Bishop of our souls: to whom, with Thee and the Holy Ghost, be honor and glory, world without end. *Amen.*

Third Sunday after Easter—Jubilate.

The Gospel, St. John xvi. 16-22. (*St. Matt.* x. 16-20.)

A little while, and ye shall not see me: and again, a little while, and ye shall see me, because I go to the Father. Then said some of his disciples among themselves, What is this that he saith unto us, A little while, and ye shall not see me: and again, a little while, and ye shall see me: and, Because I go to the Father? They said therefore, What is this that he saith, A little while? we cannot tell what he saith. Now Jesus knew that they were desirous to ask him, and said unto them, Do ye inquire among yourselves of that I said, A little while, and ye shall not see me: and again, a little while, and ye shall see me? Verily, verily, I say unto you, That ye shall weep and lament, but the world shall rejoice: and ye shall be sorrowful, but your sorrow shall be turned into joy. A woman when she is in travail hath sorrow, because her hour is come: but as soon as she is delivered of the child, she remembereth no more the anguish, for joy that a man is born into the world. And ye now therefore have sorrow: but I will see you again, and your heart shall rejoice, and your joy no man taketh from you.

The Epistle, 1 *Pet.* ii. 11-19. (*Acts* iv. 8-20.)

Dearly beloved, I beseech you as strangers and pilgrims, abstain from fleshly lusts, which war against the soul; having your conversation honest among the Gentiles: that, whereas they speak against you as evil doers, they may by your good works, which they shall behold, glorify God in the day of visitation. Submit yourselves to every ordinance of man for the Lord's sake: whether it be to the king, as supreme; or unto governors, as unto them that are sent by him for the punishment of evil doers, and for the praise of them that do

FOURTH SUNDAY AFTER EASTER.

well. For so is the will of God, that with well doing ye may put to silence the ignorance of foolish men: as free, and not using your liberty for a cloak of maliciousness, but as the servants of God. Honour all men. Love the brotherhood. Fear God. Honour the king. Servants, be subject to your masters with all fear; not only to the good and gentle, but also to the froward. For this is thankworthy, if a man for conscience toward God endure grief, suffering wrongfully.

The Collect.

God of all truth and grace, who hast caused the Sun of Righteousness to arise upon a dark and benighted world, in bringing up Thy Holy One from the grave; be pleased graciously so to illuminate the souls of Thy people with the beams of heavenly wisdom, that they may continually walk in Thy light, and know both to avoid evil and to follow after that which is good; through Jesus Christ our Lord, who liveth and reigneth with Thee and the Holy Ghost, ever one God, world without end. Amen.

Fourth Sunday after Easter—Cantate.

The Gospel, St. John xvi. 5–15. (St. Matt. x. 24–33.)

But now I go my way to him that sent me; and none of you asketh me, Whither goest thou? But because I have said these things unto you, sorrow hath filled your heart. Nevertheless I tell you the truth; It is expedient for you that I go away: for if I go not away, the Comforter will not come unto you; but if I depart, I will send him unto you. And when he is come, he will reprove the world of sin, and of righteousness, and of judgment: of sin, because they believe not on me; of righteousness, because I go to my Father, and ye see me no more; of judgment, because the prince of this world is judged. I have yet many things to say unto you, but ye cannot bear them now. Howbeit when he, the Spirit of truth, is come, he will guide you into all truth: for he shall not speak of himself; but whatsoever he shall hear, that shall he speak: and he will show you things to come. He shall glorify me: for he shall receive of mine, and shall shew it unto you. All things that the Father hath are mine: therefore said I, that he shall take of mine, and shall shew it unto you.

The Epistle, St. James i. 16–21. (1 *Thess.* ii. 9–13.)

Do not err, my beloved brethren. Every good gift and every perfect gift is from above, and cometh down from the Father of lights, with whom is no variableness, neither shadow of turning. Of his own will begat he us with the word of truth, that we should be a kind of first-fruits of his creatures. Wherefore, my beloved brethren, let every man be swift to hear, slow to speak, slow to wrath: for the wrath of man worketh not the righteousness of God. Wherefore lay apart all filthiness and superfluity of naughtiness, and receive with meekness the engrafted word, which is able to save your souls.

The Collect.

O God, the Father of lights, from whom cometh down every good and perfect gift, and who art Thyself the only satisfying portion of the souls which Thou hast made; grant us grace, we beseech Thee, to raise our thoughts and affections from earth to heaven, and to breathe continually after Thy presence; that so, in the midst of all worldly vanity and change, our hearts may surely there be fixed, where alone are to be found true joys and everlasting peace; through Jesus Christ our Lord. *Amen.*

Fifth Sunday after Easter—Rogate.

The Gospel, St. John xvi. 23-33. (*St. Luke* xi. 9-13.)

And in that day ye shall ask me nothing. Verily, verily, I say unto you, Whatsoever ye shall ask the Father in my name, he will give it you. Hitherto have ye asked nothing in my name: ask, and ye shall receive, that your joy may be full. These things have I spoken unto you in proverbs; but the time cometh, when I shall no more speak unto you in proverbs, but I shall shew you plainly of the Father. At that day ye shall ask in my name: and I say not unto you, that I will pray the Father for you: for the Father himself loveth you, because ye have loved me, and have believed that I came out from God. I came forth from the Father, and am come into the world: again, I leave the world, and go to the Father. His disciples said unto him, Lo, now speakest thou plainly, and speakest no proverb. Now are we sure that thou knowest all things, and needest not that any man should ask thee: by this we believe that thou camest forth from God. Jesus answered them, Do ye now believe? Behold, the hour cometh, yea, is now come, that ye shall be scattered, every man to his own, and shall leave me alone: and yet I am not alone, because the Father is with me. These things I have spoken unto you, that in me ye might have peace. In the world ye shall have tribulation: but be of good cheer; I have overcome the world.

The Epistle, St. James i. 22-27. (1 *Tim.* ii. 1-6.)

But be ye doers of the word, and not hearers only, deceiving your own selves. For if any be a hearer of the word, and not a doer, he is like unto a man beholding his natural face in a glass: for he beholdeth himself, and goeth his way, and straightway forgetteth what manner of man he was. But whoso looketh into the perfect law of liberty, and continueth therein, he being not a forgetful hearer, but a doer of the work, this man shall be blessed in his deed. If any man among you seem to be religious, and bridleth not his tongue, but deceiveth his own heart, this man's religion is vain. Pure religion and undefiled before God and the Father is this, To visit the fatherless and widows in their affliction, and to keep himself unspotted from the world.

The Collect.

VOUCHSAFE unto us, O Lord, the inspirations of Thy salutary grace, and quicken us according to Thy word; that knowing what is right, and approving that which is good, we may, by patient continuance in well-doing, seek for glory and honor and immortality; and so finally, having escaped the corruption that is in the world through lust, find an entrance ministered unto us abundantly into the everlasting kingdom of our Lord and Saviour Jesus Christ: to whom, with Thee and the Holy Ghost, be honor and glory, world without end. *Amen.*

Ascension Day.

The Gospel, St. Mark xvi. 14-20. (*St. Luke.* xxiv. 49-53.)

Afterward he appeared unto the eleven as they sat at meat, and upbraided them with their unbelief and hardness of heart, because they believed not them which had seen him after he was risen. And he said unto them, Go ye into all the world, and preach the gospel to every creature. He that believeth and is baptized shall be saved; but he that believeth not shall be damned. And these signs shall follow them that believe: in my name shall they cast out devils; they shall speak with new tongues; they shall take up serpents; and if they drink any deadly thing, it shall not hurt them; they shall lay hands on the sick, and they shall recover. So then after the Lord had spoken unto them, he was received up into heaven, and sat on the right hand of God. And they went forth, and preached every where, the Lord working with them, and confirming the word with signs following. Amen.

The Epistle, Acts. i. 1–11. (Ephes. i. 15–23.)

The former treatise have I made, O Theophilus, of all that Jesus began both to do and teach, until the day in which he was taken up, after that he through the Holy Ghost had given commandments unto the apostles whom he had chosen: to whom also he shewed himself alive after his passion by many infallible proofs, being seen of them forty days, and speaking of the things pertaining to the kingdom of God: and, being assembled together with them, commanded them that they should not depart from Jerusalem, but wait for the promise of the Father, which, saith he, ye have heard of me. For John truly baptized with water; but ye shall be baptized with the Holy Ghost not many days hence. When they therefore were come together, they asked of him, saying, Lord, wilt thou at this time restore again the kingdom to Israel? And he said unto them, It is not for you to know the times or the seasons, which the Father hath put in his own power. But ye shall receive power, after that the Holy Ghost is come upon you: and ye shall be witnesses unto me both in Jerusalem and in all Judea, and in Samaria, and unto the uttermost part of the earth. And when he had spoken these things, while they beheld, he was taken up; and a cloud received him out of their sight. And while they looked steadfastly toward heaven as he went up, behold, two men stood by them in white apparel; which also said, Ye men of Galilee, why stand ye gazing up into heaven? this same

Jesus, which is taken up from you into heaven, shall so come in like manner as ye have seen him go into heaven.

The Collect.

ALMIGHTY and everlasting God, who on this day didst glorify Thy Son Jesus, by receiving Him up into heaven, and setting Him at Thine own right hand, far above all principality, and power, and might, and dominion, and every name that is named, not only in this world, but also in that which is to come; work in us, we beseech Thee, such firm and abiding faith in this mystery as may raise us in heart and mind above all things here below, to dwell with Christ in heavenly places, and to possess in Him our true life; so that when He shall appear again, according to His word, we also may appear with Him in glory everlasting: to whom, with Thee and the Holy Ghost, be all worship and praise, world without end. *Amen.*

The Festival Prayer.

O LORD Jesus Christ, Thou conqueror of death and hell, who from the depths of Thy humiliation didst pass into the heavens, and art crowned with glory and honor as King of saints and eternal High Priest over the house of God; let Thy all-powerful intercessions prevail on our behalf, that, being delivered from the curse of sin, we may receive grace and strength to follow Thee with patient endurance through the sorrows and pains of earth and the darkness of the grave, and, having thus shared in Thy sufferings here, become partakers also of Thy joy and glory in the everlasting kingdom of the Father. *Amen.*

Sunday after Ascension Day—Exaudi.

The Gospel, St. John xv. 26—xvi. 1. (*St.* John vii. 33–39.)

But when the Comforter is come, whom I will send unto you from the Father, even the Spirit of truth, which proceedeth from the Father, he shall testify of me: and ye also shall bear witness, because ye have been with me from the beginning. These things have I spoken unto you, that ye should not be offended.

The Epistle, 1 Pet. iv. 7–11. (*Acts* xix. 1–7.)

But the end of all things is at hand: be ye therefore sober, and watch unto prayer. And above all things have fervent charity among yourselves: for charity shall cover the multitude of sins. Use hospitality one to another without grudging. As every man hath received the gift, even so minister the same one to another, as good stewards of the manifold grace of God. If any man speak, let him speak as the oracles of God; if any man minister, let him do it as of the ability which God giveth: that God in all things may be glorified through Jesus Christ, to whom be praise and dominion for ever and ever. Amen.

The Collect.

O God, the King of glory, who through the resurrection and ascension of our Lord Jesus Christ, hast opened the kingdom of heaven to all believers; leave us not orphans, we beseech Thee, in our weary mortal state, but send unto us the Holy Ghost, the Comforter; who may guide us always in the way of truth and peace, and bring us in the end to those mansions of rest in which Christ now dwells and reigns: to whom, with Thee and the Holy Ghost, be honor and glory, world without end. *Amen.*

Whitsunday—Pentecost.

The Gospel, *St. John* xiv. 15–31. (*Joel* ii. 28–32.)

If ye love me, keep my commandments. And I will pray the Father, and he shall give you another Comforter, that he may abide with you forever; even the Spirit of truth; whom the world cannot receive, because it seeth him not, neither knoweth him: but ye know him; for he dwelleth with you, and shall be in you. I will not leave you comfortless: I will come to you. Yet a little while, and the world seeth me no more; but ye see me: because I live, ye shall live also. At that day ye shall know that I am in my Father, and ye in me, and I in you. He that hath my commandments, and keepeth them, he it is that loveth me: and he that loveth me shall be loved of my Father, and I will love him, and will manifest myself to him. Judas saith unto him, not Iscariot, Lord, how is it that thou wilt manifest thyself unto us, and not unto the world? Jesus answered and said unto him, If a man love me, he will keep my words: and my Father will love him, and we will come unto him, and make our abode with him. He that loveth me not, keepeth not my sayings: and the word which ye hear is not mine, but the Father's which sent me. These things have I spoken unto you, being yet present with you. But the Comforter, which is the Holy Ghost, whom the Father will send in my name, he shall teach you all things, and bring all things to your remembrance, whatsoever I have said unto you. Peace I leave with you, my peace I give unto you: not as the world giveth, give I unto you. Let not your heart be troubled, neither let it be afraid. Ye have heard how I said unto you, I go away, and come again unto you. If ye loved me, ye would rejoice, because I said, I go unto the Father: for my Father is greater than I. And now I have told you before it come to pass, that, when it is come to pass, ye might believe. Hereafter I will not talk much with you: for the prince of this world cometh, and hath nothing in me. But that the world may know that I love the Father; and as the Father gave me commandment, even so I do. Arise, let us go hence.

The Epistle, Acts ii. 1–11. (*Acts* ii. 22–41.)

And when the day of Pentecost was fully come, they were all with one accord in one place. And suddenly there came a sound from heaven as of a rushing mighty wind, and it filled all the house where they were sitting. And there appeared unto them cloven tongues like as of fire, and it sat upon each of them. And they were all filled with the Holy Ghost, and began to speak with other tongues, as the Spirit gave them utterance. And there were dwelling at Jerusalem Jews, devout men, out of every nation under heaven. Now when this was noised abroad, the multitude came together, and were confounded, because that every man heard them speak in his own language. And they were all amazed and marvelled, saying one to another, Behold, are not all these which speak Galileans? and how hear we every man in our own tongue, wherein we were born? Parthians, and Medes, and Elamites, and the dwellers in Mesopotamia, and in Judea, and Cappadocia, in Pontus, and Asia, Phrygia, and Pamphylia, in Egypt, and in the parts of Libya about Cyrene, and strangers of Rome, Jews and proselytes, Cretes and Arabians, we do hear them speak in our tongues the wonderful works of God.

The Collect.

God of all peace and consolation, who didst gloriously fulfill the great promise of the Gospel, by sending down Thy Holy Ghost on the day of Pentecost, to establish the Church as the home of his continual presence and power among men; mercifully grant unto us, we beseech Thee, this same gift of the Spirit, to renew, illuminate, refresh, and sanctify our dying souls, to be over us and around us like the light and dew of heaven, and to be in us evermore as a well of water springing up into everlasting life; through Jesus Christ our Lord, to whom with Thee, and the Holy Ghost, ever one God, be honor and glory, world without end. *Amen.*

The Festival Prayer.

O HOLY Ghost, Spirit of the Father and the Son, who by Thy quickening energy hast raised us up to a new life in Christ Jesus, and dost in mercy to our infirmities condescend to dwell in our mortal bodies as Thy consecrated temples; bring forth in our hearts and lives, we beseech Thee, the fruits of love, joy, peace, long-suffering, gentleness, faith, meekness and temperance; that so walking in Thee with all holy obedience we may stand firm in the knowledge and love of the truth against the wiles of the Devil, overcome the world, and be glorified in the fellowship of the Father and the Son: to whom with Thee who art coequal and coeternal God, we ascribe all honor, thanksgiving and praise. *Amen.*

Whitmonday.

The Gospel, St. John iii. 16–21. (*St. John* iv. 13–24.)

For God so loved the world, that he gave his only begotten Son, that whosoever believeth in him should not perish, but have everlasting life. For God sent not his Son into the world to condemn the world; but that the world through him might be saved. He that believeth on him is not condemned: but he that believeth not is condemned already, because he hath not believed in the name of the only begotten Son of God. And this is the condemnation, that light is come into the world, and men loved darkness rather than light, because their deeds were evil. For every one that doeth evil hateth the light, neither cometh to the light, lest his deeds should be reproved. But he that doeth truth cometh to the light, that his deeds may be made manifest, that they are wrought in God.

The Epistle, Acts x. 34–48.

Then Peter opened his mouth, and said, Of a truth I perceive that God is no respecter of persons: but in every nation he that feareth him, and worketh righteousness, is accepted with him. The word which God sent unto the children of Israel, preaching peace by Jesus Christ: (he is Lord of all:) that word, I say, ye know, which was published throughout all Judea, and began from Galilee, after the baptism which John preached; how God anointed Jesus of Nazareth with the Holy Ghost and with power: who went about doing good and healing all that were oppressed of the devil; for God was with him. And we are witnesses of all things which he did both in the land of the Jews, and in Jerusalem; whom they slew and hanged on a tree: him God raised up the third day, and shewed him openly; not to all the people, but unto witnesses chosen before of God, even to us, who did eat and drink with him after he rose from the dead. And he commanded us to preach unto the people, and to testify that it is he which was ordained of God to be the judge of quick and dead. To him give all the prophets witness, that through his name whosoever believeth in him shall receive remission of sins. While Peter yet spake these words, the Holy Ghost fell on all them which heard the word. And they of the circumcision which believed were astonished, as many as came with Peter, because that on the Gentiles also was poured out the gift of the Holy Ghost. For they heard them speak with tongues, and magnify God. Then answered Peter, Can any man forbid water, that these should not be baptized, which have received the Holy Ghost as well as we? And he commanded them to be baptized in the name of the Lord. Then prayed they him to tarry certain days.

The Collect.

MOST glorious and blessed God, who through the Holy Ghost, hast made Thy One Catholic Church to be the Body of Christ, the fulness of Him that filleth all in all; we humbly beseech Thee to grant unto us, and to all Thy people, such strong and steadfast faith in this great mystery of grace, that being safely defended from all heresy and schism, we may ever abide in the unity of the Spirit, and so grow up into Him in all things which is the Head, even Christ: to whom, with Thee and the Holy Ghost, ever one God, be all honor and praise, world without end. *Amen.*

Trinity Sunday.

The Gospel, St. John iii. 1–15. (*St. Matt.* xxviii, 18–20.)

There was a man of the Pharisees, named Nicodemus, a ruler of the Jews: the same came to Jesus by night, and said unto him, Rabbi, we know that thou art a teacher come from God: for no man can do these miracles that thou doest, except God be with him. Jesus answered and said unto him, Verily, verily, I say unto thee, Except a man be born again, he cannot see the kingdom of God. Nicodemus saith unto him, How can a man be born when he is old? can he enter the second time into his mother's womb, and be born? Jesus answered, Verily, verily, I say unto thee, Except a man be born of water and of the Spirit, he cannot enter into the kingdom of God. That which is born of the flesh is flesh; and that which is born of the Spirit is spirit. Marvel not that I said unto thee, Ye must be born again. The wind bloweth where it listeth, and thou hearest the sound thereof, but canst not tell whence it cometh, and whither it goeth: so is every one that is born of the Spirit. Nicodemus answered and said unto him, How can these things be? Jesus answered and said unto him, Art thou a master of Israel, and knowest not these things? Verily, verily, I say unto thee, We speak that we do know, and testify that we have seen; and ye receive not our witness. If I have told you earthly things, and ye believe not, how shall ye believe, if I tell you of heavenly things? And no man hath ascended up to heaven, but he that came down from heaven, even the Son of man which is in heaven. And as Moses lifted up the serpent in the wilderness, even so must the Son of man be lifted up: that whosoever believeth in him should not perish, but have eternal life.

The Epistle, Rev. iv. 1-11. (1 *John* v. 1-12.)

After this I looked, and, behold, a door was opened in heaven: and the first voice which I heard was as it were of a trumpet talking with me; which said, Come up hither, and I will show thee things which must be hereafter. And immediately I was in the Spirit: and, behold, a throne was set in h aven, and one sat on the throne. And he that sat was to look upon like a jasper and a sardine stone: and there was a rainbow round about the throne, in sight like unto an emerald. And round about the throne were four and twenty seats: and upon the seats I saw four and twenty elders sitting, clothed in white raiment; and they had on their heads crowns of gold. And out of the throne proceeded lightnings and thunderings and voices: and there were seven lamps of fire burning before the throne, which are the seven spirits of God.

And before the throne there was a sea of glass like unto crystal: and in the midst of the throne, and round about the throne, were four beasts full of eyes before and behind. And the first beast was like a lion, and the second beast like a calf, and the third beast had a face as a man, and the fourth beast was like a flying eagle. And the four beasts had each of them six wings about him; and they were full of eyes within: and they rest not day and night, saying, Holy, holy, holy, Lord God Almighty, which was, and is, and is to come And when those beasts give glory and honor and thanks to him that sat on the throne, who liveth for ever and ever, the four and twenty elders fall down before him that sat on the throne, and worship him that liveth for ever and ever, and cast their crowns before the throne, saying, Thou art worthy, O Lord, to receive glory and honor and power: for thou hast created all things, and for thy pleasure they are and were created.

The Collect.

O God, the Creator and Saviour of the world, who hast made Thyself known in the work of man's redemption, as the Mystery of the ever adorable Trinity, Father, Son, and Holy Ghost, Three in One and One in Three; reveal in us, we beseech Thee, the full power of this faith, into which we have been planted by baptism; that being born of water and of the Spirit, we may by a life of holiness be formed into Thine image here, and rise to Thy blissful presence hereafter: there to join, with the song of the seraphim in praising Thee, world without end. Amen.

NOTE.—Instead of a Festival Prayer on Trinity Sunday, the *Te Deum* shall be chanted, or else recited antiphonally, as a substitute for the Psalm or Hymn immediately before the sermon.

But if the Holy Communion be celebrated on Trinity Sunday, or on a Sunday after Trinity and before Advent, such use of the Te Deum immediately before the Sermon shall be omitted.

First Sunday after Trinity.

The Gospel, St. Luke xvi. 19–31. (*St. Matt.* xvi. 13–20.)

There was a certain rich man, which was clothed in purple and fine linen, and fared sumptuously every day: and there was a certain beggar named Lazarus, which was laid at his gate, full of sores, and desiring to be fed with the crumbs which fell from the rich man's table: moreover the dogs came and licked his sores. And it came to pass that the beggar died, and was carried by the angels into Abraham's bosom: the rich man also died, and was buried; and in hell he lifted up his eyes, being in torments, and seeth Abraham afar off, and Lazarus in his bosom. And he cried and said, Father Abraham, have mercy on me, and send Lazarus, that he may dip the tip of his finger in water, and cool my tongue; for I am tormented in this flame. But Abraham said, Son, remember that thou in thy lifetime receivedst thy good things, and likewise Lazarus evil things: but now he is comforted, and thou art tormented. And beside all this, between us and you there is a great gulf fixed: so that they which would pass from hence to you cannot; neither can they pass to us that would come from thence. Then he said, I pray thee therefore, father, that thou wouldest send him to my father's house: for I have five brethren; that he may testify unto them, lest they also come into this place of torment. Abraham saith unto him, They have Moses and the prophets; let them hear them. And he said, Nay, father Abraham: but if one went unto them from the dead, they will repent. And he said unto him, If they hear not Moses and the prophets, neither will they be persuaded, though one rose from the dead.

The Epistle, 1 John iv. 7-21. (*Eph.* ii. 19-22.)

Beloved, let us love one another: for love is of God: and every one that loveth is born of God, and knoweth God. He that loveth not, knoweth not God; for God is love. In this was manifested the love of God toward us, because that God sent his only begotten Son into the world, that we might live through him. Herein is love, not that we loved God, but that he loved us, and sent his Son to be the propitiation for our sins. Beloved, if God so loved us we ought also to love one another. No man hath seen God at any time. If we love one another, God dwelleth in us, and his love is perfected in us. Hereby know we that we dwell in him, and he in us, because he hath given us of his Spirit. And we have seen and do testify, that the Father sent the Son to be the Saviour of the world. Whosoever shall confess that Jesus is the Son of God, God dwelleth in him, and he in God. And we have known and believed the love that God hath to us. God is love; and he that dwelleth in love dwelleth in God, and God in him. Herein is our love made perfect, that we may have boldness in the day of judgment: because as he is, so are we in this world. There is no fear in love; but perfect love casteth out fear: because fear hath torment. He that feareth, is not made perfect in love. We love him, because he first loved us. If a man say, I love God, and hateth his brother, he is a liar: for he that loveth not his brother whom he hath seen, how can he love God whom he hath not seen? And this commandment have we from him, That he who loveth God love his brother also.

The Collect.

O God, the strength of all them that put their trust in Thee, who hast not appointed us unto wrath, but to obtain salvation by our Lord Jesus Christ; because through the weakness of our mortal nature we can do no good thing without Thee, we beseech Thee to grant us the help of Thy grace, and to breathe into us that divine charity which is the fulfilling of the law; that in keeping Thy commandments we may please Thee both in will and deed, and be counted worthy, after the sufferings of this life, to reign with Christ in heaven: to whom, with Thee and the Holy Ghost, be honor and glory, world without end. *Amen.*

Second Sunday after Trinity

The Gospel, St. Luke xiv. 16-24. (St. Matt. xviii. 11-20.)

Then said he unto him, A certain man made a great supper, and bade many: and sent his servant at supper time to say to them that were bidden, Come; for all things are now ready. And they all with one consent began to make excuse. The first said unto him, I have bought a piece of ground, and I must needs go and see it: I pray thee have me excused. And another said, I have bought five yoke of oxen, and I go to prove them: I pray thee have me excused. And another said, I have married a wife, and therefore I cannot come. So that servant came, and shewed his lord these things. Then the master of the house, being angry, said to his servant, Go out quickly into the streets and lanes of the city, and bring in hither the poor, and the maimed, and the halt, and the blind. And the servant said, Lord, it is done as thou hast commanded, and yet there is room. And the lord said unto the servant, go out into the highways and hedges, and compel them to come in, that my house may be filled. For I say unto you, That none of those men which were bidden shall taste of my supper.

The Epistle, 1 John iii. 13-24. (Eph. iv. 4-16.)

Marvel not, my brethren, if the world hate you. We know that we have passed from death unto life, because we love the brethren. He that loveth not his brother abideth in death. Whosoever hateth his brother is a murderer: and ye know that no murderer hath eternal life abiding in him. Hereby perceive we the love of God, because he laid down his life for us: and we ought to lay down our lives for the brethren. But whoso hath this world's good, and seeth his brother have need and shutteth up his bowels of compassion from him, how dwelleth the love of God in him? My little children, let us not love in word, neither in tongue; but in deed and in truth. and hereby we know that we are of the truth, and shall assure our hearts before him. For if our heart condemn us, God is greater than our heart, and knoweth all things. Beloved, if our heart condemn us not, then have we confidence toward God. And whatsoever we ask, we receive of him, because we keep his commandments, and do those things that are pleasing in his sight. And this is his commandment, That we should believe on the name of his Son Jesus Christ, and love one another, as he gave us commandment. And he that keepeth his commandments dwelleth in him, and he in him. And hereby we know that he abideth in us, by the Spirit which he hath given us.

The Collect.

ALMIGHTY and everlasting God, the source of all life and joy, who, by the glad sound of the gospel, hast called us to have part in Thy kingdom and glory; shine powerfully into our hearts, we beseech Thee, by Thy word and Spirit, and draw us with the cords of Thy constraining grace; that we may heartily choose that good part which shall not be taken away from us, and give all diligence to make our calling and election sure; through Jesus Christ our Lord. *Amen.*

Third Sunday after Trinity.

The Gospel, St. Luke xv. 1–10. (*St.* John xv. 1–14.)

Then drew near unto him all the publicans and sinners for to hear him. And the Pharisees and Scribes murmured, saying, This man receiveth sinners, and eateth with them.

THIRD SUNDAY AFTER TRINITY. 117

And he spake this parable unto them, saying, What man of you, having an hundred sheep, if he lose one of them, doth not leave the ninety and nine in the wilderness, and go after that which is lost, until he find it? And when he hath found it, he layeth it on his shoulders, rejoicing. And when he cometh home, he calleth together his friends and neighbours, saying unto them, Rejoice with me; for I have found my sheep which was lost. I say unto you, that likewise joy shall be in heaven over one sinner that repenteth, more than over ninety and nine just persons which need no repentance. Either what woman having ten pieces of silver, if she lose one piece, doth not light a candle, and sweep the house, and seek diligently till she find it? And when she hath found it, she calleth her friends and her neighbours together, saying, Rejoice with me; for I have found the piece which I had lost. Likewise, I say unto you, There is joy in the presence of the angels of God over one sinner that repenteth.

The Epistle, 1 *Pet.* v. 5-11. (1 *Cor.* xii. 12-27.)

Likewise, ye younger, submit yourselves unto the elder. Yea, all of you be subject one to another, and be clothed with humility: for God resisteth the proud, and giveth grace to the humble. Humble yourselves therefore under the mighty hand of God, that he may exalt you in due time: casting all your care upon him; for he careth for you. Be sober, be vigilant; because your adversary the devil, as a roaring lion, walketh about, seeking whom he may devour: whom resist steadfast in the faith, knowing that the same afflictions are accomplished in your brethren that are in the world. But the God of all grace, who hath called us unto his eternal glory by Christ Jesus, after that ye have suffered awhile, make you perfect, stablish, strengthen, settle you. To him be glory and dominion for ever and ever. Amen.

The Collect.

O God, the Lord, strong to deliver and mighty to save, who hast been the refuge and dwelling-place of Thy people in all generations; perfect and fulfill in us, we beseech Thee, the work of Thy converting grace, and be pleased to confirm us in every good purpose and deed; that having been called into the way of righteousness, we may have power to continue steadfastly in the same until the day of Jesus Christ: to whom, with Thee and the Holy Ghost, be all honor and praise, world without end. *Amen.*

Fourth Sunday after Trinity.

The Gospel, St. Luke vi. 36–42. (*St. John* iii. 1–8.)

Be ye therefore merciful, as your Father also is merciful. Judge not, and ye shall not be judged: condemn not, and ye shall not be condemned: forgive, and ye shall be forgiven: give, and it shall be given unto you, good measure, pressed down, and shaken together, and running over, shall men give into your bosom. For with the same measure that ye mete withal it shall be measured to you again. And he spake a parable unto them, Can the blind lead the blind? shall they not both fall into the ditch? The disciple is not above his master: but every one that is perfect shall be as his master. And why beholdest thou the mote that is in thy brother's eye, but perceivest not the beam that is in thine own eye? Either how canst thou say to thy brother, Brother, let me pull out the mote that is in thine eye, when thou thyself beholdest not the beam that is in thine own eye? Thou hypocrite, cast out first the beam out of thine own eye, and then shalt thou see clearly to pull out the mote that is in thy brother's eye.

FIFTH SUNDAY AFTER TRINITY.

The Epistle, Rom. viii. 18–23. (*Gal.* iii. 26–29.)

For I reckon that the sufferings of this present time are not worthy to be compared with the glory which shall be revealed in us. For the earnest expectation of the creature waiteth for the manifestation of the sons of God. For the creature was made subject to vanity, not willingly, but by reason of him who hath subjected the same in hope, because the creature itself also shall be delivered from the bondage of corruption into the glorious liberty of the children of God. For we know that the whole creation groaneth and travaileth in pain together until now. And not only they, but ourselves also, which have the first fruits of the Spirit, even we ourselves groan within ourselves, waiting for the adoption, to wit, the redemption of our body.

The Collect.

O God, whose favor is life, and in whose presence there is fulness of peace and joy; vouchsafe unto us, we beseech Thee, such an abiding sense of the reality and glory of those things which Thou hast prepared for them that love Thee, as may serve to raise us above the vanity of this present world, both in its pleasures and in its necessary trials and pains; so that under Thy guidance and help all things here shall work together for our everlasting salvation; through Jesus Christ our Lord. *Amen.*

Fifth Sunday after Trinity.

The Gospel, St. Luke v. 1–11. (*St. John* vi. 47–59.)

And it came to pass, that, as the people pressed upon him to hear the word of God, he stood by the lake of Gennesaret, and saw two ships standing by the lake: but the fishermen were gone out of them, and were washing their nets. And he entered into one of the ships, which was Simon's, and prayed him that he would thrust out a little from the land. And he sat down, and taught the people out of the ship. Now when he had left speaking, he said unto Simon, Launch out into the deep, and let down your nets for a draught. And Simon answering said unto him, Master, we have toiled all the night, and have taken nothing: nevertheless at thy word I will let down the net. And when they had this done, they inclosed a great multitude of fishes: and their net brake. And they beckoned unto their partners, which were in the other ship, that they should come and help them. And they came and filled both the ships, so that they began to sink. When Simon Peter saw it, he fell down at Jesus' knees, saying, Depart from me; for I am a sinful man, O Lord. For he was astonished, and all that were with him, at the draught of the fishes which they had taken: and so was also James, and John, the sons of Zebedee, which were partners with Simon. And Jesus said unto Simon, Fear not; from henceforth thou shalt catch men. And when they had brought their ships to land, they forsook all, and followed him.

The Epistle, 1 Pet. iii. 8–15. (*Acts* ii. 41–47.)

Finally, be ye all of one mind, having compassion one of another, love as brethren, be pitiful, be courteous: not rendering evil for evil, or railing for railing: but contrariwise blessing; knowing that ye are thereunto called, that ye should inherit a blessing. For he that will love life, and see good days, let him refrain his tongue from evil, and his lips that they speak no guile : let him eschew evil, and do good; let him seek peace, and ensue it. For the eyes of the Lord are over the righteous, and his ears are open unto their prayers: but the face of the Lord is against them that do evil. And who is he that will harm you, if ye be followers of that which is good? But and if ye suffer for righteousness' sake, happy are ye: and be not afraid of their terror, neither be troubled; but sanctify the Lord God in your hearts: and be ready always to give an answer to every man that asketh you a reason of the hope that is in you with meekness and fear.

The Collect.

CAUSE Thy Church to arise and shine, O Lord, and let her ministers be clothed with righteousness and salvation; that Thy word which is in their hands may not return unto Thee void, but have free course and be glorified in the world; prospering in the thing whereunto Thou hast sent it, and prevailing mightily to turn men from darkness to light, and from the power of Satan unto God, that they may receive forgiveness of sins, and inheritance among them which are sanctified by faith that is in Christ: to whom, with Thee and the Holy Ghost, be honor and glory, world without end. *Amen.*

Sixth Sunday after Trinity.

The *Gospel, St. Matt.* v. 20–26. (*St Matt.* xi. 25–30.)

For I say unto you, That except your righteousness shall exceed the righteousness of the Scribes and Pharisees, ye shall in no case enter into the kingdom of heaven. Ye have heard that it was said by them of old time, Thou shalt not kill; and whosoever shall kill shall be in danger of the judgment: but I say unto you, That whosoever is angry with his brother without a cause shall be in danger of the judgment: and whosoever shall say to his brother, Raca, shall be in danger of the council: but whosoever shall say, Thou fool, shall be in danger of hell fire. Therefore if thou bring thy gift to the altar, and there rememberest that thy brother hath aught against thee; leave there thy gift before the altar, and go thy way; first be reconciled to thy brother, and then come and offer thy gift. Agree with thine adversary quickly, while thou art in the way with him; lest at any time the adversary deliver thee to the judge, and the judge deliver thee to the officer, and thou be cast into prison. Verily I say unto thee, Thou shalt by no means come out thence, till thou hast paid the uttermost farthing.

The Epistle, Rom. vi. 3–11. (*Rom.* iii. 19–28.)

Know ye not, that so many of us as were baptized into Jesus Christ were baptized into his death? Therefore we are buried with him by baptism into death: that like as Christ was raised up from the dead by the glory of the Father, even so we also should walk in newness of life. For if we have been planted together in the likeness of his death, we shall be also in the likeness of his resurrection: knowing this, that our old man is crucified with him, that the body of sin might be destroyed, that henceforth we should not serve sin. For he that is dead is freed from sin. Now if we be dead with Christ, we believe that we shall also live with him: knowing that Christ being raised from the dead dieth no more: death hath no more dominion over him. For in that he died, he died unto sin once: but in that he liveth, he liveth unto God. Likewise reckon ye also yourselves to be dead indeed unto sin, but alive unto God through Jesus Christ our Lord.

The Collect.

ALMIGHTY and everlasting God, through whose mercy we are saved by the washing of regeneration and renewing of the Holy Ghost; let this grace reign in us, we beseech Thee, as the power of a new heavenly life; whereby denying ungodliness and worldly lusts, we may live soberly, righteously, and godly, in this present world; looking for the glorious appearing of our Saviour Jesus Christ, who gave Himself for us, that He might redeem us from all iniquity, and purify unto Himself a peculiar people, zealous of good works: to whom, with Thee and the Holy Ghost, be honor and glory, world without end. *Amen.*

Seventh Sunday after Trinity.

The Gospel, St. *Mark* viii. 1–9. (*St. Luke* xv. 11–32.)

In those days the multitude being very great, and having nothing to eat, Jesus called his disciples unto him, and saith unto them, I have compassion on the multitude, because they have now been with me three days, and have nothing to eat: and if I send them away fasting to their own houses, they will faint by the way: for divers of them came from far. And his disciples answered him, From whence can a man satisfy these men with bread here in the wilderness? And he asked them, How many loaves have ye? And they said, Seven. And he commanded the people to sit down on the ground: and he took the seven loaves, and gave thanks, and brake, and gave to his disciples to set before them; and they did set them before the people. And they had a few small fishes: and he blessed, and commanded to set them also before them. So they did eat, and were filled: and they took up of the broken meat that was left seven baskets. And they that had eaten were about four thousand: and he sent them away.

The Epistle, Rom. vi. 19–23. (*Acts* ix. 1–9.)

I speak after the manner of men because of the infirmity

of your flesh: for as ye have yielded your members servants to uncleanness and to iniquity unto iniquity; even so now yield your members servants to righteousness unto holiness. For when ye were the servants of sin, ye were free from righteousness. What fruit had ye then in those things whereof ye are now ashamed? for the end of those things is death. But now being made free from sin, and become servants to God, ye have your fruit unto holiness, and the end everlasting life. For the wages of sin is death; but the gift of God is eternal life through Jesus Christ our Lord.

The Collect.

ALMIGHTY God, the Former of our bodies and Father of our spirits, in whom we live, move and have our being; shed abroad Thy love in our hearts, we beseech Thee, and cause the comfort of Thy heavenly grace to abound in us, as the earnest and pledge of joys to come; that casting away all anxious thought for the transitory things of this world, we may seek first Thy kingdom and righteousness, and labor only for that meat which endureth unto everlasting life; through Jesus Christ our Lord. *Amen.*

Eighth Sunday after Trinity.

The Gospel, St. Matt. vii. 15–21. (*St. Luke* xviii. 9–14.)

Beware of false prophets, which come to you in sheep's clothing, but inwardly they are ravening wolves. Ye shall know them by their fruits. Do men gather grapes of thorns, or figs of thistles? Even so every good tree bringeth forth good fruit; but a corrupt tree bringeth forth evil fruit. A good tree cannot bring forth evil fruit, neither can a cor-

EIGHTH SUNDAY AFTER TRINITY.

rupt tree bring forth good fruit. Every tree that bringeth not forth good fruit is hewn down, and cast into the fire. Wherefore by their fruits ye shall know them. Not every one that saith unto me, Lord, Lord, shall enter into the kingdom of heaven; but he that doeth the will of my Father which is in heaven.

The Epistle, Rom. viii. 12–17. (*Phil.* iii. 8–11.)

Therefore, brethren, we are debtors, not to the flesh, to live after the flesh. For if ye live after the flesh, ye shall die: but if ye through the Spirit do mortify the deeds of the body, ye shall live. For as many as are led by the Spirit of God, they are the sons of God. For ye have not received the spirit of bondage again to fear; but ye have received the Spirit of adoption, whereby we cry, Abba, Father. The Spirit itself beareth witness with our spirit, that we are the children of God: and if children, then heirs: heirs of God, and joint heirs with Christ; if so be that we suffer with him, that we may be also glorified together.

The Collect.

O GOD, who hast given unto us exceeding great and precious promises, that by them we might be partakers of the divine nature, having escaped the corruption that is in the world through lust; enable us, we beseech Thee, with all diligence to add to our faith virtue, knowledge, temperance, patience, godliness, brotherly kindness and charity; that, these things being in us, and abounding, we may neither be barren nor unfruitful in the knowledge of our Lord Jesus Christ: to whom, with Thee and the Holy Ghost, be honor and glory, world without end, *Amen.*

Ninth Sunday after Trinity.

The Gospel, St. Luke xvi. 1-9. (*St. Matt.* viii. 5-13.)

And he said also unto his disciples, There was a certain rich man which had a steward; and the same was accused unto him that he had wasted his goods. And he called him, and said unto him, How is it that I hear this of thee? give an account of thy stewardship; for thou mayest be no longer steward. Then the steward said within himself, What shall I do? for my lord taketh away from me the stewardship: I cannot dig; to beg I am ashamed. I am resolved what to do, that, when I am put out of the stewardship, they may receive me into their houses. So he called every one of his lord's debtors unto him, and said unto the first, How much owest thou unto my lord? And he said, An hundred measures of oil. And he said unto him, Take thy bill, and sit down quickly, and write fifty. Then said he to another, And how much owest thou? And he said, An hundred measures of wheat. And he said unto him, Take thy bill, and write fourscore. And the lord commended the unjust steward, because he had done wisely: for the children of this world are in their generation wiser than the children of light. And I say unto you, Make to yourselves friends of the mammon of unrighteousness; that, when ye fail, they may receive you into everlasting habitations.

The Epistle, 1 Cor. x. 1-13. (1 *Pet.* i. 3-9.)

Moreover, brethren, I would not that ye should be ignorant, how that all our fathers were under the cloud, and all passed through the sea; and were all baptized unto Moses in the cloud and in the sea; and did all eat the same spiritual meat; and did all drink the same spiritual drink: for they drank of that spiritual Rock that followed them: and that

Rock was Christ. But with many of them God was not well pleased: for they were overthrown in the wilderness. Now these things were our examples, to the intent we should not lust after evil things, as they also lusted. Neither be ye idolaters, as were some of them; as it is written, The people sat down to eat and drink, and rose up to play. Neither let us commit fornication, as some of them committed, and fell in one day three and twenty thousand. Neither let us tempt Christ, as some of them also tempted, and were destroyed of serpents. Neither murmur ye, as some of them also murmured, and were destroyed of the destroyer. Now all these things happened unto them for ensamples: and they are written for our admonition, upon whom the ends of the world are come. Wherefore let him that thinketh he standeth take heed lest he fall. There hath no temptation taken you, but such as is common to man: but God is faithful, who will not suffer you to be tempted above that ye are able; but will with the temptation also make a way to escape, that ye may be able to bear it.

The Collect.

O LORD GOD, our Sun, by whom light is sown for the righteous, and gladness for the upright in heart; illuminate our minds, we beseech Thee, by Thy heavenly grace, and fill them with the pure wisdom which cometh from above; that we may walk before Thee in simplicity and godly sincerity all our days, not taking counsel of the world or of the flesh, but aiming and endeavoring in all things only to know and do Thy will; through Jesus Christ our Lord. Amen.

Tenth Sunday after Trinity,

Luke ... (handwritten)

The Gospel, St. Luke xix. 41–47. (*St. Matt.* xvii. 14–21.)

And when he was come near, he beheld the city, and wept over it, saying, If thou hadst known, even thou, at least in this thy day, the things which belong unto thy peace! but now they are hid from thine eyes. For the day shall come upon thee, that thine enemies shall cast a trench about thee, and compass thee round, and keep thee in on every side, and shall lay thee even with the ground, and thy children within thee; and they shall not leave in thee one stone upon another; because thou knewest not the time of thy visitation. And he went into the temple, and began to cast out them that sold therein, and them that bought; saying unto them, It is written, My house is a house of prayer: but ye have made it a den of thieves. And he taught daily in the temple. But the chief priests and the scribes and the chief of the people sought to destroy him.

The Epistle, 1 Cor. xii. 1–11. (*Heb.* xi. 32—xii. 2.)

Now concerning spiritual gifts, brethren, I would not have you ignorant. Ye know that ye were Gentiles, carried away unto these dumb idols, even as ye were led. Wherefore I give you to understand, that no man speaking by the Spirit of God calleth Jesus accursed: and that no man can say that Jesus is the Lord, but by the Holy Ghost. Now there are diversities of gifts, but the same Spirit. And there are differences of administrations, but the same Lord. And there are diversities of operations, but it is the same God which worketh all in all. But the manifestation of the Spirit is given to every man to profit withal. For to one is given by the Spirit the word of wisdom; to another the word of knowledge by the same Spirit; to another faith by the same

Spirit; to another the gifts of healing by the same Spirit; to another the working of miracles; to another prophecy; to another discerning of spirits; to another divers kinds of tongues; to another the interpretation of tongues; but all these worketh that one and the selfsame Spirit, dividing to every man severally as he will.

The Collect. ✓

O GOD, the Father of our Lord Jesus Christ, who hast called us to renounce and forsake the world, in the service of our once crucified but now risen and gloriously exalted Saviour; be pleased, we beseech Thee, graciously so to unite our souls to Him by holy sympathy and love, that we may offer ourselves, in fellowship with His cross, a willing sacrifice to Thee on the altar of the gospel, and count it all joy to suffer for his name: who liveth and reigneth, with Thee and the Holy Ghost, ever one God, world without end. *Amen.*

Eleventh Sunday after Trinity.

The Gospel, *St. Luke* xviii. 9–14. (*St. Luke* xii. 32–40.)

And he spake this parable unto certain which trusted in themselves that they were righteous, and despised others: two men went up into the temple to pray; the one a Pharisee, and the other a publican. The Pharisee stood and prayed thus with himself, God, I thank thee, that I am not as other men are, extortioners, unjust, adulterers, or even as this publican. I fast twice in the week, I give tithes of all that I possess. And the publican, standing afar off, would not lift up so much as his eyes unto heaven, but smote upon his breast, saying, God be merciful to me a sinner. I tell you, this man went down to his house justified rather than the other: for every one that exalteth himself shall be abased; and he that humbleth himself shall be exalted.

The Epistle, 1 Cor. xv. 1-11. (*Rom.* viii. 16-26.)

Moreover, brethren, I declare unto you the gospel which I preached unto you, which also ye have received, and wherein ye stand; by which also ye are saved, if ye keep in memory what I preached unto you, unless ye have believed in vain. For I delivered unto you first of all that which I also received, how that Christ died for our sins according to the Scriptures; and that he was buried, and that he rose again the third day according to the Scriptures: and that he was seen of Cephas, then of the twelve: after that, he was seen of above five hundred brethren at once; of whom the greater part remain unto this present, but some are fallen asleep. After that, he was seen of James; then of all the apostles. And last of all he was seen of me also, as of one born out of due time. For I am the least of the apostles, that am not meet to be called an apostle, because I persecuted the church of God. But by the grace of God I am what I am: and his grace which was bestowed upon me was not in vain; but I laboured more abundantly than they all: yet not I, but the grace of God which was with me. Therefore whether it were I or they, so we preach, and so ye believed.

The Collect. ✓

O God, the High and Holy One, who inhabitest eternity, and dwellest with him also who is of a contrite and humble spirit, to revive the spirit of the humble, and to revive the heart of the contrite ones; glorify Thy grace, we beseech Thee, in the midst of our manifold infirmities and sins, and through all temptation hold us up by Thy mighty hand; that the trial of our faith, being much more precious than of gold that perisheth, though it be tried with fire, may be found unto praise, and honor, and glory, at the appearing of Jesus Christ: to whom, with Thee and the Holy Ghost, be honor and glory, world without end. *Amen.*

Twelfth Sunday after Trinity.

The Gospel, St. *Mark* vii. 31–37. (*St. Matt.* xxii. 34–40.)

And again, departing from the coasts of Tyre and Sidon, he came unto the sea of Galilee, through the midst of the coasts of Decapolis. And they bring unto him one that was deaf, and had an impediment in his speech; and they beseech him to put his hand upon him. And he took him aside from the multitude, and put his fingers into his ears, and he spit, and touched his tongue; and looking up to heaven, he sighed, and saith unto him, Ephphatha, that is, Be opened. And straightway his ears were opened, and the string of his tongue was loosed, and he spake plain. And he charged them that they should tell no man: but the more he charged them, so much the more a great deal they published it; and were beyond measure astonished, saying, He hath done all things well: he maketh both the deaf to hear, and the dumb to speak.

The Epistle, 2 *Cor.* iii. 4–11. (*John* iv. 15–21.)

And such trust have we through Christ to God-ward: not that we are sufficient of ourselves to think any thing as of ourselves; but our sufficiency is of God; who also hath made us able ministers of the New Testament; not of the letter, but of the spirit: for the letter killeth, but the spirit giveth life. But if the ministration of death, written and engraven in stones, was glorious, so that the children of Israel could not steadfastly behold the face of Moses for the glory of his countenance; which glory was to be done away: how shall not the ministration of the Spirit be rather glorious? For if the ministration of condemnation be glory, much more doth the ministration of righteousness exceed in glory. For even that which was made glorious had no glory in this respect, by reason of the glory that excelleth. For if that which was done away was glorious, much more that which remaineth is glorious.

The Collect.

O GOD, who didst will Thine Only Begotten Son to learn obedience by the things which He suffered, that being thus made perfect He might become the Author of eternal salvation unto all that obey Him; work in us, we beseech Thee, such inward conformity with His holy patience, as may cause us to have part also in His glorious power; that so, walking not after the flesh but after the Spirit, we may be able to serve Thee all our days in newness of mind and life; through Jesus Christ our Lord. *Amen.*

Thirteenth Sunday after Trinity.

The Gospel, St. Luke x. 23-37.

And he turned him unto his disciples, and said privately, Blessed are the eyes which see the things that ye see: for I tell you, that many prophets and kings have desired to see those things which ye see, and have not seen them; and to hear those things which ye hear, and have not heard them. And, behold, a certain lawyer stood up, and tempted him, saying, Master, what shall I do to inherit eternal life? He said unto him, What is written in the law? how readest thou? And he answering said, Thou shalt love the Lord thy God with all thy heart, and with all thy soul, and with all thy strength,

and with all thy mind; and thy neighbour as thyself. And
he said unto him, Thou hast answered right: this do, and
thou shalt live. But he, willing to justify himself, said unto
Jesus, And who is my neighbour? And Jesus answering
said, A certain man went down from Jerusalem to Jericho,
and fell among thieves, which stripped him of his raiment,
and wounded him, and departed, leaving him half dead.
And by chance there came down a certain priest that way:
and when he saw him, he passed by on the other side. And
likewise a Levite, when he was at the place, came and looked
on him, and passed by on the other side. But a certain
Samaritan, as he journeyed, came where he was: and when
he saw him, he had compassion on him, and went to him,
and bound up his wounds, pouring in oil and wine, and set
him on his own beast, and brought him to an inn, and took
care of him. And on the morrow when he departed, he took
out two pence, and gave them to the host, and said unto him,
Take care of him; and whatsoever thou spendest more, when
I come again, I will repay thee. Which now of these three,
thinkest thou, was neighbour unto him that fell among the
thieves? And he said, He that shewed mercy on him. Then
said Jesus unto him, Go, and do thou likewise.

The Epistle, Gal. iii. 16–22. (1 *Cor.* xiii. 1–13.)

Now to Abraham and his seed were the promises made.
He saith not, And to seeds, as of many; but as of one, And
to thy seed, which is Christ. And this I say, that the covenant, that was confirmed before of God in Christ, the law,
which was four hundred and thirty years after, cannot dis-
annul, that it should make the promise of none effect. For
if the inheritance be of the law, it is no more of promise:
but God gave it to Abraham by promise. Wherefore then
serveth the law? It was added because of transgressions,
till the seed should come to whom the promise was made;
and it was ordained by angels in the hand of a mediator.
Now a mediator is not a mediator of one, but God is one.

Is the law then against the promises of God? God forbid: for if there had been a law given which could have given life, verily righteousness should have been by the law. But the Scripture hath concluded all under sin, that the promise by faith of Jesus Christ might be given to them that believe.

The Collect.

ALMIGHTY and everlasting God, whose faithfulness reacheth unto the clouds, and whose mercy endureth for ever; be pleased to confirm and fulfil in us, we humbly beseech Thee, the covenant of Thy grace, made sure from the beginning of the world in Christ Jesus our Lord; that we may be found in Him, not having our own righteousness which is of the law, but that which is through the faith of Christ, even the righteousness of God which is by faith in Jesus Christ unto all and upon all them that believe: to whom, with Thee and the Holy Ghost, be honor and glory, world without end. *Amen.*

Fourteenth Sunday after Trinity.

The Gospel, St. *Luke* xvii. 11-19. (*St. Matt.* v. 43-48.)

And it came to pass, as he went to Jerusalem, that he passed through the midst of Samaria and Galilee. And as he entered into a certain village, there met him ten men that were lepers, which stood afar off: and they lifted up their voices, and said, Jesus, Master, have mercy on us. And when he saw them, he said unto them, Go shew yourselves unto the priests. And it came to pass, that, as they went, they were cleansed. And one of them, when he saw that he was healed, turned back, and with a loud voice glorified God, and fell down on his face at his feet, giving him thanks: and he was a Samaritan. And Jesus answering said, Were there not ten cleansed? but where are the nine? There are not found that returned to give glory to God, save this stranger. And he said unto him, Arise, go thy way: thy faith hath made thee whole.

The Epistle, Gal. v. 16-24. (*Rom.* xii. 14-21.)

This I say then, Walk in the Spirit, and ye shall not fulfil the lust of the flesh. For the flesh lusteth against the Spirit, and the Spirit against the flesh: and these are contrary the one to the other: so that ye cannot do the things that ye would. But if ye be led of the Spirit, ye are not under the law. Now the works of the flesh are manifest, which are these; adultery, fornication, uncleanness, lasciviousness, idolatry, witchcraft, hatred, variance, emulations, wrath, strife, seditions, heresies, envyings, murders, drunkenness, revellings, and such like: of the which I tell you before, as I have also told you in time past, that they which do such things shall not inherit the kingdom of God. But the fruit of the Spirit is love, joy, peace, long suffering, gentleness, goodness, faith, meekness, temperance: against such there is no law. And they that are Christ's have crucified the flesh, with the affections and lusts.

The Collect.

O GOD, who hast delivered us from the power of darkness and translated us into the kingdom of Thy dear Son, in whom we have redemption through His blood, even the forgiveness of sins; enable us by Thy grace, we earnestly beseech Thee, so to walk in the Spirit that we may not fulfil the lusts of the flesh; considering ourselves to be dead henceforth unto sin, but alive unto God through Jesus Christ our Lord: to whom, with Thee and the Holy Ghost, be honor and glory, world without end. *Amen.*

Fifteenth Sunday after Trinity.

The Gospel, St. Matt. vi. 24–34. (*St. Matt.* v. 13–20.)

No man can serve two masters: for either he will hate the one, and love the other; or else he will hold to the one, and despise the other. Ye cannot serve God and mammon. Therefore I say unto you, Take no thought for your life, what ye shall eat, or what ye shall drink; nor yet for your body, what ye shall put on. Is not the life more than meat, and the body than raiment? Behold the fowls of the air: for they sow not, neither do they reap, nor gather into barns; yet your heavenly Father feedeth them. Are ye not much better than they? Which of you by taking thought can add one cubit unto his stature? And why take ye thought for raiment? Consider the lilies of the field, how they grow; they toil not, neither do they spin: and yet I say unto you, That even Solomon in all his glory was not arrayed like one of these. Wherefore, if God so clothe the grass of the field, which to-day is, and to-morrow is cast into the oven, shall he not much more clothe you, O ye of little faith? Therefore take no thought, saying, What shall we eat? or, What shall we drink? or, Wherewithal shall we be clothed? (For after all these things do the Gentiles seek:) for your heavenly Father knoweth that ye have need of all these things. But seek ye first the kingdom of God, and his righteousness; and all these things shall be added unto you. Take therefore no thought for the morrow: for the morrow shall take thought for the things of itself. Sufficient unto the day is the evil thereof.

The Epistle, Gal. v. 25–vi–10. - (*James* ii. 14–26.)

If we live in the Spirit, let us also walk in the Spirit. Let us not be desirous of vain-glory, provoking one another, envying one another. Brethren, if a man be overtaken in a fault, ye which are spiritual, restore such an one in the spirit of meekness; considering thyself, lest thou also be tempted. Bear ye one another's burdens, and so fulfil the law of Christ. For if a man think himself to be something, when he is nothing, he deceiveth himself. But let every man prove his own work, and then shall he have rejoicing in himself alone, and not in another. For every man shall bear his own burden. Let him that is taught in the word communicate unto him that teacheth in all good things. Be not deceived; God is not mocked: for whatsoever a man soweth, that shall he also reap. For he that soweth to his flesh shall of the flesh reap corruption; but he that soweth to the Spirit shall of the Spirit reap life everlasting. And let us not be weary in well doing: for in due season we shall reap, if we faint not. As we have therefore opportunity, let us do good unto all men, especially unto them who are of the household of faith.

The Collect.

O GOD, our Father in heaven, in whose presence there is fulness of joy, and at whose right hand there are pleasures for evermore; mercifully fix our hearts on things above, and free them from all undue care and thought for the things of the present transitory world; that whilst we are here in the body, we may sow, not to the flesh, but to the Spirit, and in the end reap life everlasting; through Jesus Christ our Lord. *Amen.*

Sixteenth Sunday after Trinity.

The Gospel, St. Luke. vii. 11–17. (St. Mark xii. 41–44.)

And it came to pass the day after, that he went into a city called Nain; and many of his disciples went with him, and much people. Now when he came nigh to the gate of the city, behold, there was a dead man carried out, the only son of his mother, and she was a widow: and much people of the city was with her. And when the Lord saw her, he had compassion on her, and said unto her, Weep not. And he came and touched the bier: and they that bare him stood still. And he said, Young man, I say unto thee, Arise. And he that was dead sat up, and began to speak. And he delivered him to his mother. And there came a fear on all: and they glorified God, saying, That a great prophet is risen up among us; and, That God hath visited his people. And this rumour of him went forth throughout all Judea, and throughout all the region round about.

The Epistle, Ephes. iii. 13-21. (2 *Cor.* ix. 5-15.)

Wherefore I desire that ye faint not at my tribulations for you, which is your glory. For this cause I bow my knees unto the Father of our Lord Jesus Christ, of whom the whole family in heaven and earth is named, that he would grant you, according to the riches of his glory, to be strengthened with might by his Spirit in the inner man; that Christ may dwell in your hearts by faith; that ye, being rooted and grounded in love, may be able to comprehend with all saints what is the breadth, and length, and depth, and height; and to know the love of Christ, which passeth knowledge, that ye might be filled with all the fulness of God. Now unto him that is able to do exceeding abundantly above all that we ask or think, according to the power that worketh in us, unto him be glory in the church by Christ Jesus throughout all ages, world without end. Amen.

The Collect.

O GOD, the Father of our Lord Jesus Christ, of whom the whole family in heaven and earth is named; we beseech Thee, according to the riches of Thy glory to strengthen us with might by Thy Spirit

in the inner man, that Christ may dwell in our hearts
by faith; so that, being rooted and grounded in love,
we may be able to comprehend with all saints what
is the breadth, and length, and depth, and height,
and to know the love of Christ which passeth knowledge: to whom with Thee and the Holy Ghost be
honor and glory, world without end. *Amen.*

Seventeenth Sunday after Trinity.

The Gospel, St. Luke xiv. 1–11. (*St. Mark* x. 35–45.)

And it came to pass, as he went into the house of one of
the chief Pharisees to eat bread on the sabbath day, that they
watched him. And, behold, there was a certain man before
him which had the dropsy. And Jesus answering spake unto
the lawyers and Pharisees, saying, Is it lawful to heal on the
Sabbath day? And they held their peace. And he took him,
and healed him, and let him go; and answered them, saying,
Which of you shall have an ass or an ox fallen into a pit,
and will not straightway pull him out on the Sabbath day?
And they could not answer him again to these things. And
he put forth a parable to those which were bidden, when he
marked how they chose out the chief rooms; saying unto
them, When thou art bidden of any man to a wedding, sit
not down in the highest room; lest a more honourable man
than thou be bidden of him; and he that bade thee and him
come and say to thee, Give this man place; and thou begin
with shame to take the lowest room. But when thou art
bidden, go and sit down in the lowest room; that when he
that bade thee cometh, he may say unto thee, Friend, go up
higher: then shalt thou have worship in the presence of them
that sit at meat with thee. For whosoever exalteth himself
shall be abased; and he that humbleth himself shall be exalted.

The Epistle, Eph. iv. 1-6. (*Phil.* ii. 1-5.)

I therefore, the prisoner of the Lord, beseech you that ye walk worthy of the vocation wherewith ye are called, with all lowliness and meekness, with long suffering, forbearing one another in love; endeavouring to keep the unity of the Spirit in the bond of peace. There is one body, and one Spirit, even as ye are called in one hope of your calling; one Lord, one faith, one baptism, one God and Father of all, who is above all, and through all, and in you all.

The Collect.

ALMIGHTY and everlasting God, who didst send Thy Son into the world, not to be ministered unto, but to minister, and to give his life a ransom for many; dispose and assist us by Thy grace, most heartily we beseech Thee, to follow the example of His great humility and heavenly-minded love; that with all lowliness and meekness, and patient continuance in good works, we may adorn the Gospel of God our Saviour, and possess in our souls that true peace which the world can neither give nor take away; through Jesus Christ our Lord. *Amen.*

Eighteenth Sunday after Trinity.

The Gospel, St. Matt. xxii. 34-46. (*St. Luke* ix. 18-26.)

But when the Pharisees had heard that he had put the Sadducees to silence, they were gathered together. Then one of them, which was a lawyer, asked him a question, tempting him, and saying, Master, which is the great commandment in the law? Jesus said unto him, Thou shalt love the Lord thy God with all thy heart, and with all thy soul, and with all thy mind. This is the first and great commandment. And the second is like unto it, Thou shalt love thy neighbour as thyself. On these two commandments hang all the law and the prophets. While the Pharisees were gathered together, Jesus asked them, saying, What think ye of Christ? whose son is he? They say unto him, The son of David. He saith unto them, How then doth David in spirit call him Lord, saying, The Lord said unto my Lord, Sit thou on my right hand, till I make thine enemies thy footstool? If David then call him Lord, how is he his son? And no man was able to answer him a word, neither durst any man from that day forth ask him any more questions.

The Epistle, 1 *Cor.* i. 4–9. (2 *Cor.* iv. 8–18.)

I thank my God always on your behalf, for the grace of God which is given you by Jesus Christ; that in every thing ye are enriched by him, in all utterance, and in all knowledge; even as the testimony of Christ was confirmed in you: so that ye come behind in no gift; waiting for the coming of our Lord Jesus Christ: who shall also confirm you unto the end, that ye may be blameless in the day of our Lord Jesus Christ. God is faithful, by whom ye were called unto the fellowship of his Son Jesus Christ our Lord.

The Collect. ✓

ALMIGHTY GOD, our heavenly Father, who hast given unto us all things that pertain unto life and godliness through the glorious revelation of the Gospel; cause Thy word to dwell in us richly, we beseech Thee, and fill us with the knowledge of Thy will in all wisdom and spiritual understanding, that we may walk worthy of the Lord unto all pleasing, being fruitful in every good work, and increasing in the knowledge of God; through Jesus Christ our Lord. *Amen.*

Nineteenth Sunday after Trinity.

The Gospel, St. Matt. ix. 1-8. (*St. Matt.* v. 3-12.)

And he entered into a ship, and passed over, and came into his own city. And, behold, they brought to him a man sick of the palsy, lying on a bed: and Jesus seeing their faith said unto the sick of the palsy; Son, be of good cheer; thy sins be forgiven thee. And, behold, certain of the scribes said within themselves, This man blasphemeth. And Jesus knowing their thoughts said, Wherefore think ye evil in your hearts? For whether is easier, to say, Thy sins be forgiven thee; or to say, Arise, and walk? But that ye may know that the Son of man hath power on earth to forgive sins, (then saith he to the sick of the palsy,) Arise, take up thy bed, and go into thine house. And he arose, and departed to his house. But when the multitudes saw it, they marvelled, and glorified God, which had given such power unto men.

The Epistle, Eph. iv. 17-32. (2 *Peter* i. 1-11.)

This I say therefore, and testify in the Lord, that ye henceforth walk not as other Gentiles walk, in the vanity of their mind, having the understanding darkened, being alienated from the life of God through the ignorance that is in them, because of the blindness of their heart: who being past feeling have given themselves over unto lasciviousness, to work all uncleanness with greediness. But ye have not so learned Christ; if so be that ye have heard him, and have been taught by him, as the truth is in Jesus: that ye put off concerning the former conversation the old man, which is corrupt according to the deceitful lusts; and be renewed in the spirit of your mind; and that ye put on the new man, which after God is created in righteousness and true holiness. Wherefore putting away lying, speak every man truth with his neighbor: for we are members one of another. Be ye angry, and sin not: let not the sun go down upon your wrath:

neither give place to the devil. Let him that stole steal no more: but rather let him labour, working with his hands the thing which is good, that he may have to give to him that needeth. Let no corrupt communication proceed out of your mouth, but that which is good to the use of edifying, that it may minister grace unto the hearers. And grieve not the Holy Spirit of God, whereby ye are sealed unto the day of redemption. Let all bitterness, and wrath, and anger, and clamour, and evil speaking, be put away from you, with all malice: and be ye kind one to another, tender-hearted, forgiving one another, even as God for Christ's sake hath forgiven you.

The Collect.

O LORD, our Maker and Redeemer, the Holy One of Israel, who hast stretched forth the heavens, and laid the foundations of the earth; be pleased graciously to confirm and carry forward Thy glorious work of salvation in our hearts, causing old things to pass away and all things to become new; that looking always above and beyond this world, we may have our conversation in heaven, from whence also we look for the Saviour, the Lord Jesus Christ: who liveth and reigneth with Thee and the Holy Ghost, ever one God, world without end. *Amen.*

Twentieth Sunday after Trinity.

The Gospel, St. Matt. xxii. 1-11. (*St. Mark* xiii. 32-37.)

And Jesus answered and spake unto them again by parables, and said, The kingdom of heaven is like unto a certain king, which made a marriage for his son, and sent forth his servants to call them that were bidden to the wedding: and they would not come. Again, he sent forth other servants, saying, Tell them which are bidden, Behold, I have prepared my dinner: my oxen and my fatlings are killed, and all things are ready: come unto the marriage. But they made light of it, and went their ways, one to his farm, another to his merchandise: and the remnant took his servants, and entreated them spitefully, and slew them. But when the king heard thereof, he was wroth: and he sent forth his armies, and destroyed those murderers, and burned up their city. Then saith he to his servants, The wedding is ready, but they which were bidden were not worthy. Go ye therefore into the highways, and as many as ye shall find, bid to the marriage. So those servants went out into the highways, and gathered together all as many as they found, both bad and good: and the wedding was furnished with guests. And when the king came in to see the guests, he saw there a man which had not on a wedding garment: and he saith unto him, Friend, how camest thou in hither not having a wedding garment? And he was speechless. Then said the king to the servants, Bind him hand and foot, and take him away, and cast him into outer darkness; there shall be weeping and gnashing of teeth. For many are called, but few are chosen.

The Epistle, Eph. v. 15–21. (*Heb.* x. 32–39.)

See then that ye walk circumspectly, not as fools, but as wise, redeeming the time, because the days are evil. Wherefore be ye not unwise, but understanding what the will of the Lord is. And be not drunk with wine, wherein is excess; but be filled with the Spirit; speaking to yourselves in psalms and hymns and spiritual songs, singing and making melody in your heart to the Lord; giving thanks always for all things unto God and the Father in the name of our Lord Jesus Christ; submitting yourselves one to another in the fear of God.

The Collect.

O God, the Father everlasting, whom the glorious hosts of heaven obey, and in whose presence patriarchs, prophets, apostles, martyrs, with all the spirits of the just made perfect, continually do live; fix the eye of our faith, we beseech Thee, with clear and full vision, on the great cloud of witnesses with which we are thus compassed about in the heavenly world; that laying aside every weight, and the sin which doth so easily beset us, we may run with patience the race that is set before us, and obtain at last the crown of everlasting life; through Jesus Christ our Lord. *Amen*

Twenty-first Sunday after Trinity.

The Gospel, St. John iv. 46–54. (*St. Luke* xvi. 19–31.)

So Jesus came again into Cana of Galilee, where he made the water wine. And there was a certain nobleman, whose son was sick at Capernaum. When he heard that Jesus was come out of Judea into Galilee, he went unto him, and besought him that he would come down, and heal his son: for he was at the point of death. Then said Jesus unto him, Except ye see signs and wonders, ye will not believe. The nobleman saith unto him, Sir, come down ere my child die. Jesus saith unto him, Go thy way; thy son liveth. And the man believed the word that Jesus had spoken unto him, and he went his way. And as he was now going down, his servants met him, and told him, saying, Thy son liveth. Then inquired he of them the hour when he began to amend. And they said unto him, Yesterday at the seventh hour the fever left him. So the father knew that it was at the same hour in the which Jesus said unto him, Thy son liveth: and himself believed, and his whole house. This is again the second miracle that Jesus did, when he was come out of Judea into Galilee.

The Epistle, Eph. vi. 10–20. (*Rom.* v. 12-21.)

Finally, my brethren, be strong in the Lord, and in the power of his might. Put on the whole armour of God, that ye may be able to stand against the wiles of the devil. For we wrestle not against flesh and blood, but against principalities, against powers, against the rulers of the darkness of this world, against spiritual wickedness in high places. Wherefore take unto you the whole armour of God, that ye may be able to withstand in the evil day, and having done all, to stand. Stand therefore, having your loins girt about with truth, and having on the breastplate of righteousness; and your feet shod with the preparation of the gospel of peace; above all, taking the shield of faith, wherewith ye shall be able to quench all the fiery darts of the wicked. And take the helmet of salvation, and the sword of the Spirit, which is the word of God: praying always with all prayer and supplication in the Spirit, and watching thereunto with all perseverance and supplication for all saints; and for me, that utterance may be given unto me, that I may open my mouth boldly, to make known the mystery of the gospel, for which I am an ambassador in bonds: that therein I may speak boldly, as I ought to speak.

The Collect.

ALMIGHTY and most merciful God, whose name is a strong tower, into which the righteous runneth and is safe; lift up the standard of Thy Spirit, we beseech Thee, against the power of the enemy coming in upon us like a flood, and clothe us with the full armor of righteousness on the right hand and on the left; that we may be able to fight manfully the good fight of faith, and so finish our course with joy, in the great day when Christ, the righteous Judge, shall appear: who liveth and reigneth with Thee, in the unity of the Holy Ghost, ever one God, world without end. *Amen.*

Twenty-Second Sunday after Trinity.

The Gospel, St. Matt. xviii. 21–35. (*St. John* xi. 19–27.)

Then came Peter to him, and said, Lord, how oft shall my brother sin against me, and I forgive him? till seven times? Jesus saith unto him, I say not unto thee, Until seven times: but, Until seventy times seven. Therefore is the kingdom of heaven likened unto a certain king, which would take account of his servants. And when he had begun to reckon, one was brought unto him, which owed him ten thousand talents. But forasmuch as he had not to pay, his lord commanded him to be sold, and his wife, and children, and all that he had, and payment to be made. The servant therefore fell down, and worshipped him, saying, Lord, have patience with me, and I will pay thee all. Then the lord of that servant was moved with compassion, and loosed him, and forgave him the debt. But the same servant went out, and found one of his fellow servants, which owed him an hundred pence: and he laid hands on him, and took him by the throat, saying, Pay me that thou owest. And his fellow servant fell down at his feet, and besought him, saying, Have patience with me, and I will pay thee all. And he would not: but went and cast him into prison, till he should pay the debt. So when his fellow servants saw what was done, they were very sorry, and came and told unto their lord all that was done. Then his lord, after that he had called him, said unto him, O thou wicked servant, I forgave thee all that debt, because thou desiredst me: shouldest not thou also have had compassion on thy fellow servant, even as I had pity on thee? And his lord was wroth, and delivered him to the tormentors, till he should pay all that was due unto him. So likewise shall my heavenly Father do also unto you, if ye from your hearts forgive not every one his brother their trespasses.

The Epistle, Phil. i. 3-11. (1 *Cor.* xv. 35-50.)

I thank my God upon every remembrance of you, always in every prayer of mine for you all making request with joy, for your fellowship in the gospel from the first day until now; being confident of this very thing, that he which hath begun a good work in you will perform it until the day of Jesus Christ: even as it is meet for me to think this of you all, because I have you in my heart; inasmuch as both in my bonds, and in the defence and confirmation òf the gospel, ye all are partakers of my grace. For God is my record, how greatly I long after you all in the bowels of Jesus Christ. And this I pray, that your love may abound yet more and more in knowledge and in all judgment; that ye may approve things that are excellent; that ye may be sincere and without offence till the day of Christ; being filled with the fruits of righteousness, which are by Jesus Christ, unto the glory and praise of God.

The Collect.

O GOD, by whose wise and righteous order the whole creation groaneth and travaileth in pain together until now, as having been made subject to vanity by reason of sin; graciously help the infirmities of Thy people, we humbly beseech Thee, and raise them up through the strong power of Christian hope; that we also, who have received the first fruits of the Spirit, may not seek our rest in this mortal state, but inwardly long after that which is far better, to be with Christ in heaven: to whom, with Thee and the Holy Ghost, be honor and glory, world without end. *Amen.*

Twenty-Third Sunday after Trinity.

The Gospel, St. Matt. xxii. 15-22. (*St. Matt.* xxv. 31-46.)

Then went the Pharisees, and took counsel how they might entangle him in his talk. And they sent out unto him their disciples with the Herodians, saying, Master, we know that thou art true, and teachest the way of God in truth, neither carest thou for any man: for thou regardest not the person of men. Tell us therefore, what thinkest thou? Is it lawful to give tribute unto Cæsar, or not? But Jesus perceived their wickedness, and said, why tempt ye me, ye hypocrites? Shew me the tribute money. And they brought unto him a penny. And he saith unto them, Whose is this image and superscription? They say unto him, Cæsar's. Then saith he unto them, Render therefore unto Cæsar the things which are Cæsar's; and unto God the things that are God's. When they had heard these words, they marvelled, and left him, and went their way.

The Epistle, Phil. iii. 17-21. (*Rev.* xx. 11-15.)

Brethren, be followers together of me, and mark them which walk so as ye have us for an ensample. (For many walk, of whom I have told you often, and now tell you even weeping, that they are the enemies of the cross of Christ: whose end is destruction, whose God is their belly, and whose glory is in their shame, who mind earthly things.) For our conversation is in heaven: from whence also we look for the Saviour, the Lord Jesus Christ: who shall change our vile body, that it may be fashioned like unto his glorious body, according to the working whereby he is able even to subdue all things unto himself.

The Collect.

O GOD, to whom both power and mercy belong, and who renderest to every man according to his work; give us grace, we beseech Thee, to set Thy presence before us in all our ways, and to seek continually those things which are well pleasing in Thy sight; that we may pass through the world as pilgrims and strangers, in all holy conversation and godliness, looking for and hastening unto the second advent of the Lord Jesus, when He shall come to be glorified in His saints, and admired in all them that believe: to whom, with Thee and the Holy Ghost, be honor and glory, world without end. *Amen.*

The Fourth Sunday before Advent.

The Gospel, St. Matt. ix. 18-26. (*St. John* v. 24-29.)

While he spake these things unto them, behold, there came a certain ruler, and worshipped him, saying, My daughter is even now dead: but come and lay thy hand upon her, and she shall live. And Jesus arose, and followed him, and so did his disciples. And, behold, a woman, which was diseased with an issue of blood twelve years, came behind him, and touched the hem of his garment: for she said within herself, If I may but touch his garment, I shall be whole. But Jesus turned him about, and when he saw her, he said, Daughter, be of good comfort; thy faith hath made the whole. And the woman was made whole from that hour. And when Jesus came into the ruler's house, and saw the minstrels and the people making a noise, he said unto them, Give place: for the maid is not dead, but sleepeth. And they laughed him to scorn. But when the people were put forth, he went in, and took her by the hand, and the maid arose. And the fame hereof went abroad into all that land.

The Epistle, Col. i. 9-14. (*Rev.* xxii. 1-21.)

For this cause we also, since the day we heard it, do not cease to pray for you, and to desire that ye might be filled with the knowledge of his will in all wisdom and spiritual understanding; that ye might walk worthy of the Lord unto all pleasing, being fruitful in every good work, and increasing in the knowledge of God; strengthened with all might, according to his glorious power, unto all patience and long-suffering with joyfulness; giving thanks unto the Father, which hath made us meet to be partakers of the inheritance of the saints in light: who hath delivered us from the power of darkness, and hath translated us into the kingdom of his dear Son: in whom we have redemption through his blood, even the forgiveness of sins.

The Collect.

ALMIGHTY and most merciful God, who didst cause Thy Son to descend into the bosom of the grave, that He might destroy him that had the power of death, and deliver them who through fear of death were all their lifetime subject to bondage; work in us, we beseech Thee, such holy mortification to all the things of this world, and such lively apprehension of things unseen and eternal, as may prepare us to die without anxiety or dismay, knowing that if our earthly house of this tabernacle be dissolved, we have a building of

God, a house not made with hands, eternal in the heavens; through Jesus Christ our Lord. *Amen.*

The Third Sunday before Advent.

The Gospel, St. Matt. xxiv. 15–28. (St. John xiv. 1–4)

When ye therefore shall see the abomination of desolation, spoken of by Daniel the prophet, stand in the holy place, (whoso readeth, let him understand:) then let them which be in Judea flee into the mountains: let him which is on the house-top not come down to take any thing out of his house: neither let him which is in the field return back to take his clothes. And woe unto them that are with child, and to them that give suck in those days! But pray ye that your flight be not in the winter, neither on the sabbath day: for then shall be great tribulation, such as was not since the beginning of the world to this time, no, nor ever shall be. And except those days should be shortened, there should no flesh be saved: but for the elect's sake those days shall be shortened. Then, if any man shall say unto you, Lo, here is Christ, or there; believe it not. For there shall arise false Christs, and false prophets, and shall shew great signs and wonders; insomuch that, if it were possible, they shall deceive the very elect. Behold, I have told you before. Wherefore, if they shall say unto you, Behold, he is in the desert; go not forth: behold, he is in the secret chambers; believe it not. For as the lightning cometh out of the east, and shineth even unto the west; so shall also the coming of the Son of man be. For wheresoever the carcass is, there will the eagles be gathered together.

The Epistle, 1 Thess. iv. 13–18. (*Rev.* vii. 13–17.)

But I would not have you to be ignorant, brethren, concerning them which are asleep, that ye sorrow not, even as others which have no hope. For if we believe that Jesus died and rose again, even so them also which sleep in Jesus will God bring with him. For this we say unto you by the word of the Lord, that we which are alive and remain unto the coming of the Lord shall not prevent them which are asleep. For the Lord himself shall descend from heaven with a shout, with the voice of the archangel, and with the trump of God: and the dead in Christ shall rise first: Then we which are alive and remain shall be caught up together with them in the clouds, to meet the Lord in the air: and so shall we ever be with the Lord. Wherefore comfort one another with these words.

The Collect.

ALMIGHTY and everlasting God, the Fountain of all life and power, who hast promised to bring up again from the dead the bodies of them which sleep in Jesus; gather not our souls with sinners, we beseech Thee, but make us to be numbered with Thy saints in glory everlasting; that having been joined with them in one communion here, we may also share hereafter their joyful triumph, in the resurrection at the last day; through the same Jesus Christ, our risen and glorified Lord. *Amen.*

The Second Sunday before Advent.

The Gospel, St. Matt. xxv. 31–46. (*St. Matt.* xix. 27–30.)

When the Son of man shall come in his glory, and all the holy angels with him, then shall he sit upon the throne of his glory: and before him shall be gathered all nations: and he shall separate them one from another, as a shepherd divideth

THE SECOND SUNDAY BEFORE ADVENT.

his sheep from the goats: and he shall set the sheep on his right hand, but the goats on the left. Then shall the King say unto them on his right hand, Come, ye blessed of my Father, inherit the kingdom prepared for you from the foundation of the world: for I was an hungered, and ye gave me meat: I was thirsty, and ye gave me drink: I was a stranger, and ye took me in: naked, and ye clothed me: I was sick, and ye visited me: I was in prison, and ye came unto me. Then shall the righteous answer him, saying, Lord, when saw we thee an hungered, and fed thee? or thirsty, and gave thee drink? when we saw thee a stranger, and took thee in? or naked, and clothed thee? or when saw we thee sick, or in prison, and came unto thee? And the King shall answer and say unto them, Verily I say unto you, Inasmuch as ye have done it unto one of the least of these my brethren, ye have done it unto me. Then shall he say also unto them on the left hand, Depart from me, ye cursed, into everlasting fire, prepared for the devil and his angels. For I was anhungered, and ye gave me no meat: I was thirsty, and ye gave me no drink: I was a stranger, and ye took me not in: naked, and ye clothed me not: sick, and in prison, and ye visited me not. Then shall they also answer him, saying, Lord, when saw we thee an hungered, or athirst, or a stranger, or naked, or sick, or in prison, and did not minister unto thee? Then shall he answer them, saying, Verily I say unto you, Inasmuch as ye did it not to one of the least of these, ye did it not to me. And these shall go away into everlasting punishment: but the righteous into life eternal.

The Epistle, 2 *Thess.* i. 3–10. (*Rev* xxi. 1–8.)

We are bound to thank God always for you, brethren, as it is meet, because that your faith groweth exceedingly, and the charity of every one of you all toward each other aboundeth; so that we ourselves glory in you in the churches of God, for your patience and faith in all your persecutions and tribulations that ye endure: which is a manifest token of the righteous judgment of God, that ye may be counted worthy of the kingdom of God, for which ye also suffer: seeing it is a righteous thing with God to recompense tribulation to them that trouble you; and to you who are troubled rest with us, when the Lord Jesus shall be revealed from heaven with his mighty angels, in flaming fire taking vengeance on them that know not God, and that obey not the Gospel of our Lord Jesus Christ: who shall be punished with everlasting destruction from the presence of the Lord, and from the glory of his power; when he shall come to be glorified in his saints, and to be admired in all them that believe, (because our testimony among you was believed) in that day.

The Collect.

O GOD, who hast appointed a day in the which Thou wilt judge the world in righteousness, by that Man whom Thou hast ordained, giving assurance thereof unto all in that thou hast raised Him from the dead; grant unto us grace, we beseech Thee, to keep in mind always the power and coming of our Lord Jesus Christ, and to wait continually for His revelation from heaven; that having boldly confessed Him before men, we also may be openly acknowledged and confessed by Him when all flesh shall appear in His presence: to whom, with Thee and the Holy Ghost, be honor and glory, world without end. *Amen.*

The Sunday before Advent.

The Gospel, St. Matt. xxv. 1–13. (*St. John* xvii. 20–26.)

Then shall the kingdom of heaven be likened unto ten virgins, which took their lamps, and went forth to meet the bridegroom. And five of them were wise, and five were foolish. They that were foolish took their lamps, and took no oil with them: but the wise took oil in their vessels with their lamps. While the bridegroom tarried, they all slumbered and slept. And at midnight there was a cry made, Behold, the bridegroom cometh; go ye out to meet him. Then all those virgins arose, and trimmed their lamps. And the foolish said unto the wise, Give us of your oil; for our lamps are gone out. But the wise answered, saying, Not so; lest there be not enough for us and you: but go ye rather to them that sell, and buy for yourselves. And while they went to buy, the bridegroom came; and they that were ready went in with him to the marriage: and the door was shut. Afterward came also the other virgins, saying, Lord, Lord, open to us. But he answered and said, Verily I say unto you, I know you not. Watch therefore, for ye know neither the day nor the hour wherein the Son of man cometh.

The Epistle, 2 Pet. iii. 3-14. (*Rev.* vii. 2-12.)

Knowing this first, that there shall come in the last days scoffers, walking after their own lusts, and saying, Where is the promise of his coming? for since the fathers fell asleep, all things continue as they were from the beginning of the creation. For this they willingly are ignorant of, that by the word of God the heavens were of old, and the earth standing out of the water, and in the water: whereby the world that then was, being overflowed with water, perished: but the heavens and the earth, which are now, by the same word are kept in store, reserved unto fire against the day of judgment and perdition of ungodly men. But, beloved, be not ignorant of this one thing, that one day is with the Lord as a thousand years, and a thousand years as one day. The Lord is not slack concerning his promise, as some men count slackness; but is long-suffering to us-ward, not willing that any should perish, but that all should come to repentance. But the day of the Lord will come as a thief in the night; in the

THE SUNDAY BEFORE ADVENT.

which the heavens shall pass away with a great noise, and the elements shall melt with fervent heat, the earth also and the works that are therein shall be burned up. Seeing then that all these things shall be dissolved, what manner of persons ought ye to be in all holy conversation and godliness, looking for and hastening unto the coming of the day of God, wherein the heavens, being on fire, shall be dissolved, and the elements shall melt with fervent heat? Nevertheless we, according to his promise, look for new heavens and a new earth, wherein dwelleth righteousness. Wherefore, beloved, seeing that ye look for such things, be diligent that ye may be found of him in peace, without spot and blameless.

The Collect.

ALMIGHTY and everlasting God, by whose word the heavens and the earth, which are now, are kept in store, reserved unto fire against the day of judgment and perdition of ungodly men; make us, we beseech Thee, to be such manner of persons in all holy conversation and godliness, as they ought to be who look for such things; that when this frame of nature shall be dissolved, we may be counted worthy to behold and enjoy, according to Thy promise, the new heavens and the new earth, wherein dwelleth righteousness; through the merits and mediation of Thy Son Jesus Christ, who liveth and reigneth with Thee and the Holy Ghost, ever one God, world without end. *Amen.*

THE HOLY COMMUNION.

PREPARATION FOR THE HOLY COMMUNION.

Having taken his place at the altar, the Congregation also standing up, the Minister shall say:

The Lord is in His holy temple: let all the earth keep silence before Him. *Amen.*

God spake all these words, saying, I am the Lord thy God, which have brought thee out of the land of Egypt, out of the house of bondage.

Thou shalt have no other gods before Me.

Thou shalt not make unto thee any graven image, or any likeness of any thing that is in heaven above, or that is in the earth beneath, or that is in the water under the earth: thou shalt not bow down thyself to them, nor serve them: for I the Lord thy God am a jealous God, visiting the iniquity of the fathers upon the children unto the third and fourth generation of them that hate Me; and shewing mercy unto thousands of them that love Me, and keep My commandments.

Thou shalt not take the name of the Lord thy God in vain; for the Lord will not hold him guiltless that taketh His name in vain.

Remember the sabbath day, to keep it holy. Six days shalt thou labor, and do all thy work: but the seventh day is the sabbath of the Lord thy God: in it thou shalt not do any work, thou, nor thy son, nor thy daughter, thy manservant, nor thy maidservant, nor thy cattle, nor thy stranger that is within thy gates: for in six days the Lord made heaven and earth, the sea, and all that in them is, and rested the seventh day: wherefore the Lord blessed the sabbath day, and hallowed it.

Honor thy father and thy mother: that thy days may be long upon the land which the Lord thy God giveth thee.

Thou shalt not kill.

Thou shalt not commit adultery.

Thou shalt not steal.

Thou shalt not bear false witness against thy neighbor.

Thou shalt not covet thy neighbor's house, thou shalt not covet thy neighbor's wife, nor his manservant, nor his maidservant, nor his ox, nor his ass, nor any thing that is thy neighbor's.

Congregation. Lord, have mercy upon us, and incline our hearts to keep all these laws.

Minister. Hear also what our Lord Jesus Christ saith:

Thou shalt love the Lord thy God with all thy heart, and with all thy soul, and with all thy mind

This is the first and great commandment. And the second is like unto it: Thou shalt love thy neighbor as thyself. On these two commandments hang all the law and the prophets.

M. Let us pray.

O LORD GOD, who didst at first deliver Thy commandments from the mount which burned with fire, amid blackness, and darkness, and tempest, at which terrible sight even Moses said, I exceedingly fear and quake: we thank Thee that this same law is now published unto us from mount Zion, through the Mediator of a new and better covenant; and we humbly beseech Thee to put these words into our minds, and write them in our hearts, that we may delight in Thy law after the inward man, and serve Thee in newness of spirit, through Jesus Christ our Lord; who with Thee and the Holy Ghost liveth and reigneth, ever one God, world without end. *Amen.*

Then all shall kneel, and join in the *Litany* as follows:

M. O God the Father in heaven; have mercy upon us.

C. Have mercy upon us.

M. O God the Son, Redeemer of the world; have mercy upon us.

C. Have mercy upon us.

M. O God the Holy Ghost, proceeding from the Father and the Son; have mercy upon us.

C. Have mercy upon us.

THE HOLY COMMUNION.

M. O holy, blessed, and glorious Trinity, three Persons and one God; have mercy upon us.

C. Have mercy upon us.

M. Remember not, Lord, our offences, nor the offences of our forefathers; neither take Thou vengeance of our sins: spare us, good Lord, spare Thy people, whom Thou hast redeemed with Thy most precious blood, and be not angry with us for ever.

C. Spare us, good Lord.

M. From all evil and harm; from the power of sin, and the snares of the devil; from Thy wrath, and from everlasting damnation;

C. Good Lord, deliver us.

M. From all blindness of heart; from pride, vainglory, and hypocrisy; from envy, hatred, and malice and all uncharitableness;

C. Good Lord, deliver us.

M. From all impure lusts and desires; and from all the deceits of the world, the flesh, and the devil;

C. Good Lord, deliver us.

M. From lightning, tempest, and earthquake; from plague, pestilence, and famine; from all disasters by land and by water; from battle and murder, and from sudden death;

C. Good Lord, deliver us.

M. From tumult and riot; from sedition and rebellion; from heresy and schism; from hardness of heart, and contempt of Thy word and authority;
C. Good Lord, deliver us.

M. By the mystery of Thy holy incarnation; by Thy holy nativity and circumcision; by Thy baptism, fasting, and temptation;
C. Good Lord, deliver us.

M. By Thine agony and bloody sweat; by Thy cross and passion; by Thy precious death and burial; by Thy glorious resurrection and ascension; and by the coming of the Holy Ghost;
C. Good Lord, deliver us.

M. In all time of our tribulation; in all time of our wealth; in the hour of death, and in the day of judgment;
C. Good Lord, deliver us.

M. We sinners do beseech Thee to hear us, O Lord.
C. Son of God, we beseech Thee to hear us.

M. That it may please Thee to keep us in all time of temptation and heaviness; to comfort and help all the weak-hearted; to raise up them that fall, and finally to beat down Satan under our feet;
C. We beseech Thee to hear us, O Lord.

M. That it may please Thee to succor, help, and comfort all that are in danger, necessity, and tribulation;
C. We beseech Thee to hear us, O Lord.

M. That it may please Thee to preserve all travellers and strangers, all women in the perils of childbirth, all sick persons, and young children, and to show Thy pity upon all prisoners and captives;
C. We beseech Thee to hear us, O Lord.

M. That it may please Thee to defend and provide for the fatherless children, and widows, and all that are desolate and oppressed;
C. We beseech Thee to hear us, O Lord.

M. That it may please Thee to have mercy upon all men;
C. We beseech Thee to hear us, O Lord.

M. O Son of God, Redeemer of the world;
C. Have mercy upon us.

M. O Lamb of God, that takest away the sin of the world;
C. Have mercy upon us.

M. O Lamb of God, that takest away the sin of the world;
C. Grant us Thy peace.

O GOD, merciful Father, who despisest not the sighing

of the contrite, nor rejectest the desire of the sorrowful; be favorable to our prayers which in our afflictions that continually oppress us, we pour out before Thee; and graciously hear them, that those things which the craft of the devil or man worketh against us, may be brought to nought, and by the counsel of Thy goodness be dispersed; so that being hurt by no persecutions, we may evermore give thanks unto Thee in Thy holy Church, through Jesus Christ our Lord. *Amen.*

O GOD, from whom all holy desires, all good counsels, and all just works do proceed; give unto Thy servants that peace which the world cannot give; that our hearts may be set to obey Thy commandments, and also that we, being defended from the fear of our enemies, may by Thy protection pass our time in peace and quietness; through Jesus Christ our Lord. *Amen.*

A suitable *Psalm* or *Hymn* shall now be sung.

Then the Minister, having taken his place in the pulpit, shall proceed to deliver a brief *Sermon,* or *Exhortation.*

After the Sermon, the Minister, at the altar, shall address the communicants, and say:

BELOVED IN THE LORD: Our blessed Saviour Jesus Christ, when He was about to finish the work of our redemption, by making Himself a sacrifice for our sins upon the cross, solemnly instituted the Holy Sacrament of His own Body and Blood; that it might be the abiding memorial of His precious death; the seal of His perpetual presence in the Church by the Holy

Ghost; the mystical exhibition of His one offering of Himself made once, but of force always, to put away sin; the pledge of His undying love to His people; and the bond of His living union and fellowship with them to the end of time.

The same night, we are told, in which he was betrayed, He took bread; and when He had given thanks, He brake it, and said, Take, eat; this is My body, which is broken for you; this do in remembrance of Me. After the same manner also He took the cup, when He had supped, saying, This cup is the new testament in My blood; this do ye, as oft as ye drink it, in remembrance of Me.

It has not been without reason, therefore, that the celebration of the Holy Eucharist has ever been regarded by the Church as the inmost sanctuary of the whole Christian worship. We have to do here, not with outward signs only, but with the heavenly realities themselves which these signs represent. Our Lord Himself calls the bread His body, and the cup His blood, or the new testament in His blood. The cup of blessing which we bless, says St. Paul, is it not the communion of the blood of Christ? The bread which we break, is it not the communion of the body of Christ? And it is the same Apostle who utters, in another place, the solemn warning: Let a man examine himself, and so let him eat of that bread, and drink of that cup; for he that eateth and drinketh unworthily, eateth and drinketh judgment to himself, not discerning the Lord's body.

Being of such high and awful character. it is plain that the Lord's Supper can be rightly and safely approached only by those who are of a truly devout and religious mind. These holy mysteries are not for the irreverent, the worldly, or the profane. All who are impenitent and unbelieving, and who refuse to obey the gospel of our Lord Jesus Christ, have no right to partake of this Christian altar. They can do so only at their own peril; for coming to it thus in the spirit of hypocrisy and wickedness, they turn the blessing of the Sacrament into a curse, and that which should be a savor of life unto life is made to be for them only a savor of death unto death. They eat and drink damnation or judgment to themselves; not because they are sinners, but because they are impenitent sinners; not because they are unworthy, but because they eat and drink unworthily, not discerning the Lord's body.

If any of you who are here present, then, know yourselves to be the willing servants of sin, being without repentance and faith, and yielding yourselves to the power of worldly affections and lusts, we solemnly warn and admonish you, that ye presume not, so long as this is your character, to come to the table of the Lord. Do not pretend in this way, to join righteousness with unrighteousness, and light with darkness. Ye cannot drink the cup of the Lord, and the cup of devils; ye cannot be partakers of the Lord's table, and of the table of devils.

On the other hand, we cordially invite to this table all who are truly grieved and penitent for their sins, who look to the Lord Jesus Christ for righteousness and salvation, who abide in the fellowship of His Church, and who earnestly desire to possess His

Spirit and to walk in His steps. To all such the voice of the infinitely compassionate Redeemer Himself speaks: Come unto Me, all ye that labor, and are heavy laden, and I will give you rest. Fear not, therefore, as many of you as have this mind, to embrace the joyful and glorious privilege which is here offered for your use. Having, brethren, boldness to enter into the holiest by the blood of Jesus, by a new and living way, which He hath consecrated for us, through the veil, that is to say, His flesh; and having an High Priest over the house of God; let us draw near with a true heart, in full assurance of faith, having our hearts sprinkled from an evil conscience, and our bodies washed with pure water.

Only ye must take good heed, that your particular preparation for the Sacrament at this time be sincere and whole, according to God's command; so that no let or bar may be found in yourselves to its proper comfort and benefit. See that ye have grace, not only in general habit, but also in present exercise and power. Renew your repentance and faith. Be in perfect charity with all men. Put away from you the leaven of malice and wickedness. Remember earnestly your past offences and shortcomings, that ye may humble yourselves, with true hearty confession, under the mighty hand of Him, who alone has power to exalt you in His own good time. Thus, clothed in the robes of salvation, you will be able to compass God's holy altar with thankfulness and joy, and to share the full benefit of its one offering for sin, while you feed on the sacrifice at the same time as the bread of everlasting life. For in this most comfortable Sacrament of the Body and Blood of our Saviour Jesus Christ, we have exhibited to us at once, both the forgiveness of sins through His death, and the gift of immortality through His glorious resurrection; according to His own word: Verily, verily, I say unto you, Except ye eat the flesh of the Son of Man, and drink His blood, ye have no life in you. Whoso eateth My flesh, and drinketh My blood, hath eternal life; and I will raise him up at the last day. For My flesh is meat indeed, and My blood is drink indeed. He that eateth My flesh, and drinketh My blood, dwelleth in Me, and I in him. As the living Father hath sent Me, and I live by the Father; so he that eateth Me, even he shall live by Me. This is that bread which came down from heaven: not as your fathers did eat manna, and are dead; he that eateth of this bread shall live for ever.

Ye then, beloved brethren in the Lord, who have looked earnestly into your own hearts, and who find in yourselves these good dispositions of penitence and faith, with the sincere desire and purpose of forsaking all sin and following after all Christian holiness, approach with me now to the throne of grace, and make your humble confession to Almighty God.

All kneeling.

ALMIGHTY GOD, Father of our Lord Jesus Christ, Maker of all things, Judge of all men; we cast ourselves down at Thy feet, with deep humiliation and heartfelt penitent grief, in view of our manifold sins and great unrighteousness, whereby we have provoked against ourselves most justly Thine indignation and wrath. We have sinned against Thee in thought, word, and deed. We have broken Thy holy laws. We have come short of Thy righteousness and glory, in all our ways. Our lives bear testimony against us, and our own hearts condemn us, as being prone to all evil, and backward to all good. We have abused Thy mercies, and made light of Thy judgments. We have turned aside from Thy covenant; and have not been faithful and diligent, as we ought to have been, in using the helps of Thy grace for our eternal salvation. We acknowledge and bewail before Thee, the corruption of our nature, the vanity of our minds, the waywardness of our hearts, the wanderings and apostasies of our whole fallen life. Righteousness belongeth unto Thee, O Lord; and unto us only confusion of face. But unto Thee, O Lord our God, belong also mercies and forgivenesses, though we have rebelled against Thee. For Thou, Lord, art good, and ready to forgive, and plenteous in mercy unto all them that call upon Thee. Look upon us, therefore, O righteous and holy Father, with an eye of pity and compassion, as we now humble ourselves, with sincere confession, before the throne of Thy heavenly grace; and for the sake of Thy Son Jesus Christ, speak pardon and peace to our souls. Let Thy mercy be upon us, O Lord, according as we hope in Thee. And with the full pardon of our past sins, be pleased also to quicken us, we beseech Thee, in the way of righteousness, and uphold us with Thy free Spirit; that we may walk worthy henceforth of the vocation wherewith we are called, and ever hereafter serve and please Thee in newness of life, to the honor and glory of Thy holy name, through Jesus Christ our Lord. Amen.

Then shall the Minister rise, and pronounce to the Congregation, still kneeling, the following Declaration of Pardon.

HEARKEN now unto the comforting assurance of the grace of God, promised in the Gospel to all that repent and believe: As I live, saith the Lord God, I have no pleasure in the death of the wicked, but that the wicked turn from his way and live. God so loved the world, that He gave His only begotten Son, that whosoever believeth in Him should not perish, but have everlasting life.

Unto as many of you, therefore, beloved in the Lord, as have now made confession of your sins unto God with hearty repentance and sincere faith, being resolved to turn from them, and to follow after righteousness and true holiness in time to come, I declare, by the authority of the Gospel, that all your sins are remitted and forgiven, through the perfect satisfaction of the most holy passion and death of our Lord Jesus Christ. *Amen.*

Then shall the Congregation rise, and join in singing a Doxology; after which the service shall be concluded with this Benediction:

The God of peace, who brought again from the dead our Lord Jesus, the great Shepherd of the sheep, through the blood of the everlasting covenant, make you perfect in every good work, to do His will, working in you that which is well-pleasing in His sight, through Jesus Christ: to whom be glory for ever and ever. *Amen.*

THE HOLY COMMUNION.

[The Sacrament of the Lord's Supper shall be administered publicly in the Church, in every Congregation, at least twice a year, and if possible oftener.]

HAVING taken his place at the altar, the Congregation also standing up, the Minister shall say as follows:

In the name of the Father, and of the Son, and of the Holy Ghost. *Amen.*

DEARLY BELOVED IN THE LORD: If we say that we have no sin, we deceive ourselves, and the truth is not in us; but if we confess our sins, God is faithful and just to forgive us our sins, and to cleanse us from all unrighteousness. Let us therefore humble ourselves before the throne of Almighty God, our heavenly Father, and confess our manifold sins and transgressions with lowly and contrite hearts, that we may obtain forgiveness of the same through the merits of our Lord Jesus Christ.

Then the Minister and Congregation shall kneel, and repeat the following *Confession.*

ALMIGHTY God, our heavenly Father, who dost admit Thy people unto such wonderful communion, that partaking of the Body and Blood of Thy dear Son, they should dwell in Him, and He in them; we unworthy sinners, approaching to Thy presence, and beholding Thy glory, do abhor ourselves, and repent in dust and ashes. We have sinned, we have sinned, we have grievously sinned against Thee, in thought, in word, and in deed, provoking most justly Thy wrath and indignation against us. The remembrance of our transgressions and shortcomings fills us with sorrow and shame. Yet now, O most merciful Father, have mercy upon us; for the sake of Jesus Christ, forgive us all our sins; purify us, by the inspiration of Thy Holy Spirit, from all inward uncleanness; enable us heartily to forgive others, as we beseech Thee to forgive us; and grant that we may ever hereafter serve and please Thee in newness of life; to the honor and glory of Thy name, through Jesus Christ our Lord. Amen.

<small>Then shall the Minister rise, and pronounce to the Congregation, still kneeling, the following *Declaration of Pardon.*</small>

HEARKEN now unto the comforting assurance of the grace of God, promised in the Gospel to all that repent and believe: As I live, saith the Lord God, I have no pleasure in the death of the wicked, but that the wicked turn from his way and live. God so loved the world, that He gave His only begotten Son, that whosoever believeth in Him should not perish, but have everlasting life.

Unto as many of you, therefore, beloved brethren,

as truly repent of your sins, and believe in the Lord Jesus Christ, with full purpose of new obedience, I announce and declare, by the authority and in the name of Christ, that your sins are forgiven in heaven, according to His promise in the Gospel, through the perfect merit of Jesus Christ our Lord.

Here, and at the end of every Collect and Prayer, the Congregation shall say:

Amen.

The Congregation shall now rise, and join with the Minister in repeating the *Nicene creed;* immediately after which shall be sung, chanted, or recited, the *Gloria in Excelsis;* all in the following order.

WE BELIEVE in one God, the Father Almighty, Maker of heaven and earth, of all things visible and invisible:

And in one Lord Jesus Christ, the only begotten Son of God, begotten of the Father before all worlds, God of God, Light of Light, very God of very God; begotten not made; of one substance with the Father, by whom all things were made: who for us men and for our salvation came down from heaven, and was incarnate by the Holy Ghost of the Virgin Mary, and was made man: who was also crucified for us under Pontius Pilate, and suffered, and was buried; and the third day rose again according to the Scriptures; and ascended into heaven, and sitteth at the right hand of the Father; and shall come again with glory to judge the quick and the dead; of whose kingdom there shall be no end.

And we believe in the Holy Ghost, the Lord, the Giver of life, who proceedeth from the Father and the

Son, who with the Father and the Son together is worshipped and glorified, who spake by the prophets; in one holy catholic and apostolic Church. We confess one baptism for the remission of sins; we look for the resurrection of the dead, and the life of the world to come. Amen.

Minister. Praise ye the Lord.
Congregation. The Lord's name be praised.

GLORY be to God on high, and on earth peace, good will toward men. We praise Thee, we bless Thee, we worship Thee, we glorify Thee, we give thanks to Thee for Thy great glory, O Lord God, heavenly King, God the Father Almighty.

O Lord, the only begotten Son, Jesus Christ; O Lord God, Lamb of God, Son of the Father, that takest away the sin of the world, have mercy upon us. Thou that takest away the sin of the world, have mercy upon us. Thou that takest away the sin of the world, receive our prayer. Thou that sittest at the right hand of God the Father, have mercy upon us.

For Thou only art holy; Thou only art the Lord; Thou only, O Christ, with the Holy Ghost, art most high in the glory of God the Father. Amen.

Then shall the Minister read the proper *Gospel* and *Epistle* for the day.

After the reading, the service shall proceed thus, the Congregation rising:

M. Glory be to the Father, and to the Son, and to the Holy Ghost:

C. As it was in the beginning, is now, and ever shall be, world without end. Amen.

M. The Lord be with you.

C. And with thy spirit.

M. Let us pray.

Here shall be offered the *Collect* for the day and the *Festival Prayer.*

A suitable *Psalm* or *Hymn* shall then be sung.

After this, the Minister having taken his place in the pulpit, shall proceed to deliver a brief *Sermon.* Or, instead of this, he may read a lesson of moderate length, taken from the Holy Gospels, on the history of Christ's Passion and Death.

Then shall follow a collection of the *Offerings* of the people, to be devoted to the service of the poor, or to some benevolent purpose; during which the Minister, standing at the altar, shall read some of the following *Sentences* from the Holy Scriptures.

He which soweth sparingly shall reap also sparingly; and he which soweth bountifully shall reap also bountifully.

Every man according as he purposeth in his heart, so let him give; not grudgingly, or of necessity: for God loveth a cheerful giver. As it is written, He hath dispersed abroad; he hath given to the poor: his righteousness remaineth forever.

Charge them that are rich in this world, that they be not high-minded, nor trust in uncertain riches, but in the living God, who giveth us richly all things to enjoy; that they do good, that they be rich in good works, ready to distribute, willing to communicate; laying up in store for themselves a good foundation against the time to come, that they may lay hold on eternal life.

To do good and to communicate forget not: for with such sacrifices God is well pleased.

Whoso hath this world's good, and seeth his brother have need, and shutteth up his bowels of compassion from him, how dwelleth the love of God in him?

He that hath pity upon the poor lendeth unto the Lord; and that which he hath given will He pay him again.

I have shewed you all things, how that so laboring ye ought to support the weak, and to remember the words of the Lord Jesus, how He said, It is more blessed to give than to receive.

<small>The collection shall be brought by the Deacons, in a proper vessel provided for the purpose, to the Minister; who shall then reverently place it upon the altar, as an oblation presented unto God.</small>

<small>After this, the Minister shall uncover and expose to view the vessels containing the Bread and Wine for the use of the Holy Sacrament, and proceed as follows:</small>

M. Let us pray.

ALMIGHTY and everlasting God, who by the blood of Thy dear Son hast consecrated for us a new and living way into the holiest of all; cleanse our minds, we beseech Thee, by the inspiration of Thy Holy Spirit, that we, Thy redeemed people, drawing near unto Thee in these holy mysteries, with a true heart and undefiled conscience, in full assurance of faith, may offer unto Thee an acceptable sacrifice in righteousness, and worthily magnify Thy great and glorious name; through Jesus Christ our Lord. *Amen.*

<small>Then shall the Minister pronounce, slowly and solemnly, either the whole, or some part, of the following selection of passages from the *Holy Scriptures.*</small>

Surely He hath borne our griefs, and carried our sorrows: yet we did esteem Him stricken, smitten of God, and afflicted. But He was wounded for our transgressions, He was bruised for our iniquities: the chastisement of our peace was upon Him; and with His stripes we are healed. All we like sheep have gone astray; we have turned every one to his own way; and the Lord hath laid on Him the iniquity of us all.

In this was manifested the love of God toward us, because that God sent His only begotten Son into the world, that we might live through Him. Herein is love, not that we loved God, but that He loved us, and sent His Son to be the propitiation for our sins.

Abide in Me, and I in you. As the branch cannot bear fruit of itself, except it abide in the vine; no more can ye, except ye abide in Me. I am the vine, ye are the branches: he that abideth in Me, and I in him, the same bringeth forth much fruit: for without Me ye can do nothing.

I am the living bread which came down from heaven. If any man eat of this bread, he shall live for ever: and the bread which I will give is My flesh, which I will give for the life of the world. The Jews therefore strove among themselves, saying, How can this man give us His flesh to eat? Then Jesus said unto them, Verily, verily, I say unto you, except ye eat the flesh of the Son of man, and drink His blood, ye have no life in you.

Whoso eateth My flesh, and drinketh My blood, hath eternal life; and I will raise him up at the last day. For My flesh is meat indeed, and My blood is drink indeed. He that eateth My flesh, and drinketh My blood, dwelleth in Me, and I in him. As the living Father hath sent Me, and I live by the Father: so he that eateth Me, even he shall live by Me. This is that bread which came down from heaven: not as your fathers did eat manna, and are dead: he that eateth of this bread shall live for ever.

<small>Then, the whole Congregation rising, the service shall proceed:</small>

M. The Lord be with you.
C. And with thy spirit.
M. Lift up your hearts.
C. We lift them up unto the Lord.
M. Let us give thanks unto the Lord our God.
C. It is meet and right so to do.

It is very meet, right, and our bounden duty, that we should at all times, and in all places, give thanks unto Thee, Lord God Almighty, Father, Son, and Holy Ghost.

Before the mountains were brought forth, or ever Thou hadst formed the earth and the world, even from everlasting to everlasting, Thou art God.

Thou didst in the beginning create all things for Thyself. By Thy word were the heavens made, and all the host of them by the breath of Thy mouth. The armies of the invisible world, angels and archangels, thrones, dominions, principalities and powers; the glorious firmament on high, sun, moon and stars; the earth and the fulness thereof; all are the work of Thy hands, and all are upheld by Thee continually in their appointed order and course.

Thou also at the first didst make man in Thine own image, and after Thine own likeness, and didst set him over the works of Thy hands, endowing him with the excellent gift of righteousness, and forming him for immortality. And when afterwards, through the fraud and malice of Satan, he fell by transgression from that first estate, Thou didst not leave him still to perish utterly in his fall, but wast pleased to raise him up again and to restore him to the joyful hope of everlasting life, by the promise of redemption through Jesus Christ; who, being God of God, very God of very God, dwelling in the bosom of the Father with unspeakable blessedness from all eternity, at last, when the fulness of the time was come, came down from heaven, and became man, for us men and for our salvation.

For all Thy mercies and favors, known to us and unknown, we give Thee thanks. But most of all, we praise Thee, the Father everlasting, for the gift of Thine adorable, true, and only Son, our Saviour Jesus Christ, who by His appearing hath abolished death and brought life and immortality to light through the Gospel. We bless Thee for His holy incarnation; for His life on earth; for His precious sufferings and death upon the cross; for His resurrection from the dead; and for His glorious ascension to Thy right hand. We bless Thee for the giving of the Holy Ghost; for the institution of the Church; for the means of grace; for the hope of everlasting life; and for the glory which shall be brought unto us at the coming, and in the kingdom, of Thy dear Son.

Thee, mighty God, heavenly King, we magnify and praise. With patriarchs and prophets, apostles and martyrs; with the holy Church throughout all the world; with the heavenly Jerusalem, the joyful assembly and congregation of the first-born on high; with the innumerable company of angels round about

Thy throne, the heaven of heavens, and all the powers therein; we worship and adore Thy glorious name, joining in the song of the Cherubim and Seraphim:

Here let the people join aloud in the *Seraphic Hymn.*

Holy, Holy, Holy, Lord God of Sabaoth; heaven and earth are full of the majesty of thy glory. Hosanna in the highest! Blessed is He that cometh in the name of the Lord. Hosanna in the highest!

Then the Minister shall proceed:

THE LORD JESUS, THE SAME NIGHT IN WHICH HE WAS BETRAYED [here he shall take some of the bread into his hands], TOOK BREAD; AND WHEN HE HAD GIVEN THANKS, HE BRAKE IT [here he shall break the bread], AND SAID, TAKE, EAT, THIS IS MY BODY WHICH IS BROKEN FOR YOU; THIS DO IN REMEMBRANCE OF ME.

AFTER THE SAME MANNER ALSO [here he shall take the cup into his hands], HE TOOK THE CUP, WHEN HE HAD SUPPED, SAYING, THIS CUP IS THE NEW TESTAMENT IN MY BLOOD; THIS DO YE AS OFTEN AS YE DRINK IT, IN REMEMBRANCE OF ME.

Let us pray.

ALMIGHTY God, our heavenly Father, send down, we beseech Thee, the powerful benediction of Thy Holy Spirit upon these elements of bread and wine, that being set apart now from a common to a sacred and mystical use, they may exhibit and represent to us with true effect the Body and Blood of Thy Son, Jesus Christ; so that in the use of them we may be made, through the power of the Holy Ghost, to partake really and truly of His blessed life, whereby only we can be saved from death, and raised to immortality at the last day. *Amen.*

AND be pleased now, O most merciful Father, graciously to receive at our hands this memorial of the blessed sacrifice of Thy Son; in union with which we here offer and present unto Thee, O Lord, the reasonable sacrifice of our own persons; consecrating ourselves, on the altar of the Gospel, in soul and body, property and life, to Thy most blessed service and praise. Look upon us through the mediation of our great High Priest. Make us accepted in the Beloved; and let His name be as a pure and holy incense, through which all our worship may come up before Thee, as the odor of a sweet smell, a sacrifice acceptable, well pleasing to God. *Amen.*

REMEMBER in mercy, we beseech Thee, Thy Church militant throughout the whole earth. Let her ministers be clothed with righteousness, and her priests with salvation. Build up her desolations; restore her disorders; heal her divisions; and grant unto her prosperity, safety, unity and peace. *Amen.*

WE commend unto Thee especially this particular church and congregation, pastor, elders, deacons, and people, beseeching Thee to accept their piety and faith, and to increase toward them Thy heavenly grace, so that they may come behind in no gift, waiting for the coming of our Lord Jesus Christ. *Amen.*

WE pray for all estates of men in Christian lands; for kings, princes, and governors, and for the people committed to their charge and care; especially for Thy servant the President of the United States, and for all the rulers of this land and nation. Make us a righteous people, and give us power to serve Thee in quietness and peace. *Amen.*

VOUCHSAFE unto us, we beseech Thee, favorable weather, that the fruits of the earth may ripen and be gathered in for us in due season; and be pleased of Thy great goodness to preserve us from war, pestilence, and famine. *Amen.*

SEND forth Thy light and Thy truth unto the ends of the earth; cause the glorious Gospel of Thy grace to be proclaimed among all nations; and powerfully incline the hearts of men everywhere, that they may hear and obey the joyful sound. *Amen.*

REGARD in tender compassion those among Thy people, who are called to suffer heavy affliction, or sore temptation and trial of any kind: and be Thou graciously nigh unto them with Thy divine help, according to all their need. *Amen.*

ESPECIALLY do we commend unto Thee those departing this life. Let the arms of Thy love be round about them in their last hour; defend them against the assaults of the Devil; enable them joyfully to commit their spirits into Thy hands; and so receive them to Thy rest. *Amen.*

O God, the Father of our Lord Jesus Christ, of whom the whole family in heaven and earth is named; we rejoice before Thee in the blessed communion of all Thy saints, wherein Thou givest us also to have part. We praise Thee for the holy fellowship of patriarchs and prophets, apostles and martyrs, and the whole glorious company of the redeemed of all ages, who have died in the Lord, and now live with Him for evermore. We give thanks unto Thee for Thy great grace and many gifts bestowed on those who have thus gone before us in the way of salvation, and by whom we are now compassed about, in our Christian course, as a cloud of witnesses looking down upon us from the heavenly world. Enable us to follow their faith, that we may enter at death into their joy; and so abide with them in rest and peace, till both they and we shall reach our common consummation of redemption and bliss in the glorious resurrection of the last day. *Amen.*

Here let the people join aloud in the *Lord's Prayer.*

Our Father who art in heaven, Hallowed be Thy name. Thy kingdom come. Thy will be done in earth, as it is in heaven. Give us this day our daily bread. And forgive us our debts, as we forgive our debtors. And lead us not into temptation. But deliver us from evil. For Thine is the kingdom, and the power, and the glory, for ever. Amen.

M. The peace of our Lord Jesus Christ be with you all.

C. Amen.

THE HOLY COMMUNION.

Here the Holy Communion shall take place. While a sacramental hymn is sung, the people shall present themselves in front of the altar, reverently and devoutly standing. The officiating Minister shall first receive the Communion in both kinds himself, and administer the same to his assistants; and he shall then proceed with their help to administer it, first to the elders and deacons, and afterward to the people; distributing first the bread and then the cup.

Giving the bread, the Minister shall say:

The bread which we break, is the Communion of the body of Christ.

Giving the cup, the Minister shall say:

The cup of blessing which we bless, is the Communion of the Blood of Christ.

After the people have communed in both kinds, the Minister shall say:

MAY the Holy Communion of the Body and Blood of our Lord and Saviour Jesus Christ, keep and preserve you, each one, in body, soul, and spirit, unto everlasting life. *Amen.*

Depart in peace.

When all have communed, the Minister shall say:

Let us pray.

ALMIGHTY and everlasting God, we give Thee most hearty thanks for the great goodness Thou hast shown toward us at this time, in vouchsafing to feed us, through these holy mysteries, with the spiritual food of the most precious body and blood of Thy Son our Saviour Jesus Christ; assuring us thereby, that we are very members incorporate in the mystical body of Thy Son, and heirs through hope of Thine everlasting kingdom, by the merits of His most blessed death and passion. And we most humbly beseech Thee, O heavenly Father, so to assist us with Thy grace, that we may continue in that holy fellowship, and do all such good works as Thou hast prepared for us to walk in; through Jesus Christ our Lord, to whom, with Thee and the Holy Ghost, be all honor and glory, world without end. *Amen.*

Then shall be said, or chanted, the *Ambrosian Hymn* (Te Deum laudamus), as follows:

M. WE praise Thee, O God:

C. We acknowledge Thee to be the Lord.

M. All the earth doth worship Thee, the Father everlasting.

C. To Thee all angels cry aloud; the heavens and all the powers therein.

M. To Thee cherubim and seraphim continually do cry:

C. Holy, Holy, Holy, Lord God of Sabaoth.

M. Heaven and earth are full of the majesty of Thy glory.

C. The glorious company of the apostles praise Thee.

M. The goodly fellowship of the prophets praise Thee.

C. The noble army of martyrs praise Thee.

M. The holy Church, thoroughout all the world, doth acknowledge Thee,

C. The Father of an infinite majesty;

M. Thine adorable, true, and only Son;

C. Also, the Holy Ghost, the Comforter.

M. Thou art the King of glory, O Christ.

C. Thou art the everlasting Son of the Father.

M. When Thou tookest upon Thee to deliver man, Thou didst humble Thyself to be born of a Virgin.

C. When Thou hadst overcome the sharpness ot death, Thou didst open the kingdom of heaven to all believers.

M. Thou sittest at the right hand of God, in the glory of the Father.

C. We believe that Thou shalt come to be our Judge.

M. We therefore pray Thee, help Thy servants, whom Thou hast redeemed with Thy precious blood.

C. Make them to be numbered with Thy saints in glory everlasting.

M. O Lord, save Thy people, and bless Thy heritage.

C. Govern them, and lift them up forever.

M. Day by day we magnify Thee;

C. And we worship Thy name ever, world without end.

M. Vouchsafe, O Lord, to keep us this day without sin.

C. O Lord, have mercy upon us, have mercy upon us.

M. O Lord, let Thy mercy be upon us, as our trust is in Thee.

C. O Lord in Thee have I trusted; let me never be confounded.

<small>After which the Minister shall close the whole service with this *Benediction*.</small>

The peace of God, which passeth all understanding, keep your hearts and minds in the knowledge and love of God, and of His Son Jesus Christ, our Lord: and the blessing of God Almighty, the Father, the Son, and the Holy Ghost, be amongst you, and remain with you always. *Amen.*

HOLY BAPTISM.

BAPTISM OF INFANTS.

[Children, one or both of whose parents are members of the Church are entitled to Baptism.
Baptism shall be performed in the Church, except for good reason.
Sponsors may be admitted in Baptism; but the parents themselves must be present and answer to the questions in the Service.
Members of the Church may present orphan children for Baptism, assuming the proper vows.]

When there are children to be baptized, they shall be brought to the altar, by the parents or sponsors, immediately after the Gloria in Excelsis in the Lord's Day Service.

Pure water having been provided in the font, or some other clean vessel, fit and decent for the sacred ordinance, the Minister, standing near it, shall say:

DEARLY BELOVED: Our Lord and Saviour Jesus Christ, after His resurrection, and shortly before His ascension to the right hand of God the Father Almighty, instituted the Holy Sacrament of Baptism for the remission of sins, saying to His disciples: All power is given unto Me in heaven and in earth. Go ye, therefore, and teach all nations, baptizing them in the name of the Father, and of the Son, and of the Holy Ghost; teaching them to observe all things whatsoever I have commanded you: and, lo, I am with you alway, even unto the end of the world.

Hear, also, what is written in another place: And they brought young children to Him, that He might touch them; and His disciples rebuked them that brought them. But when Jesus saw it, He was much displeased, and said, Suffer the little children to come unto Me, and forbid them not; for of such is the kingdom of God. Verily, I say unto you, Whosoever, shall not receive the kingdom of God as a little child, he shall not enter therein. And He took them up in His arms, put His hands upon them, and blessed them.

Therefore, taking encouragement from these words, and firmly believing that the promise of the New Covenant is to our children, no less than to ourselves, let us call upon God the Father, in the name of our Lord Jesus Christ, that of His bounteous mercy He may grant to *this child*, through the Holy Sacrament of Baptism, that which by nature *he* cannot have; that being washed from *his* sins, and delivered from the power of the Devil, *he* may be made a member of Christ's Holy Church unto eternal salvation.

Here the Congregation shall rise, and continue standing until the Baptism is ended.

ALMIGHTY and everlasting God, who of Thy great mercy didst save Noah and his family in the ark by water; and also didst safely lead the children of Israel, Thy people, through the Red Sea, figuring thereby Thy holy Baptism; and by the Baptism of Thy well beloved Son, Jesus Christ, in the river Jordan, didst sanctify water to the mystical washing away of sin: we beseech Thee for Thine infinite mercies, graciously to look upon *this child*, to wash *him*, and sanctify *him* with the Holy Ghost, that *he* being delivered from Thy wrath, may be received into the ark of Christ's Church, and being steadfast in faith, joyful through hope, and rooted in charity, may so pass the waves of this troublesome world, that finally *he* may come to the land of everlasting life; there to reign with Thee, world without end, through Jesus Christ our Lord. *Amen.*

Then the Minister shall address the parents or sponsors as follows:

DEARLY BELOVED: You present *this child* here, and do seek for *him* deliverance from the power of the Devil, the remission of sin, and the gift of a new and spiritual life by the Holy Ghost, through the Sacrament of Baptism, which Christ hath ordained for the communication of such great grace. These benefits God, on his part, will most surely bestow, for the sake of His well beloved Son: wherefore, in the presence of God and these witnesses, I require of you, who are the sureties of *this child*, that on *his* part, and for *him*, who cannot answer for *himself*, you do now make that confession of unfeigned faith, out of a pure conscience, which Almighty God shall accept and answer, by vouchsafing His holy Baptism.

Then shall the Minister address to the parents or sponsors, the following questions, to which the answer shall be given audibly by each one.

Dost thou, in the name of this child, renounce the Devil with all his ways and works, the world with its vain pomp and glory, and the flesh with all its sinful desires?

Ans. I do.

Dost thou believe in God the Father Almighty, Maker of heaven and earth?

And in Jesus Christ His only begotten Son our Lord; who was conceived by the Holy Ghost, born of the Virgin Mary; suffered under Pontius Pilate, was crucified, dead, and buried; descended into hades; the third day rose from the dead; ascended into heaven, and sitteth at the right hand of God the Father Almighty; from whence He shall come to judge the quick and the dead?

And in the Holy Ghost; the holy catholic Church; the communion of saints; the forgiveness of sins; the resurrection of the body, and the life everlasting?

Ans. I believe.

Wilt thou that this child be baptized in this faith?
Ans. I will.

Dost thou promise to bring up this child in the nurture and admonition of the Lord, and in the doctrines and duties of our holy religion?
Ans. I do.

Then, taking the child on his arm, or leaving it in the arms of the parent or sponsor, the Minister shall say:

Name this child.

Thereupon, pronouncing the name aloud, he shall baptize it with a free application of water, saying:

N. I baptize thee, in the name of the Father, and of the Son, and of the Holy Ghost. *Amen.*

Then the Minister shall restore the child to the parents or sponsors and say:

Let us give thanks.

WE yield Thee hearty thanks, most merciful Father, that it hath pleased Thee, through the mystery of Thy holy Baptism, to deliver *this child* from the power of darkness, and to translate *him* into the kingdom of Thy dear Son, in whom we have redemption through His blood, even the forgiveness of sins. And we humbly beseech Thee to grant that *he,* being dead unto sin, and living unto righteousness, and being buried with Christ in His death, may crucify the old man, and utterly abolish the whole body of sin; and that as *he is* made *partaker* of the death of Thy Son, *he* may also be made *partaker* of His resurrection; so that finally, with the residue of Thy holy Church, *he* may be *an inheritor* of Thine everlasting kingdom; through Jesus Christ our Lord. *Amen.*

OUR Father who art in heaven, Hallowed be Thy name. Thy kingdom come. Thy will be done in earth, as it is in heaven. Give us this day our daily bread. And forgive us our debts, as we forgive our debtors. And lead us not into temptation. But deliver us from evil. For Thine is the kingdom, and the power, and the glory, for ever. Amen.

Then the Minister shall address the parents or sponsors, as follows:

DEARLY BELOVED IN THE LORD: Forasmuch as you have now dedicated *this child* by Baptism to the service of the Triune God, you must remember that it is your duty to train *him* up, by precept and example, in the true knowledge and fear of God according to the articles of the Christian faith and doctrine, as contained in the Old and New Testament, and in the symbols of the Church. Especially is it your duty, so soon as *he* shall be able to learn, to remind *him* often of *his* baptismal vows and obligations, and in particular to teach *him* the Lord's Prayer, the Apostles' Creed, and the Ten Commandments, that *he* may know how to pray, what to believe, and how to live. Finally, you are to see to it, that *he* be brought at the proper time to the Minister, to be instructed in the Catechism, and prepared for Confirmation and the Holy Communion; that *he* may heartily renew *his* baptismal vows, renounce in *his* own name the world, the flesh, and the Devil, profess Jesus Christ, and ever honor this profession by a holy life and conversation, to the glory of God, and the salvation of *his* soul.

Then shall the Minister pronounce this *Benediction:*

The peace of God, which passeth all understanding, keep your heart and mind, through Christ Jesus. *Amen.*

PRIVATE BAPTISM OF INFANTS.

In case of private Baptism, the form provided for use in the church shall be employed, unless sickness require the use of a shorter form, when the Minister addressing the parents or sponsors, shall proceed as follows:

DEARLY BELOVED: You present *this child* here, and do seek for *him* deliverance from the power of the Devil, the remission of sin, and the gift of a new and spiritual life by the Holy Ghost, through the Sacrament of Baptism, which Christ hath ordained for the communication of such great grace. These benefits God, on His part, will most surely bestow, for the sake of His well beloved Son: wherefore, in the presence of God and these witnesses, I require of you, who are the sureties of *this child*, that on *his* part and for *him*, who cannot answer for *himself*, you do now make that confession of unfeigned faith, out of a pure conscience, which Almighty God shall accept and answer, by vouchsafing His holy Baptism.

Then shall the Minister address to the parents or sponsors, the following questions, to which the answer shall be given audibly, by each one.

Dost thou, in the name of this child, renounce the Devil with all his ways and works, the world with its vain pomp and glory, and the flesh with all its sinful desires?

Ans. I do.

Dost thou believe in God the Father Almighty, Maker of heaven and earth?

And in Jesus Christ His only begotten Son our Lord; who was conceived by the Holy Ghost, born of the Virgin Mary; suffered under Pontius Pilate, was crucified, dead, and buried; descended into hades; the third day rose from the dead; ascended into heaven, and sitteth at the right hand of God the Father Almighty; from whence He shall come to judge the quick and the dead?

And in the Holy Ghost; the holy catholic Church; the communion of saints; the forgiveness of sins; the resurrection of the body, and the life everlasting?

Ans. I believe.

Wilt thou that this child be baptized in this faith?

Ans. I will.

Dost thou promise to bring up this child in the nurture and admonition of the Lord, and in the doctrines and duties of our holy religion?

Ans. I do.

Then, taking the child on his arm, or leaving it in the arms of the parent or sponsor, the Minister shall say:

Name this child.

Thereupon, pronouncing the name aloud, he shall baptize it with a free application of water, saying:

N. I baptize thee in the name of the Father, and of the Son, and of the Holy Ghost. *Amen.*

Then the Minister shall restore the child to the parents or sponsors, and say:

Let us give thanks.

WE yield Thee hearty thanks, most merciful Father, that it hath pleased Thee, through the mystery of Thy holy Baptism, to deliver *this child* from the power of darkness, and to translate *him* into the kingdom of Thy dear Son, in whom we have redemption through His blood, even the forgiveness of sins. And we humbly beseech Thee to grant that *he*, being dead unto sin, and living unto righteousness, and being buried with Christ in His death, may crucify the old man, and utterly abolish the whole body of sin; and that as *he is* made *partaker* of the death of Thy Son, *he* may also be made *partaker* of His resurrection; so that finally, with the residue of Thy holy Church, *he* may be *an inheritor* of Thine everlasting kingdom; through Jesus Christ our Lord. *Amen.*

OUR Father who art in heaven, Hallowed be Thy name. Thy kingdom come. Thy will be done in earth, as it is in heaven. Give us this day our daily bread. And forgive us our debts, as we forgive our debtors. And lead us not into temptation. But deliver us from evil. For Thine is the kingdom, and the power, and the glory, for ever. Amen.

Then shall the Minister pronounce this Benediction:

The peace of God, which passeth all understanding, keep your heart and mind, through Christ Jesus. *Amen.*

BAPTISM OF ADULTS

[Before adults are baptized, the Minister and Elders shall be satisfied that they understand the fundamental truths of the Christian religion, and are governed by them in their lives.

Adults must be baptized publicly, either in the church, or elsewhere, in the presence of a worshipping assembly. The Minister shall unite the rite of Confirmation with their Baptism, by laying his hands upon them, and pronouncing the Benediction, as in the Office of Confirmation.]

When adults are to be baptized, they shall present themselves at the altar, after the Gloria in Excelsis in the Lord's Day Service.

Pure water having been provided in the font, or some other clean vessel, fit and decent for the sacred ordinance, the Minister, standing near it, shall begin thus:

DEARLY BELOVED: That you may know and rightly understand, from God's holy word, the meaning and importance of the Sacrament of Baptism, hear first what Jesus said to Nicodemus: Verily, verily, I say unto thee, Except a man be born of water and of the Spirit, he cannot enter into the kingdom of God. That which is born of the flesh is flesh; and that which is born of the Spirit is spirit. Marvel not that I said unto thee, Ye must be born again. The wind bloweth where it listeth, and thou hearest the sound thereof, but canst not tell whence it cometh, and whither it goeth: so is every one that is born of the Spirit.

Hear also the words of the institution of this Sacrament: He said unto His disciples, Go ye into all the world, and preach the gospel to every creature. He that believeth and is baptized, shall be saved; but he that believeth not, shall be damned.

You see from these words of our Saviour, Jesus Christ, that we are all by nature in a sinful and lost condition, and cannot enter into the kingdom of God except by a new birth of water and of the Spirit; and that there is no salvation without faith in Jesus Christ, and a child-like submission to His ordinances. You see, moreover, that the ordinary way of entering into the covenant of grace, according to God's appointment, is the Sacrament of holy Baptism, by which we are divinely assured of the remission of our sins, and become partakers of the gift of the Holy Ghost. Hence, also, St. Peter, on the day of Pentecost, after preaching the gospel of Christ's death and resurrection, called upon the hearers, saying: Repent, and be baptized, every one of you, in the name of Jesus Christ, for the remission of sins, and ye shall receive the gift of the Holy Ghost. For the promise is unto you, and to your children, and to all that are afar off, even as many as the Lord our God shall call.

Then addressing the Congregation, he shall say:

THEREFORE, taking encouragement from these words, let us, as many as are here present, call upon God the Father, in the name of our Lord Jesus Christ, that of His bounteous mercy He may grant to *this person*, through the holy Sacrament of Baptism, that which

BAPTISM OF ADULTS. 199

by nature *he* cannot have; that being washed from *his* sins, and delivered from the power of the Devil, *he* may be made *a member* of Christ's holy Church, unto eternal salvation.

<small>Here the Congregation shall rise, and remain standing until the Baptism is ended.</small>

ALMIGHTY and everlasting God, who of Thy great mercy didst save Noah and his family in the ark by water; and also didst safely lead the children of Israel, Thy people, through the Red Sea, figuring thereby Thy holy Baptism; and by the Baptism of Thy well beloved Son, Jesus Christ, in the river Jordan, didst sanctify water to the mystical washing away of sin: we beseech Thee, for Thine infinite mercies, graciously to look upon *this person*, to wash *him*, and sanctify *him* with the Holy Ghost, that *he* being delivered from Thy wrath, may be received into the ark of Christ's Church, and being steadfast in faith, joyful through hope, and rooted in charity, may so pass the waves of this troublesome world, that finally *he* may come to the land of everlasting life, there to reign with Thee, world without end; through Jesus Christ our Lord. *Amen.*

<small>Then the Minister shall address the person or persons to be baptized:</small>

DEARLY BELOVED: You are come hither seeking deliverance from the power of the Devil, the remission of sin, and the gift of a new and spiritual life by the Holy Ghost, through the Sacrament of Baptism, which Christ hath ordained for the communication of such great grace. These benefits God, on His part, will most surely bestow, for the sake of His well beloved Son : wherefore, in the presence of God and these witnesses, I require of you, that you, on your part, do now make that confession of unfeigned faith, out of a pure conscience, which Almighty God shall accept and answer, by vouchsafing His holy Baptism.

<small>Then shall the Minister address to the person or persons to be baptized the following questions, to which the answer shall be given audibly by each one.</small>

Dost thou renounce the Devil with all his ways and works, the world with its vain pomp and glory, and the flesh with all its sinful desires?
Ans. I do.

Dost thou believe in God the Father Almighty, Maker of heaven and earth?

And in Jesus Christ His only begotten Son our Lord; who was conceived by the Holy Ghost, born of the Virgin Mary; suffered under Pontius Pilate, was crucified, dead, and buried; descended into hades; the third day rose from the dead; ascended into heaven, and sitteth at the right hand of God the Father Almighty; from whence he shall come to judge the quick and the dead?

And in the Holy Ghost; the holy catholic Church; the communion of saints; the forgiveness of sins; the resurrection of the body, and the life everlasting?
Ans. I believe.

Wilt thou be baptized in this faith?
Ans. I will.

BAPTISM OF ADULTS. 201

Dost thou promise to follow Christ, and to keep His commandments, all the days of thy life?

Ans. I do.

Then shall the Minister ask the name of the Catechumen, and requiring him to kneel down, shall baptize him, saying:

N. I baptize thee in the name of the Father, and of the Son, and of the Holy Ghost. *Amen.*

Then shall the Minister lay his hands on the head of the person baptized, and confirm him, saying:

The very God of peace sanctify you wholly; and I pray God your whole spirit, and soul, and body, be preserved blameless unto the coming of our Lord Jesus Christ. *Amen.*

Then the person or persons rising, the Minister shall proceed:

Let us give thanks.

WE yield Thee hearty thanks, most merciful Father, that it hath pleased Thee, through the mystery of Thy holy Baptism, to deliver *this person* from the power of darkness, and to translate *him* into the kingdom of Thy dear Son, in whom we have redemption through His blood, even the forgiveness of sins. And we humbly beseech Thee to grant that *he,* being dead unto sin, and living unto righteousness, and being buried with Christ in His death, may crucify the old man, and utterly abolish the whole body of sin; and that as *he is* made *partaker* of the death of Thy Son, *he* may also be made *partaker* of His resurrection; so that finally, with the residue of Thy holy Church, *he* may be *an inheritor* of Thine everlasting kingdom; through Jesus Christ our Lord. *Amen.*

Our Father who art in heaven, Hallowed be Thy name. Thy kingdom come. Thy will be done in earth, as it is in heaven. Give us this day our daily bread. And forgive us our debts, as we forgive our debtors. And lead us not into temptation. But deliver us from evil. For Thine is the kingdom, and the power, and the glory, for ever. Amen.

<small>Then shall the Minister pronounce this *Benediction*:</small>

And now may the God of all grace, who hath called us unto His eternal glory by Christ Jesus, after that ye have suffered awhile, make you perfect, stablish, strengthen, settle you: to Him be glory and dominion forever and ever. *Amen.*

CONFIRMATION.

[It is the duty of the baptized children of the Church to become Catechumens, as soon as they are old enough to commit to memory the Catechism, and to be benefited by the Pastor's instructions. In no case ought their attendance to be delayed beyond their thirteenth year. Their Catechization looks forward to their Confirmation, which forms its solemn completion.

Before Confirmation is administered, the Minister and Elders shall be satisfied that the candidate understands the fundamental truths of the Christian religion, and is governed by them in his life.]

After a *Sermon*, or an *Address*, the Minister shall read the names of the Catechumens, who shall then present themselves at the altar; whereupon the Minister shall begin thus:

Following the example of the holy Apostles, and those who succeeded them, the Church bestows upon those who have been baptized, either as adults or in their infancy, after they have been properly instructed, the blessing of Confirmation, by prayer and the laying on of hands.

The laying on of hands was first practised as a religious act by devout parents upon their children, whereby they imparted unto them the parental blessing, and confirmed them in faith and piety. By the laying on of hands also, such as were called to be public ministers in the Church were invested with the authority and grace of the sacred office; and so also by the same solemn act, the Apostles of our Lord communicated the gift of the Holy Ghost for the confirmation of believers after their baptism.

Then, addressing the Catechumens, he shall say:

DEARLY BELOVED: As children of your heavenly Father, called to a holy priesthood in the Church, to offer up spiritual sacrifices to God by Jesus Christ, you are now to receive the solemn rite of Confirmation by the laying on of hands, as your full and formal consecration to His holy service.

In this sacred ordinance, you on your part renew and ratify the promise and vow made in your baptism; whilst the Church, in God's stead, claims you publicly for His service, blesses you in His name, and confirms you in His covenant, invoking upon you in larger measure the Holy Ghost, by whose help alone you are able to fulfil your vows by leading holy and obedient lives.

Then shall the Minister address to the Catechumens the following questions, to which the answer shall be given audibly by each one.

Dost thou now, in the presence of God and of this Congregation, renew the solemn promise and vow made in your name at your baptism? Dost thou ratify and confirm the same, and acknowledge thyself bound to believe and to do all those things which your parents then undertook for you?

Ans. I do.

Dost thou renounce the Devil with all his ways and works, the world with its vain pomp and glory, and the flesh with all its sinful desires?

Ans. I do.

Then the Minister shall say:

Profess now your faith before God and this congregation.

<small>Here, the Congregation standing, the Catechumens led by the Minister shall repeat the *Apostles' Creed*, as follows:</small>

I BELIEVE in God the Father Almighty, Maker of heaven and earth:

And in Jesus Christ His only begotten Son our Lord; who was conceived by the Holy Ghost, born of the Virgin Mary; suffered under Pontius Pilate; was crucified, dead, and buried; He descended into hades; the third day He rose from the dead; He ascended into heaven, and sitteth at the right hand of God the Father Almighty; from thence He shall come to judge the quick and the dead.

I believe in the Holy Ghost; the holy catholic Church; the communion of saints; the forgiveness of sins; the resurrection of the body, and the life everlasting. Amen.

Minister. Our help is in the name of the Lord;

Congregation. Who hath made heaven and earth.

M. Blessed be the name of the Lord;

C. Henceforth, world without end.

M. Lord, hear our prayer;

C. And let our cry come unto Thee.

M. Let us pray.

ALMIGHTY and everlasting God, who out of infinite mercy in Christ Jesus, hast caused these Thy servants to be born again of water and of the Holy Ghost, and hast given unto them the remission of their sins; strengthen them, we beseech Thee, O Lord, through the Holy Ghost, the Comforter; and daily increase in them the manifold gifts of Thy grace, the spirit of wisdom and understanding, the spirit of counsel and might, the spirit of knowledge and of the fear of the Lord, now and forever. *Amen.*

<small>Then, the Congregation still standing, the Catechumens shall kneel, and the Minister, laying his hand on the head of each one successively, shall say:</small>

The very God of peace sanctify you wholly; and I pray God your whole spirit, and soul, and body, be preserved blameless unto the coming of our Lord Jesus Christ. *Amen.*

Here all shall kneel.

M. Let us pray.

ALMIGHTY GOD, our heavenly Father, we render Thee thanks for the great mercy Thou hast been pleased to show toward these Thy servants, by giving them power this day publicly to own and accept for themselves Thy covenant of salvation made with them before in the sacrament of Baptism, and by confirming unto them at this time the same grace through the solemn benediction of Thy holy Church. And now, O Lord, we beseech Thee to verify and fulfil in them the truth of this glorious covenant unto the end, that as they have been introduced into the kingdom of our Lord and Saviour Jesus Christ, and made to have part in its privileges and hopes, they may be constantly kept in the same by the power of the Holy Ghost, through faith, unto everlasting life. Fortify them against the assaults of sin and hell. Let not Satan prevail against them. Keep them from the evil that is in the world. Help them to walk in the Spirit, that they may not fulfil the lusts of the flesh. Defend them from all heresy and schism, from all apostasy and unbelief. Let them never draw back to perdition. Make them faithful unto death, that no man may take from them their crown. And grant, O most merciful Father, that having continued thus steadfast in faith and hope to the end, they may be counted worthy to be joined with Thy saints in heaven, and to have part with them finally in the resurrection of the dead; through Jesus Christ our Lord. *Amen.*

Then the Minister shall dismiss the Catechumens, saying:

The peace of God which passeth all understanding, keep your heart and mind, through Christ Jesus. *Amen.*

MARRIAGE.

At the day and time appointed, the persons to be married shall come into the body of the Church, or shall be ready in some proper house, with their friends and neighbors; and there standing together, the Man on the right hand, and the Woman on the left, the Minister shall say:

In the name of the Father, and of the Son, and of the Holy Ghost. *Amen.*

DEARLY BELOVED: We are assembled, in the sight of God and of His holy angels, to join together this man and this woman in the bonds of Matrimony; which is an honorable estate, instituted of God in the time of man's innocency, confirmed by the teaching of our blessed Saviour, and compared by St. Paul to the mystical union, which subsists between Christ and His Church.

Into this holy estate these two persons are come to be joined. Therefore, if any man can show any just cause why they may not be lawfully joined together, let him now speak, or else hereafter forever hold his peace.

And then addressing the persons to be married, he shall say:

I charge you each and both, as ye will answer before God at the day of judgment, if either of you know any reason why ye may not be lawfully joined together in matrimony, confess it now. For be well assured, that all those who are brought together, contrary to the word of God, are not joined together of God; neither is their marriage lawful.

If no impediment be alleged, the Minister shall say unto the man:

M. Wilt thou take this woman to be thy wedded wife?

Wilt thou love her, comfort her, honor, and keep her in sickness and in health; and, forsaking every other, cleave to her only, so long as ye both shall live?

The man shall answer:

I will.

Then shall the Minister say unto the woman:

N. Wilt thou take this man to be thy wedded husband?

Wilt thou obey him, love, honor, and keep him in sickness and in health; and, forsaking every other, cleave to him only, so long as ye both shall live?

The woman shall answer:

I will.

When a ring is used, the man shall give the ring to the woman, which the Minister taking from her shall deliver again to the man, who shall then place it upon the third finger of the woman's left hand, and holding it there, shall say after the Minister:

With this ring I thee wed: in the name of the Father, and of the Son, and of the Holy Ghost. Amen.

Then shall the Minister say:

As a seal to this holy vow, give each other the right hand.

Then the Minister, laying his hand upon the joined hands of the pair, shall say:

FORASMUCH as you, *M.* and *N.* have consented together in holy wedlock, and have witnessed the same before God and this company, I pronounce you man and wife, in the name of the Father, and of the Son, and of the Holy Ghost. *Amen.*

Those whom God hath joined together, let not man put asunder.

Let us pray.

O GOD, who by Thy mighty power hast made all things of nothing; who also didst appoint that out of man, created after Thine own image and similitude, woman should take her beginning; and knitting them together, didst teach that it should never be lawful to put asunder those whom Thou by matrimony hadst made one: look mercifully upon these Thy servants, that both this man may love his wife, according to Thy word, (as Christ did love His spouse the Church, who gave Himself for it, loving and cherishing it even as His own flesh,) and also that this woman may be loving and faithful to her husband; and in all quietness, sobriety, and peace, be a follower of holy and godly matrons. O Lord, bless them both, and grant them to inherit Thine everlasting kingdom; through Jesus Christ our Lord. *Amen.*

OUR Father who art in heaven, Hallowed be Thy name. Thy kingdom come. Thy will be done in earth, as it is in heaven. Give us this day our daily bread. And forgive us our debts, as we forgive our debtors. And lead us not into temptation. But deliver us from evil. For Thine is the kingdom, and the power, and the glory, for ever. Amen.

<small>Then shall he bless them:</small>

GOD the Father, God the Son, God the Holy Ghost, bless, preserve, and keep you; the Lord mercifully with His favor look upon you, and fill you with all spiritual benediction and grace; that ye may so live together in this life, that in the world to come ye may have life everlasting. *Amen.*

<small>After which, if the service be in the church, and there be no sermon declaring the duties of marriage, the Minister shall read as follows:</small>

ALL YE that are married, or that intend to take the excellent estate of matrimony upon you, hear what the Holy Scripture doth say as touching the duty of husbands towards their wives, and wives towards their husbands.

Saint Paul, in his Epistle to the Ephesians, the fifth Chapter, doth give this commandment to all married men: Husbands, love your wives, even as Christ also loved the Church, and gave Himself for it; that He might sanctify and cleanse it with the washing of water, by the word; that He might present it to Himself a glorious Church, not having spot, or wrinkle, or any such thing; but that it should be holy, and without blemish. So ought men to love their wives as their own bodies. He that loveth his wife loveth himself. For no man ever yet hated his own flesh, but nourisheth and cherisheth it, even as the Lord the Church: for we are members of His body, of His flesh, and of His bones. For this cause shall a man leave his father and mother, and shall be joined unto his wife; and they two shall be one flesh. This is a great mystery; but I speak concerning Christ and the Church. Nevertheless, let every one of you in particular so love his wife, even as himself.

Likewise the same St. Paul, writing to the Colossians, speaketh thus to all men that are married: Husbands, love your wives, and be not bitter against them.

Hear also what Saint Peter, the Apostle of Christ, who was himself a married man, saith unto them that are married: Ye husbands, dwell with your wives according to knowledge; giving honor unto the wife, as unto the weaker vessel, and as being heirs together of the grace of life, that your prayers be not hindered.

Hitherto ye have heard the duty of the husband toward the wife. Now likewise, ye wives, hear and learn your duties toward your husbands, even as it is plainly set forth in Holy Scripture.

Saint Paul, in the afore-named Epistle to the Ephesians, teacheth you thus: Wives, submit yourselves unto your own husbands, as unto the Lord. For the husband is the head of the wife, even as Christ is the head of the Church: and He is the Saviour of the body. Therefore as the Church is subject unto Christ, so let the wives be to their own husbands in every thing. And again he saith: Let the wife see that she reverence her husband.

And in his Epistle to the Colossians, Saint Paul giveth you this short lesson: Wives, submit yourselves unto your own husbands, as it is fit in the Lord.

Saint Peter also doth instruct you very well, thus saying: Ye wives, be in subjection to your own husbands; that, if any obey not the word, they also may without the word be won by the conversation of the wives; while they behold your chaste conversation coupled with fear. Whose adorning let it not be that outward adorning of plaiting the hair, and of wearing of gold, or of putting on of apparel; but let it be the hidden man of the heart, in that which is not corruptible, even the ornament of a meek and quiet spirit, which is in the sight of God of great price. For after this manner in the old time the holy women also, who trusted in God, adorned themselves, being in subjection unto their own husbands: even as Sara obeyed Abraham, calling him lord: whose daughters ye are, as long as ye do well, and are not afraid with any amazement.

After which the Minister shall close the service with this Benediction:

The grace of the Lord Jesus Christ, and the love of God, and the communion of the Holy Ghost, be with you all. *Amen.*

ORDINATION AND INSTALLATION.

ORDINATION OF MINISTERS.

After the Sermon, the presiding Minister, having taken his place at the altar, shall begin thus:

Let us pray:

MEET us, O Lord, in all our doings, with Thy most gracious favor, and further us with Thy continual help; that in all our works begun, continued, and ended in Thee, we may glorify Thy holy name, and finally by Thy mercy attain unto everlasting life; through Jesus Christ our Lord. *Amen.*

Here the Candidate for Ordination, his name being distinctly announced, shall be requested to present himself before the altar; whereupon the Minister shall address the Congregation, as follows:

DEARLY BELOVED IN THE LORD: Almighty God, whom it hath pleased by His Spirit and word to gather and preserve to Himself continually, out of the whole human race, a Church chosen to everlasting life, hath given to all the members of the same, both ministers and people, a common interest in its welfare. For this reason, it hath ever been the practice, that in the ordination of those who have been called to the office of the holy Ministry, the people also should have an opportunity to express their voice. Now, therefore, in order that we may be assisted in the case before us by your knowledge and past observation of him who is here present for admission to this office, we call upon you, to the end that if you know any just cause or impediment, because of which he ought not to be ordained to the Christian Ministry, you do come forward in God's name, and make it known.

If no objection be offered, after a sufficient pause, he shall address the Candidate, and say:

DEARLY BELOVED BROTHER: It is now our part, solemnly and for the last time, before proceeding to lay upon you irrevocably the burden and responsibility of the holy Ministry, to remind you how great is the dignity of the office, and how weighty and momentous also are the duties which it involves.

The office is of divine origin, and of truly supernatural character and force; flowing directly from the Lord Jesus Christ Himself, as the fruit of His resurrection and triumphant ascension into heaven, and being designed by Him to carry forward the purposes of His grace upon the earth, in the salvation of men by the Church, to the end of time.

All power, we hear Him saying after He had risen from the dead, is given unto Me in heaven and in earth; Go ye, therefore, and teach all nations, baptizing them in the name of the Father, and of the Son, and of the Holy Ghost; teaching them to observe all things whatsoever I have commanded you: and lo, I am with you alway, even unto the end of the world.

To this answers in full what is written also by St. Paul: Wherefore He saith, When He ascended up on high, He led captivity captive, and gave gifts unto men. Now that He ascended, what is it but that He also descended first into the lower parts of the earth? He that descended is the same also that ascended up far above all heavens, that He might fill all things. And He gave some, apostles; and some, prophets; and some, evangelists; and some, pastors and teachers; for the perfecting of the saints, for the work of the ministry, for the edifying of the body of Christ; till we all come in the unity of the faith, and of the Son of God, unto a perfect man, unto the measure of the stature of the fulness of Christ.

Consider well, dear brother in Christ, how much all this means, as declaring and setting forth the true nature and significance of the holy office. The first Ministers were the Apostles, who were called and commissioned immediately by Jesus Christ Himself. They in turn ordained and set apart other suitable men, as pastors and teachers over the churches which they had gathered and established in different places; and these again, in the same way appointed and sent forth others to carry onward and forward still the true succession of this office; which, being regularly transmitted in this way from age to age in the Christian Church, has come down finally to our time. The solemnity of ordination, through which this transmission flows, is not merely an impressive ceremony, by which the right of such as are called of God to the Ministry is owned and confessed by the Church; but it is to be considered rather as their actual investiture with the very power of the office itself, the sacramental seal of their heavenly commission, and a symbolical assurance from on high, that their consecration to the service of Christ is accepted, and that the Holy Ghost will most certainly be with them in the faithful discharge of their official duties.

These duties are of the same order with the high origin of the office, and its glorious design. The Ministers of Christ are set in the world to be at once the representatives of His authority, and the ambassadors of His grace. As My Father hath sent Me, He says, even so send I you. He that heareth you, heareth Me; and he that despiseth you, despiseth Me; and he that despiseth Me, despiseth Him that sent Me. Let a man so account of us, says St. Paul, as of the ministers of Christ and stewards of the mysteries of God. Again: We are ambassadors for Christ, as though God did beseech you by us. To them it belongs to baptize, to preach the word, to administer the holy Sacrament of the Lord's Supper. They are appointed to wait upon and serve the Church, which is the spouse of Jesus Christ, His body mystical; to offer before Him the prayers and supplications of His people; to feed, to instruct, to watch over and guide the sheep and lambs of His flock, whom He hath purchased with His own blood. They are charged also with the government of the Church, and with the proper use of its discipline, in the way both of censure and absolution, according to that awfully mysterious and solemn word: I will give unto thee the keys of the kingdom of heaven; and whatsoever thou shalt bind on earth, shall be bound in heaven; and whatsoever thou shalt loose on earth, shall be loosed in heaven.

Such being the character of the office to which you are now called, beloved brother in the Lord, and such the high and arduous nature of its duties, it is easy to see with what seriousness and godly fear, with what solemn forethought, with what holy caution, you should approach unto it, as you are now doing, in the present transaction; and with how great care and study also you ought to apply yourself, that you may appear hereafter to have been worthy of being put into the Christian Ministry, by being found faithful to its mighty trust. Know, at the same time, that for this you are by no means sufficient of yourself. All proper sufficiency here is from God alone; to whom therefore you should pray earnestly, through the mediation of our only Saviour Jesus Christ, for the heavenly assistance of the Holy Ghost; that giving yourself wholly to this office, with daily meditation, and study of the Scriptures, you may be able to make full proof of your ministry, being nourished up in the words of faith and good doctrine, and showing yourself a pattern to others in piety and godly living. In doing this, thou shalt both save thyself, and them that hear thee. And when the Chief Shepherd shall appear, you shall receive a crown of glory that fadeth not away.

And now, that this congregation of Christ may also understand your views and will in these things, and that you may yourself also the more feel the binding force of what you thus publicly profess and promise, we call upon you to make answer plainly to these following questions, which we now propose to you in the name of God and of His Church.

Do you receive the Holy Scriptures as being the true and proper word of God, the ultimate rule and measure of the whole Christian faith?

Ans. I do.

Do you believe in one God the Father; and in one Lord Jesus Christ, the only begotten Son of the Father; and in one Holy Ghost, proceeding from the Father and the Son, and with the Father and the Son one God Almighty?

Do you believe the Incarnation of our Lord Jesus Christ, the Son of God, whereby being perfect God He became also perfect Man; suffered for our salvation, descended into hades, rose again from the dead, and now sitteth at the right hand of God the Father Almighty, from whence He shall come to judge the quick and the dead?

And do you believe in one holy catholic Church, in which is given one true Baptism for the remission of sins?

Ans. I do.

Do you receive the confessional system of the Heidelberg Catechism as being in harmony with the Bible, and the ancient Christian Creeds?

Ans. I do.

Are you truly persuaded in your heart, that you are called of God to the office of the holy Ministry, and do you desire and expect to receive, through the laying on of our hands, the gift and grace of the Holy Ghost, which shall enable you to fulfil this heavenly commission and trust?

Ans. Such is my persuasion, and such my desire and hope.

Do you acknowledge the rightful authority of this Church, from which you are now to receive ordination, as being a true part in the succession of the Church Catholic; and do you promise to exercise your ministry in the same with faithful diligence, showing all proper regard for its laws and ordinances, and all suitable obedience to its lawful government in the Lord?

Ans. So I confess, and so I promise.

Here the Candidate shall be directed to kneel; the Ministers shall lay their right hands severally upon his head, and the presiding Minister shall say;

IN the name of the Lord Jesus Christ, the Chief Shepherd and Bishop of the Church, and trusting in the power of His grace, we ordain, consecrate, and appoint you to the Ministry of reconciliation, to proclaim His gospel, to dispense His holy Sacraments, to administer Christian discipline in His Church, and to be wholly set apart as an instrument to His use in the salvation of our fallen race, and to this end may the blessing of God Almighty, the Father, the Son, and the Holy Ghost, rest upon and abide with you always. *Amen.*

He shall then rise, when each of the Ministers in turn shall give him the right hand of fellowship, saying:

We give you the right hand of fellowship, to take part with us in this Ministry.

Or this:

Our fellowship is with the Father, and with the Son, and with the Holy Ghost.

Or this:

The grace of our Lord Jesus Christ, the love of God the Father, and the fellowship of the Holy Ghost, be with you always.

When the new Minister is to be installed at the same time as Pastor of the Charge in which he is ordained, the Installation services shall now go forward according to the form provided for that purpose. If there be no Installation, the presiding Minister shall here say:

Let us pray, beloved brethren, to God the Father Almighty, that He may be pleased to multiply His heavenly gifts upon this His servant, whom He hath called to the office of the holy Ministry, through Jesus Christ our Lord. *Amen.*

Then kneeling down:

ALMIGHTY God, most merciful Father, who of Thine infinite goodness hast given Thine only Son Jesus Christ to be our Redeemer, and the Author of everlasting life; who after that He had completed our redemption, and was ascended into heaven, poured down His gifts abundantly upon men, making some apostles, some prophets, some evangelists, some pastors and teachers, for the edifying and perfecting of His body the Church; send down, we beseech Thee, the anointing of the Holy Ghost upon the head of this Thy servant, who has now been set apart in Thy name, through the solemn act of ordination, to the office of teacher and ruler in Christ's Church. Grant unto him, O most merciful Father, such fulness of Thy grace, that he may be a faithful and wise steward whom Thou settest over Thy household, using the authority Thou givest him, not unto destruction, but unto salvation; that he may be an able minister of the New Testament, knowing how he ought to behave himself in the house of God, a workman that needeth not to be ashamed, rightly dividing the word of truth; that he may be a true preacher of righteousness; a faithful leader of the blind, and of them that are out of the way; a light unto those who are in darkness; a watchful guardian over Thy fold, and a follower of the true Shepherd who giveth His life for the sheep. Make his feet beautiful to publish the gospel of peace, and to bring glad tidings of good things. Give him power to preach not himself, but Christ Jesus the Lord, and himself the servant of all for Jesus' sake. May he be an example of the believers, in word, in conversation, in charity, in spirit, in faith, in purity. So may he in all things fulfil his ministry unblamably and unreprovably in Thy sight, that he may be prepared to stand without shame before the judgment seat of Christ, and thus, finishing his course with joy, be received unto glory and immortality in Thine eternal kingdom, where they that turn many to righteousness shall shine as the stars for ever and ever. Hear us for the sake of Jesus Christ Thy Son our Lord, who liveth and reigneth with Thee and the Holy Ghost, ever one God, world without end. *Amen.*

The Congregation shall then rise and join in singing a *Doxology*, after which the whole service shall be concluded with this *Benediction:*

The God of peace, who brought again from the dead our Lord Jesus Christ, the great Shepherd of the sheep, through the blood of the everlasting covenant, make you perfect in every good work to do His will, working in you that which is well pleasing in His sight, through Jesus Christ: to whom be glory for ever and ever. *Amen.*

INSTALLATION OF AN ORDAINED MINISTER IN A PARTICULAR CHARGE.

Immediately after the Ordination of the new Minister, if this take place on the same occasion, or in any other case after the sermon, the presiding Minister, having taken his place at the altar, shall address the Congregation as follows:

DEARLY BELOVED IN THE LORD: You have called *N. N.*, now present, an ordained Minister (*or*, who has now been ordained a Minister), to become your Pastor. He has consented to accept the call. After full inquiry and deliberation, the Classis of *M.* under whose supervision and care you stand, has resolved that the proposed settlement ought to take place; and being here accordingly, by its appointment and order, at the present time, for that purpose, we now proceed to institute and install him, in the name of the Lord, as the Pastor of this Charge.

Let us pray.

ALMIGHTY God, by whose holy inspiration and guidance, Thine Apostles, in the first days of Thy Church, did, for the fulfilling of their charge, ordain others also, who, under them, might take part in the care and government of Thy flock; grant, we beseech Thee, that all those who are placed by Thine authority over the several congregations of Thy people, may be endowed with Thy heavenly grace, and may so faithfully serve Thee in their office and administration, and watch over the souls under their charge, that at the appearing of our Lord Jesus Christ, they may present the people committed to their care a holy and glorious flock, giving an account of them with joy, and not with grief; through the same our Lord Jesus Christ, who liveth and abideth with Thee and the Holy Ghost, one God, world without end. *Amen.*

Then shall he read, either the whole or some part of, the following passages of *Scripture.*

Verily, verily, I say unto you, He that entereth not by the door into the sheepfold, but climbeth up some other way, the same is a thief and a robber. But he that entereth in by the door is the shepherd of the sheep. To him the porter openeth; and the sheep hear his voice: and he calleth his own sheep by name, and leadeth them out. And when he putteth forth his own sheep, he goeth before them, and the sheep follow him: for they know his voice. And a stranger will they not follow, but will flee from him: for they know not the voice of strangers. This parable spake Jesus unto them: but they understood not what things they were which he spake unto them. Then said Jesus unto them again, Verily, verily, I say unto you, I am the door of the sheep. All that ever came before me are thieves and robbers: but the sheep did not hear them. I am the door: by me if any man enter in, he shall be saved, and shall go in and out, and find pasture. The thief cometh not, but for to steal, and to kill, and to destroy: I am come that they might have life, and that they might have it more abundantly. I am the good shepherd: the good shepherd giveth his life for the sheep. But he that is an hireling, and not the shepherd, whose own the sheep are not, seeth the wolf coming, and leaveth the sheep, and fleeth: and the wolf catcheth them, and scattereth the sheep. The hireling fleeth, because he is an hireling, and careth not for the sheep. I am the good shepherd, and know my sheep, and am known of mine. As the Father knoweth me, even so know I the Father: and I lay down my life for the sheep. And other sheep I have, which are not of this fold: them also I must bring, and they shall hear my voice; and there shall be one fold, and one shepherd.

Jesus saith to Simon Peter, Simon, son of Jonas, lovest thou me more than these? He saith unto him, Yea, Lord; thou knowest that I love thee. He saith unto him, Feed my lambs. He saith to him again the second time, Simon, son of Jonas, lovest thou me? He saith unto him, Yea, Lord; thou knowest that I love thee. He saith unto him, Feed my sheep. He saith unto him the third time, Simon, son of Jonas, lovest thou me? Peter was grieved because he said unto him the third time, Lovest thou me? And he said unto him, Lord, thou knowest all things; thou knowest that I love thee. Jesus saith unto him, Feed my sheep.

This is a true saying, If a man desire the office of a bishop, he desireth a good work. A bishop then must be blameless, the husband of one wife, vigilant, sober, of good behavior, given to hospitality, apt to teach; not given to wine, no

P

striker, not greedy of filthy lucre; but patient, not a brawler, not covetous; one that ruleth well his own house, having his children in subjection with all gravity; (for if a man know not how to rule his own house, how shall he take care of the church of God?) not a novice, lest being lifted up with pride he fall into the condemnation of the devil. Moreover he must have a good report of them which are without; lest he fall into reproach and the snare of the devil.

And from Miletus Paul sent to Ephesus, and called the elders of the church. And when they were come to him, he said unto them, Ye know, from the first day that I came into Asia, after what manner I have been with you at all seasons, serving the Lord with all humility of mind, and with many tears, and temptations, which befel me by the lying in wait of the Jews: and how I kept back nothing that was profitable unto you, but have shewed you, and have taught you publicly, and from house to house, testifying both to the Jews, and also to the Greeks, repentance toward God, and faith toward our Lord Jesus Christ. And now, behold, I go bound in the spirit unto Jerusalem, not knowing the things that shall befall me there: save that the Holy Ghost witnesseth in every city, saying that bonds and afflictions abide me. But none of these things move me, neither count I my life dear unto myself, so that I might finish my course with joy, and the ministry, which I have received of the Lord Jesus, to testify the gospel of the grace of God. And now, behold, I know that ye all, among whom I have gone preaching the kingdom of God, shall see my face no more. Wherefore I take you to record this day, that I am pure from the blood of all men. For I have not shunned to declare unto you all the counsel of God. Take heed therefore unto yourselves, and to all the flock, over the which the Holy Ghost hath made you overseers, to feed the church of God, which he hath purchased with his own blood.

Be thou an example of the believers, in word, in conversation, in charity, in spirit, in faith, in purity. Till I come, give attendance to reading, to exhortation, to doctrine. Neglect not the gift that is in thee, which was given thee by prophecy, with the laying on of the hands of the presbytery. Meditate upon these things; give thyself wholly to them; that thy profiting may appear to all. Take heed unto thyself, and unto the doctrine; continue in them: for in doing this thou shalt both save thyself, and them that hear thee.

The elders which are among you I exhort, who am also an elder, and a witness of the sufferings of Christ, and also a partaker of the glory that shall be revealed: feed the flock of God which is among you, taking the oversight thereof, not by constraint, but willingly; not for filthy lucre, but of a ready mind; neither as being lords over God's heritage, but being ensamples to the flock. And when the chief Shepherd shall appear, ye shall receive a crown of glory that fadeth not away.

And we beseech you, brethren, to know them which labor among you, and are over you in the Lord, and admonish you; and to esteem them very highly in love for their work's sake. And be at peace among yourselves.

Remember them which have the rule over you, who have spoken unto you the word of God: whose faith follow, considering the end of their conversation; Jesus Christ the same yesterday, and to-day, and forever.

Obey them that have the rule over you, and submit yourselves; for they watch for your souls, as they that must give account, that they may do it with joy, and not with grief: for that is unprofitable for you.

The Congregation shall now rise, and the Pastor elect having presented himself before the altar, the presiding Minister shall address him thus:

AND now, beloved brother in Christ, in full view of the great solemnity of the trust as it is thus set forth by the lively oracles of God, are you willing and ready to take upon yourself the charge of this flock?

Ans. I am, God being my helper.

Do you promise and engage, on your part, that being set as Pastor of this people, you will endeavor faithfully to discharge among them all the duties of your ministry, exercising the authority you hold as a true commission from our Lord Jesus Christ, with becoming recollection of His presence, according to His commandments, and in due subjection to the rule that is over you in this church?

Ans. I promise so to do, with God's help.

Then addressing the Church and Congregation, he shall say:

DEARLY BELOVED: Ye have heard the solemn vows and engagements now taken by him whom you have called to be your Pastor; now, then, we demand of you, do ye on your part receive him in this character and office, promising to show towards him such love, honor, and fit obedience in the Lord, as are due to an overseer and guide placed over you by the Lord Jesus Christ Himself, the Chief Shepherd and Bishop of souls?

Ans. We do.

On the ground of this mutual engagement, we do now, by the authority which has been delegated to us for that purpose, solemnly install you, *N. N.*, as Pastor of this people, committing them by this act as a part of Christ's flock, to your spiritual oversight and care. In the name of the Father, and of the Son, and of the Holy Ghost. *Amen.*

Then addressing the Congregation, the presiding Minister shall say:

LET us pray, beloved brethren, to the Triune God, the fountain of all grace and glory, that He may be pleased to sanctify with His heavenly blessing, the Pastoral relation which has now been formed in His name. *Amen.*

AN ORDAINED MINISTER. 229

Then kneeling down:

ALMIGHTY God, most merciful Father, who of Thine infinite goodness hast given Thine only Son Jesus Christ to be our Redeemer and the Author of everlasting life; who after that He had completed our redemption, and was ascended into heaven, poured down His gifts abundantly upon men, making some apostles, some prophets, some evangelists, some pastors and teachers, for the edifying and perfecting of the Church; send down, we beseech Thee, the Holy Ghost upon Thy servant, whom Thou hast been pleased now to set over this people in the office of Bishop and Pastor; and so replenish him with the truth of Thy doctrine, and endue him with innocency of life, that he may faithfully serve before Thee, to the glory of Thy great name, and the benefit of Thy holy Church; through Jesus Christ our only Mediator and Advocate. *Amen.*

O HOLY Jesus, who hast purchased to Thyself an universal Church, and hast promised to be with the ministers of apostolic succession to the end of the world, be graciously pleased to bless the ministry and service of him who is now appointed to offer the sacrifices of prayer and praise to Thee in this house, which is called by Thy name. May the words of his mouth, and the meditation of his heart, be always acceptable in Thy sight, O Lord, our strength and our Redeemer. *Amen.*

AND Thou, O God the Holy Ghost, Sanctifier of the faithful, visit, we pray Thee, this Congregation with

Thy love and favor; enlighten their minds more and more with the light of the everlasting gospel; graft in their hearts a love of the truth; increase in them true religion; nourish them with all goodness; and of Thy great mercy keep them in the same, O blessed Spirit, whom with the Father and the Son together we worship and glorify as one God, world without end. *Amen.*

<small>Then the Congregation shall rise, and join in singing a *Doxology;* after which the whole service shall be concluded with this *Benediction:*</small>

The God of peace, who brought again from the dead our Lord Jesus Christ, the great Shepherd of the sheep, through the blood of the everlasting covenant, make you perfect in every good work to do His will, working in you that which is well pleasing in His sight, through Jesus Christ: to whom be glory for ever and ever. *Amen.*

ORDINATION AND INSTALLATION OF ELDERS AND DEACONS.

[When Elders only are to be set in office without Deacons, or Deacons only without Elders, such parts merely of the following form are to be used as relate to that particular case. So also, if the case calls for Installation only, all the persons elected to office having been previously ordained, there must be a like omission of what forms the Ordination act.]

After the *Sermon*, the Minister, having taken his place at the altar, shall say:

Let us pray.

Meet us, O Lord, in all our doings with Thy most gracious favor, and further us with Thy continual help; that in all our works, begun, continued, and ended in Thee, we may glorify Thy holy name, and finally, by Thy mercy, attain everlasting life; through Jesus Christ our Lord. *Amen.*

Here the persons to be set in office, their names being distinctly announced, shall be requested to present themselves before the altar; whereupon the Minister shall address the Congregation as follows:

DEARLY BELOVED IN THE LORD: These persons have been solemnly chosen and called by you, as a Christian Congregation, to take part as Elders and Deacons in the care and service of this church. They have accepted your call. No one has come forward to urge any just objection to their being set in office. I therefore proceed, in the name of the Lord, to ordain such of them as have not been ordained to the same degree before, and to set all of them apart, each in his own office, to the work of the ministry among you, and in your behalf.

<small>Then addressing the Candidates, he shall say:</small>

BRETHREN: As it is a great honor to bear office in the Lord's house, so is it at the same time also a high and solemn trust, which no one should take upon him rashly or lightly. For no such office, is of merely human origin or authority. There are diversities of gifts, and differences of administrations, in the Church; but all proceed from the same Lord, through the power of one and the same Spirit. Men may be chosen and called to their particular ministry by the voice of their fellow-men; but their ministry itself comes to them, not from earth, but from heaven; not from the people they serve, but from God. Its rights and powers, its duties and responsibilities, all flow from that jurisdiction of Christ in His Church, which is the fruit of His glorious resurrection, and which is to be regarded as a new order of life and power in the world, extending with real unbroken succession, from the day of Pentecost onward continually to the end of time. You may see thus how much is comprehended in your present ordination and induction into office; and how needful it is that you should magnify your ministry, and make high account of its duties, as a service to be fulfilled unto God, and not simply unto men.

ELDERS are appointed to assist and support the Ministers of the word in the general government of the Church. They form, with the Minister, in each particular ecclesiastical charge, a council in common for the spiritual supervision of the flock which is committed to their care. They are bound to take part, accordingly, in the work of the Ministry, so far as it has to do with this pastoral oversight and rule. They are to be the advisers and counsellors of the Minister in his episcopal trust; they are to be to him as hands and eyes, acting with him and for him, and representing his presence throughout the congregation. It is their province to go before the flock in the way of Christian example, to watch over it in the Lord, to take an active interest in its spiritual welfare, to feel a responsibility for its condition, to be at hand in all circumstances with spiritual aid for its necessities and wants. It belongs to them, in virtue of their office, to visit the sick and the afflicted, to instruct the ignorant, to admonish such as are out of the way, to warn the unruly, to command and rebuke with authority in Christ's name. To them, moreover, in conjunction with the Pastor, belongs the whole discipline of the Church, its power of the keys, as exercised both in the form of censure and in the form of absolution.

The office of DEACONS has regard especially to the wants of the poor. To them it belongs, accordingly, to help the Pastor, and to supply his place, in those church ministrations which are directed immediately towards the more outward needs of the general household of faith. On them falls the honorable charge of looking after the desolate and poor, and of seeing that the charities of the Church are applied with proper effect to their weekly and daily wants. In this service, at the same time, they must not lose sight of the true spiritual character of their office; which, however it may be thus occupied with outward and temporal things, remains always a proper branch of the Christian Ministry, the last scope and purpose of which in all things can only be the eternal salvation of men in the world to come. Hence it is that so much stress is laid, in the New Testament, on the character and life of those who are called to take part in this work. They must be men of honest report, full of the Holy Ghost and wisdom, who may be able, both by word and example, to help forward the great purpose of the Gospel, making their ministrations to the bodily necessities of the poor the occasion and means of a still better benefit to their souls. St. Paul also, writing on this subject, in his first Epistle to Timothy, requires of them expressly virtues and merits of like sort with those which are needful for the office of the Ministry in its most exalted character.

And now, brethren, having well considered the nature and design of these sacred offices, to the use of which you have been called respectively by the voice of this Congregation, do you accept the call as coming to you from God, and are you willing to undertake the work and service it sets before you, in the name and for the glory of our common Lord and Master Jesus Christ?

Ans. Yes.

OF ELDERS AND DEACONS. 235

Do you receive the Holy Scriptures as being the inspired word of God? Do you consent to the ancient and primitive symbol commonly called the Apostles' Creed, as being a true expression of the foundation articles of the Christian Faith? And do you own the doctrines of the Heidelberg Catechism, as flowing from the Bible in the sense of the same Creed?

Ans. I do.

Do you promise to exercise your ministry, as *Elders* or *Deacons*, among this people, with faithful diligence according to what you have now declared to be the rule and measure of your faith; showing all proper regard for the lawful authority of the Church, and taking heed to your own lives, that you may adorn the gospel of God our Saviour by a walk and conversation answerable to the place you occupy in Christ's house?

Ans. I so promise, trusting in God's help.

Here those who have not been previously ordained to the office in which they are now called to serve, shall be directed to kneel; whereupon the Minister shall proceed to *ordain* them, laying his right hand upon each one in succession, and saying:

Take thou authority to execute the office of Elder [*or,* Deacon] in the Church of God; which office I now solemnly commit unto thee, in the name of the Father, and of the Son, and of the Holy Ghost. *Amen.*

Then shall they rise; after which the Minister shall go on immediately to *install,* or clothe with actual charge in the Congregation, all who are before him for this purpose, both those now ordained, and any who may have been ordained before, making use of the following form:

In the name of the Lord Jesus Christ, and by the authority belonging to me in His Church, I now install you in the charge and service to which you have been called by this Congregation; and may the blessing of God Almighty, Father, Son, and Holy Ghost, rest upon you, abide with you, and strengthen you in your ministry always with all might through the Spirit, unto every good word and work. *Amen.*

Let us pray.

ALMIGHTY and most merciful God, our heavenly Father, who hast been pleased of Thy great goodness, to call *these* Thy *servants* to office and power in Thy Church, send down upon *them*, we beseech Thee, the Holy Ghost; by whose most blessed inspiration alone *they* can be made able to fulfill the ministry now committed unto *them*, and to use rightly therein the gift of Thy manifold grace. Let every fruit of the Spirit appear and abound in *them*, to the ornament of the gospel and the glory of Thy great name. Make *them* wise and faithful, humble, tender, modest, and yet bold, constant, patient, and persevering in their appointed work. In all *their* walk and conversation may Thy precepts shine forth; that, holding the testimony of a good conscience, *they* may abide in Christ firm and steadfast, and show forth a good example unto all Thy flock. So may *they* purchase to *themselves* a good degree and great boldness in the faith; through Jesus Christ our Lord, who liveth and reigneth with Thee, in the unity of the Holy Ghost, one God, world without end. *Amen.*

OF ELDERS AND DEACONS. 237

The Congregation shall now join in singing a Doxology, after which the whole service shall be concluded with this Benediction:

The God of peace, who brought again from the dead our Lord Jesus Christ, the great Shepherd of the sheep, through the blood of the everlasting covenant, make you perfect in every good work to do His will, working in you that which is well pleasing in His sight, through Jesus Christ: to whom be glory for ever and ever. *Amen.*

EXCOMMUNICATION AND RESTORATION.

EXCOMMUNICATION.

[If any member give offence to the Church by open sin, he shall first be admonished by the Minister, or an Elder privately; and afterwards, if he does not amend, in the presence of one or more witnesses. The admonition may be repeated, according to the nature of the case. If this discipline fail of its end, the offender is to be suspended, or separated from the use of the sacraments, and the prayers of the Congregation requested on his behalf. Should he still persist in his errors and sins, the proper steps shall be taken for his excommunication.

If, however, the offence be one of more than ordinary heinousness, the offender may be excommunicated, after due examination of the case, without previous admonition and suspension.]

The time having been announced beforehand, and the people exhorted to intercede with God, if by any means the offender may be brought to true repentance, the solemn act of Excommunication shall take place, in presence of the assembled congregation, as follows. The Minister, standing at the altar in company with the Elders, shall say:

DEARLY BELOVED IN THE LORD.: We have on several occasions made known to you, that *N. N.*, a member of this church, has been leading an immoral and ungodly life [*or*, has been holding and teaching false doctrine—*or*, has been holding and teaching false doctrine and leading an immoral and ungodly life], and has thus by *his* sin given great offence to the Church of Christ, to the end that by your prayers to God on *his* behalf, *he* might be brought to repentance, and so be freed from the bonds of the Devil. According to the command of our Lord, we have kindly told *him* *his* fault, both alone and in the presence of one or two witnesses; we have warned *him* of the end of *his* heinous offences against God and the Church, and admonished *him* to repent. But it is with deep sorrow of heart we announce to you, that thus far we have received no evidence of true repentance and reformation of life. On the contrary, *he* has hardened *his* heart, and daily increases *his* guilt by continuing in stubborness and disobedience.

Wherefore, in order that this corrupt member may not endanger the whole body, and that the name of God be not blasphemed among us through *him*, we are now in duty bound, by the command of our Lord, to proceed to the use of the last remedy, and cut *him* off from the communion of the Church.

We, therefore, the Minister and Elders of this church, assembled in the name and by the authority of our Lord Jesus Christ, do hereby announce to you all that N. N., because *he* will not forsake *his* sin, is excommunicated from the Church of God ; *he* is separated and cut off from the communion of saints, and from the use of the Sacraments, so long as he continues impenitent.

Moreover, we admonish you, dearly beloved, that you hold no fellowship with this person, so that *he* may be led to a deep sense of *his* fall and separation from the Church of Christ. We beseech you, however, not to treat *him* as an enemy; but admonish *him* and pray for *him*, that *he* may be brought to repentance, and restored to the communion of the Church. Remember also that ye yourselves are beset by temptation; and let the fall of this *man* be an example unto you, and a warning of your danger.

Ye have seen how *he* began to depart from the ways of truth and righteousness, and by degrees fell away more and more into error and sin, until Satan led *him* captive at his will. Observe, therefore, how cunning the great adversary of souls is, in leading men to destruction. The Devil, as a roaring lion, walketh about, seeking whom he may devour. Wherefore, let him that thinketh he standeth take heed lest he fall. Be sober; watch and pray, lest ye enter into temptation. Let every one be truly sorrowful for his sins, that God may not humble us again by the fall of any other member of this church. Beloved brethren, let your fellowship be with the Father, and with His Son Jesus Christ; and be ye steadfast, unmovable, always abounding in the work of the Lord.

Let us pray.

O RIGHTEOUS GOD, most merciful Father, we bewail our sins before Thy most high Majesty, and confess that we have deserved the sorrow and pain which we have felt in the separation of a member from Thy Church. For Christ's sake, be Thou gracious unto us; forgive our iniquities, over which we mourn; and work in our hearts a godly sorrow for sin, that we may fear the judgments which Thou dost send upon the stiff-necked and rebellious. And as Thou hast no pleasure in the death of the sinner, but wilt have all men to be converted and live; and as the door of Thy Church is always open to those who return to Thee with true penitence; we pray, O most merciful Father, for grace to walk before Thee in all holiness, and with humility and love to admonish *him*, upon whom this judgment has now come, that through Thy good Spirit, *he* may be brought to repentance, and restored to Thy favor. May we soon have cause to rejoice over *him* for whom we now have sorrow of heart, that Thy name may be praised, through Jesus Christ our Lord. *Amen.*

RESTORATION.

When an excommunicated person asks to be restored to the communion of the Church, the Minister and Elders shall make diligent inquiry into his state of mind and manner of life; and if he give sufficient evidence of being truly penitent, the Minister shall make the following announcement to the Congregation, at least one week before the time appointed for his restoration.

BELOVED IN THE LORD: It is my privilege to announce to you to-day, that N. N., who was cut off from our communion, has, by this remedy, as also by good admonitions and your Christian prayers, come so far, that, being ashamed of *his* sins, he now desires to be restored to the fellowship of the Church.

We have made diligent inquiry into *his* spiritual state and manner of life, and have good reason to believe that *he* has forsaken *his* wickedness, and turns to the Lord with a broken and a contrite heart. Since then, we are in duty bound, by the command of God, to receive such persons with joy, and yet it is necessary to proceed herein according to good order, we do hereby make known to you that we propose, on [Here the Minister shall name the time,] to loose *him* from the bond of excommunication, and restore *him* to the fellowship of the Church; except any one of you may know any just cause why this ought not to be done;

in which case it will be your duty to give us notice thereof in due time. Meanwhile, let every one thank the Lord for the mercy shown to this erring *brother*, and beseech Him to perfect His work in *him* to *his* eternal salvation. *Amen.*

At the appointed time, if no impediment be alleged, the Penitent coming forward, shall kneel before the altar, and the Minister, standing in company with the Elders, shall say to the Congregation:

BELOVED BRETHREN: We have, on a previous occasion, informed you of the repentance of *N. N.*, who was cut off from our communion, in order, that with your knowledge and approval, *he* might be restored to the fellowship of the Church. And inasmuch as no one has, in the meantime, brought any charge against *him*, we now proceed to *his* formal and solemn restoration.

Our Lord Jesus Christ declares that whatsoever His ministers shall loose on earth, shall be loosed in heaven; whereby He gives us to understand that, when any person is excommunicated from the Church, *he* is not at once cut off thereby from all hope of being saved, but may again be loosed from the bonds of condemnation. And as God declares in His word, that He has no pleasure in the death of the wicked, but that the wicked turn from his way and live, the Church always hopes for the conversion of her backslidden children, and keeps her bosom open for those who truly repent. Accordingly, the holy Apostle Paul commands that the Corinthian offender, who by his direction had been cut off from the Church, should be again received and comforted, lest perhaps such a one might be swallowed up with overmuch sorrow.

Our Lord teaches us also, that such absolution, being pronounced according to the word of God, is by Him accounted sure and firm: for Christ saith, Whosoever sins ye remit, they are remitted unto them. Wherefore no one, who truly repents, ought to doubt in the least that *he* is assuredly received by God in mercy.

Then, addressing the Penitent, he shall say:

Now, therefore I ask thee, *N. N.*, dost thou declare with all thy heart, before God and His Church, that thou art sincerely sorry for the sin and stubbornness for which thou hast been justly excommunicated, and dost thou desire to be restored to the communion of the Church of Christ, and promise henceforth to live in all godliness, according to the command of the Lord?

Ans. I do.

Then the Minister shall further say:

And now, in the name and by the authority of Christ and His Church, I announce to you the pardon of your sins; release you from the bond of excommunication; receive you and restore you to the fellowship of Christ, the communion of saints, and the use of the holy Sacraments. The God of all grace, who hath had pity upon you, and who hath given you repentance unto life, confirm you therein unto the end, through Jesus Christ our Lord. *Amen.*

RESTORATION. 245

Here the Penitent shall rise:

Seeing then, beloved *brother*, that God hath received you into grace, be careful to watch henceforward continually, that Satan, the world, and your flesh, may not cause you to fall again into sin. Bring forth fruits meet for repentance; and, as God has forgiven you much, love Him much, and walk before Him in newness of life.

And ye, brethren, receive this penitent with joy and tenderness; praise God for *his* return, and rejoice ye with the angels of heaven over this sinner who comes to-day to repentance; for *he* was dead and is alive again, *he* was lost and is found. Since God has forgiven and received *him,* let no one despise *him;* look no longer upon *him* as a stranger, but love *him* as a brother, and count *him* a fellow-citizen with the saints, and of the household of God. But let each one also profit by the example of *his* fall. Put on the whole armor of God, that ye may be able to stand against the wiles of the devil. For we wrestle not against flesh and blood, but against principalities, against powers, against the rulers of the darkness of this world, against spiritual wickedness in high places. Wherefore, take unto you the whole armor of God, that ye may be able to withstand in the evil day, and having done all to stand.

Let us return thanks unto the Lord.

O GRACIOUS GOD, our heavenly Father, we thank Thee through Jesus Christ Thy Son, that it hath pleased Thee to grant unto our *brother*, who is here present, repentance unto life, and to give us occasion to rejoice over *his* conversion. We beseech Thee to ratify in heaven, that which we have now done in *his* behalf on the earth. May *he* be more and more assured in *his* heart of the pardon of *his* sins, that thereby *he* may be comforted and animated for Thy service. Restore unto *him* the joy of Thy salvation; and let Thy free Spirit uphold *him*, that he may walk in Thy ways steadfastly all the days of *his* life. As *he* has offended many by *his* sins, so may *he* edify many by *his* conversion. And grant us all grace, we beseech Thee, that we may learn from this example to hold sin in abhorrence, and to fear Thee. Deliver us in the hour of temptation. Suffer none of us to draw back, nor to fall into sin, and dishonor Thy Church; but help us to hold fast our profession, and abide faithful unto the end, that we may receive the crown of life. All which we ask through Jesus Christ our Lord, to whom with Thee and the Holy Ghost, be honor and glory, world without end. *Amen.*

Then the Minister addressing *him*, shall say:

Depart in peace.

VISITATION AND COMMUNION OF THE SICK.

VISITATION OF THE SICK.

When any one is sick, notice thereof shall be given to the Minister, or, if any circumstance prevent his attendance, to one of the Elders of the Church, who, coming to the sick person, shall carefully inquire into his spiritual state.

[If the sick person be not baptized, he shall be immediately instructed as to his duty in this respect, and urged to become obedient to the faith, and enter into covenant with God. To this end the following Scripture passages shall be read and explained to him: Matt. xxviii. 18–20; Mark xvi. 16; John iii. 5; Acts ii. 38–41; Rom. vi. 3–12; Gal. iii. 27; Col. ii. 12; Titus iii. 5; 1 Peter iii. 21. If the sick person give evidence of true repentance and faith, the Minister shall baptize him in the presence of one or more Elders of the Church.]

When the necessary examination has been made, and the proper instructions and exhortations have been given, the Minister, or Elder, shall say:

DEARLY BELOVED: Be fully persuaded that Almighty God is the Lord of life and of death, and that all His creatures are so in His hands, that without His will they cannot so much as move. Wherefore, know certainly that this is God's visitation, coming not by chance, but by His fatherly hand. Know also that He will make whatever afflictions He sends upon us in this vale of tears, if they be received in the right spirit, and used in the right way, turn out to our advantage: for He is able to do it, being Almighty God, and willing also, being a faithful Father.

That your present afflictions may be sanctified to you, humble yourself with continual repentance for all your sins under the mighty hand of God. Acknowledge His faithfulness and love, and endeavor to bear your sickness with true Christian patience, trusting in His mercy through Jesus Christ, our Lord. Resign yourself wholly to His will, while you look and wait for His salvation, either in your restoration to health, or in your translation to the joys of heaven.

That you may be further instructed in regard to God's will concerning you in this your sickness, and receive such encouragement and consolation as you need, listen to those things which are written for our learning, that we, through patience and comfort of the Scriptures, might have hope.

<small>Here shall be read or repeated some suitable portions of Holy Scripture. The following are given for direction and help.</small>

I.

Affliction cometh not forth of the dust, neither doth trouble spring out of the ground.

Behold, happy is the man whom God correcteth: therefore despise not thou the chastening of the Almighty: for He maketh sore, and bindeth up: He woundeth, and His hands make whole. He shall deliver thee in six troubles: yea, in seven there shall no evil touch thee.

Behold, I have refined thee, but not with silver; I have chosen thee in the furnace of affliction.

I will bring them through the fire, and will refine them as silver is refined, and will try them as gold is tried: they shall call on My name, and I will hear them: I will say, It is My people: and they shall say, The Lord is my God.

Ye have forgotten the exhortation which speaketh unto you as unto children, My son, despise not thou the chastening of the Lord, nor faint when thou art rebuked of Him: for whom the Lord loveth He chasteneth, and scourgeth every son whom He receiveth. If ye endure chastening, God dealeth with you as with sons; for what son is he whom the father chasteneth not? But if ye be without chastisement, whereof all are partakers, then are ye bastards, and not sons. Furthermore, we have had fathers of our flesh which corrected us, and we gave them reverence: shall we not much rather be in subjection unto the Father of spirits and live? For they verily for a few days chastened us after their own pleasure; but He for our profit, that we might be partakers of His holiness. Now no chastening for the present seemeth to be joyous, but grievous: nevertheless, afterward it yieldeth the peaceable fruit of righteousness unto them which are exercised thereby. Wherefore lift up the hands which hang down, and the feeble knees.

For I reckon that the sufferings of this present time are not worthy to be compared with the glory which shall be revealed in us.

II.

Before I was afflicted I went astray: but now have I kept Thy word. Thou art good, and doest good; teach me Thy statutes. It is good for me that I have been afflicted; that I might learn Thy statutes. I know, O Lord, that Thy judgments are right, and that Thou in faithfulness hast afflicted me. Let, I pray Thee, Thy merciful kindness be for my comfort, according to Thy word unto Thy servant. Let Thy tender mercies come unto me, that I may live: for Thy law is my delight.

We glory in tribulations also; knowing that tribulation worketh patience; and patience, experience; and experience, hope: and hope maketh not ashamed; because the love of God is shed abroad in our hearts by the Holy Ghost which is given unto us.

We are chastened of the Lord, that we should not be condemned with the world.

For which cause we faint not; but though our outward man perish, yet the inward man is renewed day by day.

For our light affliction, which is but for a moment, worketh for us a far more exceeding and eternal weight of glory; while we look not at the things which are seen, but at the things which are not seen; for the things which are seen are temporal; but the things which are not seen are eternal.

III.

The Lord is my Shepherd; I shall not want. He maketh me to lie down in green pastures: He leadeth me beside the still waters. He restoreth my soul: He leadeth me in the paths of righteousness for His name's sake. Yea, though I walk through the valley of the shadow of death, I will fear no evil: for Thou art with me; Thy rod and Thy staff they comfort me. Thou preparest a table before me in the presence of mine enemies: Thou anointest my head with oil; my cup runneth over. Surely goodness and mercy shall follow me all the days of my life: and I will dwell in the house of the Lord forever.

For we know that if our earthly house of this tabernacle were dissolved, we have a building of God, an house not made with hands, eternal in the heavens. For in this we groan, earnestly desiring to be clothed upon with our house which is from heaven: if so be that being clothed we shall not be found naked. For we that are in this tabernacle do groan, being burdened: not for that we would be unclothed, but clothed upon, that mortality might be swallowed up of life. Now He that hath wrought us for the self-same thing is God, who also hath given unto us the earnest of the Spirit. Therefore we are always confident, knowing that, whilst we are at home in the body, we are absent from the Lord: (for we walk by faith, not by sight:) we are confident, I say, and willing rather to be absent from the body, and to be present with the Lord. Wherefore we labor, that, whether present or absent, we may be accepted of Him.

IV.

For me to live is Christ, and to die is gain. What I shall choose I wot not. For I am in a strait betwixt two, having a desire to depart, and to be with Christ; which is far better.

For I am now ready to be offered, and the time of my departure is at hand. I have fought a good fight, I have finished my course, I have kept the faith: henceforth there is laid up for me a crown of righteousness, which the Lord, the righteous Judge, shall give me at that day: and not to me only, but unto all them also that love His appearing. And the Lord shall deliver me from every evil work, and will preserve me unto His heavenly kingdom: to whom be glory for ever and ever. Amen.

V.

Though I walk in the midst of trouble, Thou wilt revive me.

O God, who is like unto Thee! Thou, which hast showed me great and sore troubles, shalt quicken me again, and shalt bring me up again from the depths of the earth.

For His anger endureth but a moment; in His favor is life: weeping may endure for a night, but joy cometh in the morning.

For the Lord will not cast off forever: but though He cause grief, yet will He have compassion according to the multitude of His mercies. For He doth not afflict willingly, nor grieve the children of men.

For a small moment have I forsaken Thee; but with great mercies will I gather thee. In a little wrath I hid my face from thee for a moment; but with everlasting kindness will I have mercy on thee, saith the Lord thy Redeemer. For the mountains shall depart, and the hills be removed; but my kindness shall not depart from thee, neither shall the covenant of my peace be removed, saith the Lord that hath mercy on thee.

Then the Minister, or Elder, shall pray with and for the sick person, slowly and distinctly rehearsing, in the first place, the *Apostles' Creed*, using afterward one or other of the following prayers, as the case may require, and closing with the *Lord's Prayer*.

◀ *A General Prayer for the Sick.*

O LORD God, in whose hand is the soul of every living thing, and the breath of all mankind; regard with tender compassion this Thy servant, whom it hath pleased Thee to visit with bodily affliction and disease. Be graciously near to *him* in the hour of *his* need. Grant unto *him*, we beseech Thee, true repentance for all *his* sins, a firm and steady trust in the merits of Thy Son, Jesus Christ, and grace to be in perfect charity with all men. Enable *him* to cast all *his* cares on Thee, and to yield *himself* with childlike submission to Thy righteous will.

God of all power and grace, bless, we entreat Thee, the means used for *his* recovery, rebuke the violence of disease, and raise *him* up from *his* bed of pain, that being delivered by Thy compassion *he* may walk before Thee in newness of life. But if, O most wise and merciful Father, this sickness should be unto death, grant *him*, we humbly implore Thee, a comfortable release from all *his* sufferings. Let the arms of Thine everlasting love be around *him*, and, when flesh and heart shall fail, be Thou the strength of *his* heart and *his* portion for evermore: through the mediation and merits of Thy Son, Jesus Christ, our Lord. *Amen.*

A Prayer for a Sick Person not prepared for Death.

MOST merciful Saviour, who, when hanging on the cross, didst grant repentance and faith to the dying thief, and hast assured us in Thy holy word, that Thou desirest not the death of the sinner, but that whosoever cometh unto Thee Thou wilt in no wise cast him out; look down, we beseech Thee, in tender compassion upon *him*, who now looks up to Thee from *his* bed of suffering and distress. Lamb of God, that takest away the sin of the world, have mercy upon *him*. Hear *his* prayer and wash *him* from *his* sins in Thy most precious blood. Give *him* strength against all *his* temptations and heal the maladies of *his* soul. Break not the bruised reed, nor quench the smoking flax. Shut not up Thy tender mercies in displeasure; but make him to hear of joy and gladness, that the bones which Thou hast broken may rejoice. Deliver *him* from fear of the Enemy, and lift up the light of Thy countenance upon *him*, and give *him* peace.

Hear us, merciful Saviour, who, with the Father and the Holy Ghost, livest and reignest, ever one God, world without end. *Amen.*

A Prayer for a Sick Child.

O ALMIGHTY God and merciful Father, to whom alone belong the issues of life and death; look down from heaven, we humbly beseech Thee, with the eyes of mercy upon this child, now lying upon the bed of sickness. Visit *him*, O Lord, with Thy salvation, deliver *him* in Thy good appointed time from *his* bodily pain, and save *his* soul for Thy mercies' sake; that if it shall be Thy pleasure to prolong *his* days here on earth, *he* may live to Thee, and be an instrument of Thy glory, by serving Thee faithfully, and doing good in *his* generation; or else receive *him* into those heavenly habitations, where the souls of those who sleep in the Lord Jesus, enjoy perpetual rest and felicity. Grant this, O Lord, for Thy mercies' sake, in the name of Thy Son, our Lord Jesus Christ, who liveth and reigneth with Thee and the Holy Ghost, ever one God, world without end. *Amen.*

Prayer for a Departing Soul.

ALMIGHTY God, with whom do live the spirits of just men made perfect, we humbly commend our departing *brother*, into Thy hands, as into the hands of a faithful Creator and most merciful Saviour; beseeching Thee that *his* soul may be precious in Thy sight. Wash *him*, we pray Thee, in the blood of that immaculate Lamb that was slain to take away the sins of the world; that whatsoever defilements *he* may have contracted in the midst of this miserable and wicked world, through the lusts of the flesh or the wiles of Satan, being purged and done away, *he* may be presented pure and without spot before Thee. Vouchsafe to *him* a quiet passage, and guide *him* through the valley of the shadow of death. Place *him* in the habitations of light and peace, in the company of Thy saints and faithful people who are gone before; and in the resurrection of the just do Thou make *him* partaker of the heavenly inheritance; there to reign with Thy holy apostles, with the goodly company of prophets and martyrs, and with all Thy saints, in glory and blessedness, for ever and ever. *Amen.*

A Litany for the Dying.

O God the Father in heaven; have mercy upon us.
Have mercy upon us.

O God the Son, Redeemer of the world; have mercy upon us.
Have mercy upon us.

VISITATION OF THE SICK. 255

O God the Holy Ghost, the Comforter; have mercy upon us.
Have mercy upon us.

Remember not, Lord, our offences, nor the offences of our forefathers. Spare us, good Lord; spare Thy servant before Thee, whom Thou hast redeemed with Thy precious blood.
Spare *him*, good Lord.

From all evil and harm; from the power of sin, and the snares of the devil; from Thy wrath, and from everlasting damnation;
Good Lord, deliver *him*.

By the mystery of Thy holy incarnation; by Thine agony and bloody sweat; by Thy cross and passion; by Thy precious death and burial; by Thy glorious resurrection and ascension; and by the coming of the Holy Ghost: in the hour of death and in the day of judgment;
Good Lord, deliver *him*.

We sinners do beseech Thee to hear us.
Son of God, we beseech Thee to hear us.

That it may please Thee to uphold *him* with Thy free Spirit; to grant *him* true repentance; to forgive *him* all *his* sins; to strengthen and confirm *him* in Thy grace; and to beat down Satan under *his* feet.
We beseech Thee to hear us, O Lord.

O Son of God, Redeemer of the world;
Hear us.

O Lamb of God, that takest away the sin of the world;
Have mercy upon *him*.

O Lamb of God, that takest away the sin of the world;
Grant *him* Thy peace.

O Lord God, our heavenly Father, who hast no pleasure in the death of the wicked, but that the wicked turn from his way and live, we heartily beseech Thee to regard this sick person with an eye of compassion; suffer *him* not to be overwhelmed by any pains of body, or any anguish of soul; but grant unto *him* in this world Thy pardon and peace, and in the world to come life everlasting; through the abounding merits and the glorious mediation of Jesus Christ our Lord. *Amen.*

COMMUNION OF THE SICK.

[If any member of the Church, through sickness or infirmity, be not able to come to the house of God, and yet is anxious to receive the Communion, it may be administered to him privately; in which case, timely notice thereof must be given to the Minister. One other person at least should commune with the sick; and one or more of the Elders ought to be present.

The Sacrament may also be administered to sick persons who have not been communicants, provided they have proper views of its nature, right dispositions of heart, and are first baptized and confirmed.]

The elements having been placed upon a decently covered table, the Minister shall say:

Grace be unto you, and peace from God our Father, and from the Lord Jesus Christ. *Amen.*

DEARLY BELOVED IN THE LORD: Forasmuch as in the providence of God, you are deprived of the privilege of receiving the Holy Communion in the church, and your heart nevertheless longs for the enjoyment of this blessing and grace, be encouraged and comforted by the words of the Lord Jesus: Where two or three are gathered together in My name, there am I in the midst of them.

That you may not partake unworthily of this holy Sacrament, consider well, and lay rightly to heart, the exhortation and warning of the Apostle Paul: Let a man examine himself, and so let him eat of that Bread and drink of that Cup. For he that eateth and drinketh unworthily, eateth and drinketh damnation to himself, not discerning the Lord's body.

Hear also how St. John encourages those who are truly penitent, saying: If we confess our sins, He is faithful and just to forgive us our sins, and to cleanse us from all unrighteousness.

And again it is written: If thou shalt confess with thy mouth the Lord Jesus, and shalt believe in thy heart that God hath raised Him from the dead, thou shalt be saved. For with the heart man believeth unto righteousness, and with the mouth confession is made unto salvation.

<small>Then the Minister and all present shall kneel, and repeat the following *Confession*.</small>

ALMIGHTY God, our heavenly Father, who dost admit Thy people unto such wonderful communion, that partaking of the Body and Blood of Thy dear Son, they should dwell in Him, and He in them; we unworthy sinners, approaching to Thy presence, and beholding Thy glory, do abhor ourselves, and repent in dust and ashes. We have sinned, we have sinned, we have grievously sinned against Thee, in thought, in word, and in deed, provoking most justly Thy wrath and indignation against us. The remembrance of our transgressions and shortcomings fills us with sorrow and shame. Yet now, O most merciful Father, have mercy upon us; for the sake of Jesus Christ, forgive us all our sins; purify us, by the inspiration of Thy Holy Spirit, from all inward uncleanness; enable us heartily to forgive others, as we beseech Thee to forgive us; and grant that we may ever hereafter serve and please Thee in newness of life; to the honor and glory of Thy name, through Jesus Christ our Lord. Amen.

<small>Then shall the Minister rise, and pronounce to those assembled, still kneeling, the following *Declaration of Pardon*.</small>

HEARKEN now unto the comforting assurance of the grace of God, promised in the Gospel to all that repent and believe: As I live, saith the Lord God, I have no pleasure in the death of the wicked, but that the wicked turn from his way and live. God so loved the world, that He gave His only begotten Son, that whosoever believeth in Him should not perish, but have everlasting life.

Unto as many of you, therefore, beloved brethren, as truly repent of your sins, and believe in the Lord Jesus Christ, with full purpose of new obedience, I announce and declare, by the authority and in the name of Christ, that your sins are forgiven in heaven, according to His promise in the Gospel, through the perfect merit of Jesus Christ our Lord. *Amen.*

<small>Then, all standing, the Minister shall say:</small>

Now join with us, whilst we, as many as are here present, make confession of our holy catholic faith.

I BELIEVE in God the Father Almighty, Maker of heaven and earth: And in Jesus Christ His only begotten Son our Lord; who was conceived by the Holy Ghost, born of the Virgin Mary; suffered under Pontius Pilate, was crucified, dead and buried; He descended into hades; the third day he rose from the dead; He ascended into heaven, and sitteth at the right hand of God the Father Almighty; from thence He shall come to judge the quick and the dead.

I believe in the Holy Ghost; the holy catholic Church; the communion of saints; the forgiveness of sins; the resurrection of the body, and the life everlasting. Amen.

M. Let us pray.

OUR Father who art in Heaven, Hallowed be Thy name. Thy kingdom come. Thy will be done in earth, as it is in heaven. Give us this day our daily bread. And forgive us our debts, as we forgive our debtors. And lead us not into temptation. But deliver us from evil. For Thine is the kingdom, and the power, and the glory, for ever. Amen.

Here, if desirable, a hymn or psalm may be sung.

If the elements have already been consecrated in the Church, the Minister shall proceed thus:

THE Lord Jesus, the same night in which He was betrayed, took bread; and when He had given thanks,

He brake it, and said, Take, eat, this is My Body which is broken for you; this do in remembrance of Me.

After the same manner also, He took the cup, when He had supped, saying, This cup is the New Testament in My Blood; this do ye, as oft as ye drink it, in remembrance of Me.

[If the elements have *not* been consecrated in the Church, the Minister shall consecrate in manner and form as follows:

THE LORD JESUS, THE SAME NIGHT IN WHICH HE WAS BETRAYED [here he shall take some of the bread into his hands] TOOK BREAD; AND WHEN HE HAD GIVEN THANKS, HE BRAKE IT [here he shall break the bread] AND SAID, TAKE, EAT; THIS IS MY BODY, WHICH IS BROKEN FOR YOU; THIS DO IN REMEBERANCE OF ME.

AFTER THE SAME MANNER ALSO [here he shall take the cup into his hands] HE TOOK THE CUP, WHEN HE HAD SUPPED, SAYING, THIS CUP IS THE NEW TESTAMENT IN MY BLOOD; THIS DO YE, AS OFT AS YE DRINK IT, IN REMEMBRANCE OF ME.

Let us pray.

ALMIGHTY God, our heavenly Father, send down, we beseech Thee, the powerful benediction of Thy Holy Spirit upon these elements of bread and wine, that being set apart now from a common to a sacred and mystical use, they may exhibit and represent to us with true effect the Body and Blood of Thy Son, Jesus Christ; so that in the use of them we may be made, through the power of the Holy Ghost, to partake really and truly of His blessed life, whereby only we can be saved from death, and raised to immortality at the last day. *Amen.*]

In administering the elements, the Minister shall give first to those who communicate with the sick, and then to the sick person.

Giving the bread, the Minister shall say:

The bread which we break, is the Communion of the Body of Christ.

Giving the cup, the Minister shall say:

The cup of blessing which we bless, is the Communion of the Blood of Christ.

When all have communed, the Minister shall say:

Let us pray.

ALMIGHTY and everlasting God, we give Thee most hearty thanks for the great goodness Thou hast shown toward us at this time, in vouchsafing to feed us, through these holy mysteries, with the spiritual food of the most precious body and blood of Thy Son, our Saviour Jesus Christ; assuring us thereby, that we are very members incorporate in the mystical body of Thy Son, and heirs through hope of Thine everlasting kingdom, by the merits of His most blessed death and passion. And we most humbly beseech Thee, O heavenly Father, so to assist us with Thy grace, that we may continue in that holy fellowship, and do all such good works as Thou hast prepared for us to walk in; through Jesus Christ our Lord, to whom, with Thee and the Holy Ghost, be all honor and glory, world without end. *Amen.*

The Minister shall close the service with this *Benediction:*

The peace of God, which passeth all understanding, keep your hearts and minds in the knowledge and love of God, and of His Son Jesus Christ, our Lord; and the blessing of God Almighty, the Father, the Son, and the Holy Ghost, be amongst you, and remain with you always. *Amen.*

THE BURIAL OF THE DEAD.

THE BURIAL OF MEMBERS OF THE CHURCH.

The Minister, going before the corpse, on entering the church and passing slowly along the aisle or, if there be no service in the church, on entering the graveyard, shall solemnly say:

I AM the resurrection and the life, saith the Lord; he that believeth in Me, though he were dead, yet shall he live: and whosoever liveth and believeth in Me, shall never die.

None of us liveth to himself, and no man dieth to himself; for whether we live, we live unto the Lord, and whether we die, we die unto the Lord: whether we live therefore or die, we are the Lord's: for to this end Christ both died and rose, and revived, that He might be Lord both of the dead and living.

And now is Christ risen from the dead, and become the first fruits of them that slept.

O death, where is thy sting? O grave, where is thy victory? Thanks be to God, which giveth us the victory through our Lord Jesus Christ! *Amen.*

[If the service be not held in the church, the following office as far as to the rubric directing the funeral to proceed to the grave, shall be omitted.]

BURIAL OF MEMBERS OF THE CHURCH.

Then, the Minister having taken his place at the altar, and all standing, the *Ninetieth Psalm* shall be chanted, or said, as follows:

Minister. Lord, Thou hast been our dwelling place in all generations.

Congregation. Before the mountains were brought forth, or ever Thou hadst formed the earth and the world, even from everlasting to everlasting, Thou art God.

M. Thou turnest man to destruction; and sayest, Return, ye children of men.

C. For a thousand years in Thy sight are but as yesterday when it is past, and as a watch in the night.

M. Thou carriest them away as with a flood; they are as a sleep: in the morning they are like grass which groweth up.

C. In the morning it flourisheth, and groweth up; in the evening it is cut down, and withereth.

M. For we are consumed by Thine anger, and by Thy wrath are we troubled.

C. Thou hast set our iniquities before Thee, our secret sins in the light of Thy countenance.

M. For all our days are passed away in Thy wrath: we spend our years as a tale that is told.

C. The days of our years are three score years and ten; and if by reason of strength they be four score years, yet is their strength labor and sorrow; for it is soon cut off, and we fly away.

M. Who knoweth the power of Thine anger? even according to Thy fear, so is Thy wrath.

C. So teach us to number our days, that we may apply our hearts unto wisdom.

Here the following *Lesson* (1 Cor. xv. 20-58,) shall be read.

Now is Christ risen from the dead, and become the first-fruits of them that slept. For since by man came death, by man came also the resurrection of the dead. For as in Adam all die, even so in Christ shall all be made alive. But every man in his own order: Christ the first-fruits; afterward they that are Christ's at his coming. Then cometh the end, when he shall have delivered up the kingdom to God, even the Father; when he shall have put down all rule and all authority and power. For he must reign, till he hath put all enemies under his feet. The last enemy that shall be destroyed is death. For he hath put all things under his feet. But when he saith, All things are put under him, it is manifest that he is excepted, which did put all things under him. And when all things shall be subdued unto him, then shall the Son also himself be subject unto him that put all things under him, that God may be all in all.

Else what shall they do which are baptized for the dead, if the dead rise not at all? Why are they then baptized for the dead?

And why stand we in jeopardy every hour? I protest by your rejoicing which I have in Christ Jesus our Lord, I die daily. If after the manner of men I have fought with beasts at Ephesus, what advantageth it me, if the dead rise not? let us eat and drink; for to-morrow we die. Be not deceived: evil communications corrupt good manners. Awake to righteousness, and sin not; for some have not the knowledge of God: I speak this to your shame.

But some man will say, How are the dead raised up? and

with what body do they come? Thou fool, that which thou sowest is not quickened, except it die: and that which thou sowest, thou sowest not that body that shall be, but bare grain, it may chance of wheat, or of some other grain: but God giveth it a body as it hath pleased him, and to every seed his own body. All flesh is not the same flesh: but there is one kind of flesh of men, another flesh of beasts, another of fishes, and another of birds. There are also celestial bodies, and bodies terrestrial: but the glory of the celestial is one, and the glory of the terrestrial is another. There is one glory of the sun, and another glory of the moon, and another glory of the stars: for one star differeth from another star in glory. So also is the resurrection of the dead. It is sown in corruption; it is raised in incorruption: it is sown in dishonor; it is raised in glory: it is sown in weakness; it is raised in power: it is sown a natural body; it is raised a spiritual body. There is a natural body, and there is a spiritual body. And so it is written, The first man Adam was made a living soul; the last Adam was made a quickening spirit. Howbeit that was not first which is spiritual, but that which is natural; and afterward that which is spiritual. The first man is of the earth, earthy: the second man is the Lord from heaven. As is the earthy, such are they also that are earthy: and as is the heavenly, such are they also that are heavenly. And as we have borne the image of the earthy, we shall also bear the image of the heavenly. Now this I say, brethren, that flesh and blood cannot inherit the kingdom of God; neither doth corruption inherit incorruption.

Behold, I show you a mystery; we shall not all sleep, but we shall all be changed, in a moment, in the twinkling of an eye, at the last trump: for the trumpet shall sound, and the dead shall be raised incorruptible, and we shall be changed. For this corruptible must put on incorruption, and this mortal must put on immortality.

So when this corruptible shall have put on incorruption,

and this mortal shall have put on immortality, then shall be brought to pass the saying that is written, Death is swallowed up in victory. O death, where is thy sting? O grave, where is thy victory? The sting of death is sin; and the strength of sin is the law. But thanks be to God, which giveth us the victory, through our Lord Jesus Christ. Therefore, my beloved brethren, be ye steadfast, unmoveable, always abounding in the work of the Lord, forasmuch as ye know that your labor is not in vain in the Lord.

Then the Minister shall say:

Let us pray.

ALMIGHTY GOD, with whom do live the spirits of those who depart hence in the Lord, and with whom the souls of the faithful, after they are delivered from the burden of the flesh, are in joy and felicity; we give Thee hearty thanks for the good examples of all those Thy servants, who, having finished their course in faith, do now rest from their labors. And we beseech Thee, that we, with all those who are departed in the true faith of Thy holy name, may have our perfect consummation and bliss, both in body and soul, in Thy eternal and everlasting glory; through Jesus Christ our Lord. *Amen.*

O THOU ever-blessed Mediator, who wast dead, but livest forever, of whom the whole family in heaven and earth is named, and who hast knit all Thy saints in one communion unto life eternal, in that mystical body of which Thou art the glorious and ever-living Head; grant us grace so to follow Thy blessed saints, who have gone before us, in the faith and fellowship of Thy holy Church, that we may come to those unspeakable joys, which Thou hast prepared for all that love Thee, from the foundation of the world. *Amen.*

O HOLY and ever-blessed Spirit, who art one with the Father and the Son, and who dwellest in all Thy saints, to comfort and quicken them; comfort us, we beseech Thee, in the prospect of death, with the hope of the resurrection of the just, and abide in us, that these mortal bodies may be quickened, and fashioned like unto our Saviour's glorious body, according to the working whereby He is able even to subdue all things unto Himself. *Amen.*

O HOLY and adorable Trinity, Father, Son, and Holy Ghost, Creator, Redeemer, and Sanctifier of our bodies and souls, we humbly confess our sins, and acknowledge them as the cause of our misery and death; and that, on account of our sins, Thou art justly displeased. Yet, through infinite mercy in Jesus Christ, we implore Thee, blot out our transgressions, wash us from our iniquity, and cleanse us from our sin. O Lord God most holy, O Lord most mighty, O holy and most merciful Saviour, deliver us not into the bitter pains of eternal death. *Amen.*

THOU knowest, Lord, the secrets of our hearts: shut not Thy merciful ears to our prayer; but spare us, Lord most holy, O God most mighty, O holy and merciful Saviour, Thou most worthy Judge eternal, suffer us not, at our last hour, for any pains of death, to fall from Thee. But keep us in everlasting fel lowship with the Church triumphant, and let us rest together in Thy presence from our labors; through Jesus Christ our Lord, who liveth and reigneth with Thee and the Holy Ghost, ever one God, world without end. *Amen.*

<small>Here may follow a short *Sermon* or *Exhortation;* after which the Minister shall say:</small>

Let us pray.

ALMIGHTY and most merciful God, the consolation of the sorrowful, and the support of the weary, who dost not willingly grieve or afflict the children of men; look down in tender love and pity, we beseech Thee, upon Thy servants, the bereaved household, whose joy is turned into mourning; and according to the multitude of Thy mercies be pleased to uphold, strengthen, and comfort them, that they may not faint under Thy fatherly chastening, but find in Thee their strength and refuge; through Jesus Christ our Lord. *Amen.*

OUR Father who art in heaven, Hallowed be Thy name. Thy kingdom come. Thy will be done in earth, as it is in heaven. Give us this day our daily bread. And forgive us our debts, as we forgive our debtors. And lead us not into temptation. But deliver us from evil. For Thine is the kingdom, and the power, and the glory for ever. Amen.

<small>After which the funeral shall proceed to the grave.</small>

BURIAL OF MEMBERS OF THE CHURCH. 271

At the grave, when the coffin has been let down, the Minister shall say:

In the name of the Father, and of the Son, and of the Holy Ghost. *Amen.*

I know that my Redeemer liveth, and that He shall stand at the latter day upon the earth: and though after my skin worms destroy this body, yet in my flesh shall I see God; whom I shall see for myself, and mine eyes shall behold, and not another.

I would not have you to be ignorant, brethren, concerning them which are asleep, that ye sorrow not, even as others which have no hope. For if we believe that Jesus died and rose again, even so them also which sleep in Jesus will God bring with Him.

The Lord gave, and the Lord hath taken away; blessed be the name of the Lord.

Let us pray.

ALMIGHTY GOD, who by the death of Thy Son Jesus Christ hast destroyed death; by His rest in the tomb hast sanctified the graves of the saints; and by His glorious resurrection hast brought life and immortality to light, so that all who die in Him abide in hope as to their bodies, and in joy as to their souls; receive, we beseech Thee, our unfeigned thanks for that victory over death and the grave which He has obtained for us and for all who sleep in Him; and keep us who are still in the body, in everlasting fellowship with all that wait for Thee on earth, and with all that are around Thee in heaven, in union with Him who is the Resurrection and the Life: who liveth and reign-

.eth with Thee and the Holy Ghost, ever one God, world without end. *Amen.*

FORASMUCH as it hath pleased Almighty God, in His wise providence, to take out of this world the soul of our deceased *brother,* we therefore commit *his* body to the ground; earth to earth, ashes to ashes, dust to dust: looking for the general resurrection in the last day, and the life of the world to come; through Jesus Christ our Lord. *Amen.*

I heard a voice from heaven, saying unto me, Write, Blessed are the dead which die in the Lord from henceforth: yea, saith the Spirit, that they may rest from their labors; and their works do follow them.

Let us pray.

M. Lord, have mercy upon us.
C. Christ, have mercy upon us.

M. Lord, have mercy upon us.
C. Christ, hear us.

M. Lord God, the Son, in the bosom of the Father, Saviour of the world;
C. Be gracious unto us.

M. By Thy human birth; by Thy prayers and tears; by all the troubles of Thy life; by the grief and anguish of Thy soul; by Thine agony and bloody sweat; by Thy bonds and scourgings; by Thy crown of thorns; by Thine ignominious crucifixion; by Thy sacred wounds and precious blood; by Thine atoning death; by Thy rest in the grave; by Thy glorious resurrection and ascension; by Thy sitting at the right hand of God; by Thy power to save;

C. Hear us, and save us, Lord Jesus.

M. O Lamb of God, that takest away the sin of the world;

C. Have mercy upon us, and grant us Thy peace. Amen.

After which the Minister shall close the service with the *Apostolic Benediction.*

The grace of our Lord Jesus Christ, and the love of God, and the communion of the Holy Ghost, be with you all. *Amen.*

THE BURIAL OF CHILDREN.

To be used at the grave.

Man that is born of a woman is of few days, and full of trouble. He cometh forth like a flower, and is cut down; he fleeth also as a shadow, and continueth not.

Jesus saith, Suffer the little children to come unto Me, and forbid them not: for of such is the kingdom of God. Verily I say unto you, Whosoever shall not receive the kingdom of God as a little child, he shall not enter therein.

Weep not, saith the Lord, the child is not dead, but sleepeth. If we believe that Jesus died and rose again, even so them also which sleep in Jesus will God bring with Him.

Let us pray.

ALMIGHTY God, who by the death of Thy Son Jesus Christ hast destroyed death; by His rest in the tomb hast sanctified the graves of the saints; and by His glorious resurrection hast brought life and immortality to light, so that all who die in Him abide in hope as to their bodies, and in joy as to their souls; receive, we beseech Thee, our unfeigned thanks for that victory over death and the grave which He has obtained for us and for all who sleep in Him; and keep us who are still in the body, in everlasting fellowship with all that wait for Thee on earth, and with all that are around Thee in heaven, in union with Him who is the Resurrection and the Life: who liveth and reigneth with Thee and the Holy Ghost, ever one God, world without end. *Amen.*

Forasmuch as it hath pleased Almighty God, in His wise providence to take out of this world the soul of this deceased child, we therefore commit *his* body to the ground; earth to earth, ashes to ashes, dust to dust: looking for the general resurrection in the last day, and the life of the world to come. *Amen.*

Let us pray.

M. Lord, have mercy upon us.
C. Christ, have mercy upon us.

M. Lord, have mercy upon us.
C. Christ, hear us.

M. Lord God, the Son, in the bosom of the Father, Saviour of the world;
C. Be gracious unto us.

M. By Thy human birth; by Thy prayers and tears; by all the troubles of Thy life; by the grief and anguish of Thy soul; by Thine agony and bloody sweat; by Thy bonds and scourgings; by Thy crown of thorns; by Thine ignominious crucifixion; by Thy sacred wounds and precious blood; by Thine atoning death; by Thy rest in the grave; by Thy glorious resurrection and ascension; by Thy sitting at the right hand of God; by Thy power to save;

C. Hear us, and save us, Lord Jesus.

M. O Lamb of God, that takest away the sin of the world;

C. Have mercy upon us, and grant us Thy peace. Amen.

<small>After which the Minister shall close the service with the *Apostolic Benediction.*</small>

The grace of our Lord Jesus Christ, and the love of God, and the communion of the Holy Ghost, be with you all. *Amen.*

A BURIAL SERVICE.

To be used at the grave.

Man that is born of a woman is of few days, and full of trouble. He cometh forth like a flower, and is cut down; he fleeth also as a shadow, and continueth not.

All flesh is as grass, and all the glory of man as the flower of the grass. In the morning it flourisheth, and groweth up: in the evening it is cut down and withereth. We are strangers before Thee, and sojourners, as were all our fathers: our days on earth are as a shadow, and there is none abiding. For what is your life? It is even a vapor, that appeareth for a little time, and then vanisheth away.

In the midst of life we are in death: of whom may we seek for succor, but of Thee, O Lord, who for our sins art justly displeased?

Yet, O Lord God most holy, O Lord most mighty, O holy and most merciful Saviour, deliver us not into the bitter pains of eternal death.

Thou knowest, Lord, the secrets of our hearts: shut not Thy merciful ears to our prayers; but spare us, Lord most holy. O God most mighty, O holy and merciful Saviour, thou most worthy Judge eternal, suffer us not, at our last hour, for any pains of death to fall from Thee.

The hour is coming, in the which all that are in the graves shall hear His voice, and come forth. Until that day of the glorious revelation of the great God and our Saviour, we commit this body to the ground: earth to earth; ashes to ashes; dust to dust. *Amen.*

Let us pray.

M. Lord, have mercy upon us.
C. Christ, have mercy upon us.

M. Lord, have mercy upon us.
C. Christ, hear us.

M. Lord God, the Son, in the bosom of the Father, Saviour of the world;
C. Be gracious unto us.

M. By Thy human birth; by Thy prayers and tears; by all the troubles of Thy life; by the grief and anguish of Thy soul; by Thine agony and bloody sweat; by Thy bonds and scourgings; by Thy crown of thorns; by Thine ignominious crucifixion; by Thy sacred wounds and precious blood; by Thine atoning death; by Thy rest in the grave; by Thy glorious resurrection and ascension; by Thy sitting at the right hand of God; by Thy power to save;
C. Hear us, and save us, Lord Jesus.

M. O Lamb of God, that takest away the sin of the world;
C. Have mercy upon us, and grant us Thy peace. Amen.

The Minister shall close the service with the *Apostolic Benediction.*

The grace of the Lord Jesus Christ, and the love of God, and the communion of the Holy Ghost, be with you all. *Amen.*

A SERVICE TO BE USED AT SEA.

The service shall begin with the singing of a *Hymn;* after which all shall kneel, and repeat the following *Confession.*

ALMIGHTY and most merciful God, our heavenly Father, we cast ourselves down before Thee, under a deep sense of our unworthiness and guilt. We have grievously sinned against Thee, in thought, in word, and in deed. We have come short of Thy glory. We have broken Thy commandments, and turned aside every one of us from the way of life; and in us there is no soundness nor health. Yet now, O most merciful Father, hear us when we call upon Thee with penitent hearts; and for the sake of Thy Son, Jesus Christ, have mercy upon us. Pardon our sins, and grant us Thy peace. Take away our guilt. Purify us, by the inspiration of Thy Holy Spirit, from all inward uncleanness; and make us able and willing to serve Thee in newness of life, to the glory of Thy holy name, through Jesus Christ our Lord. Amen.

Then a *Lesson,* taken from the "Order of Scripture Readings for the Family," shall be read.

All standing up, shall now join in repeating the *Apostles' Creed.*

I BELIEVE in God the Father Almighty, Maker of heaven and earth:

And in Jesus Christ His only begotten Son our Lord; who was conceived by the Holy Ghost, born of the Virgin Mary; suffered under Pontius Pilate, was crucified, dead, and buried; He descended into hades; the third day He rose from the dead; He ascended into heaven, and sitteth at the right hand of God the Father Almighty; from thence He shall come to judge the quick and the dead.

I believe in the Holy Ghost; the holy catholic Church; the communion of saints; the forgiveness of sins; the resurrection of the body, and the life everlasting. Amen.

After which the following prayers shall be used.

ALMIGHTY GOD, Father of all mercies, we, Thine unworthy servants, do give Thee most humble and hearty thanks for all Thy goodness and loving-kindness to us, and to all men. We praise Thee for our creation, preservation, and all the blessings of this life; but above all, for thine inestimable love in the redemption of the world by our Lord Jesus Christ; for the means of grace, and for the hope of glory. And, we beseech Thee, give us such due sense of all Thy mercies, that our hearts may be unfeignedly thankful, and that we may show forth Thy praise, not only with our lips, but in our lives; by giving up ourselves to Thy service, and by walking before Thee in holiness and righteousness all our days; through Jesus Christ our Lord, to whom, with Thee and the

Holy Ghost, be all honor and glory, world without end. *Amen.*

A Morning Prayer.

O LORD, our heavenly Father, Almighty and everlasting God, who hast safely brought us to the beginning of this day: defend us in the same with thy mighty power; and grant that this day we fall into no sin, neither run into any kind of danger; but that all our doings, being ordered by Thy governance, may be righteous in Thy sight; through Jesus Christ our Lord. *Amen.*

An Evening Prayer.

ALMIGHTY and everlasting God, be pleased to watch over us this night, and to spread the wings of Thy protection about us. Lighten our darkness, and by Thy great mercy deliver us from all perils and dangers, from every adverse working of the devil, from idle thoughts and wicked imaginations. Bring us, we beseech Thee, in safety to the morning hours, that thou mayest receive our praise at all times; through Jesus Christ our Lord. *Amen.*

O MOST powerful Lord God, King of kings, and Lord of lords, who alone ordainest the powers that be; take under Thy most gracious government and guidance, we beseech Thee, Thy servants, the President of the United States, our Legislators and Judges, and all others in authority; and so enrich them with heavenly wisdom and grace, that they may attain Thine everlasting favor, and we lead quiet and peaceable lives, in all godliness and honesty; through Jesus Christ our Lord. *Amen.*

O ETERNAL Lord God, who alone spreadest out the heavens, and rulest the raging of the sea, and hast compressed the waters with bounds, until day and night come to an end: be pleased to receive into Thine Almighty and most gracious protection the persons of us Thy servants, and the ship [*or* fleet] in which we serve. Preserve us from the dangers of the deep, and from the violence of enemies; [that we may be a safeguard unto our country, and a security for such as do business in the mighty waters;] that in due season we may return to our homes with a thankful remembrance of our mercies; and that finally, having passed the sea of this troublous life, we may enter the haven of eternal rest, through Him, who is our only refuge and Saviour, Jesus Christ our Lord. *Amen.*

Here any other prayers may be introduced.

ALMIGHTY God, who hast given us grace at this time, with one accord to make our common supplications unto Thee, and dost promise that where two or three are gathered together in Thy name, Thou wilt grant their requests; fulfil now, O Lord, the desires and petitions of Thy servants, as may be most expedient for them, granting us in this world knowledge of Thy truth, and in the world to come life everlasting. *Amen.*

OUR Father who art in heaven, Hallowed be Thy name. Thy kingdom come. Thy will be done in earth, as it is in heaven. Give us this day our daily bread. And forgive us our debts, as we forgive our debtors. And lead us not into temptation. But deliver us from evil. For Thine is the kingdom, and the power, and the glory, for ever. Amen.

PRAYERS AND THANKSGIVINGS FOR SPECIAL OCCASIONS AT SEA.

On commencing a Voyage.

O MOST powerful Lord God, who didst carry the hosts of Israel through the sea, singing the praise of Thy name; let Thy grace, going before and attending on our voyage, find for us a pathway upon the waters, and be to us our solace in setting sail; our guiding star on the way; our wand of peace among tempests; the shield of our defence against enemies; our harbor in shipwreck, and the anchor of our hope; that so we may come at length to the desired haven, both in this life and in the life immortal; through Jesus Christ our Lord. *Amen.*

During Storms at Sea.

O MOST glorious and gracious Lord God, who dwellest in heaven, but beholdest all things below; look down, we beseech Thee, and hear us, calling out of the depth of misery, and out of the jaws of this death, which is ready now to swallow us up: save, Lord, or we perish. The living, the living shall praise Thee. O send Thy word of command to rebuke the raging winds and the roaring sea; that we, being delivered from this distress, may live to serve Thee, and glorify Thy name all the days of our life; through the infinite merits of our blessed Saviour, Thy Son our Lord Jesus Christ. *Amen.*

In Time of War.

O ALMIGHTY God, Supreme Ruler and Governor of all things, who art a strong tower of defence to them that fear Thee, and whose power no creature is able to resist: unto Thee do we make our humble cry in this the hour of our country's need. To Thee it belongeth justly to punish sinners, and to be merciful to those who repent. Save and deliver us, we humbly beseech Thee, from the hands of our enemies; abate their pride, assuage their malice, and confound their devices; that we, being armed with Thy defence, may be preserved evermore from all perils, to glorify Thee, who art the only Giver of all victory; through the merits of Thy Son, Jesus Christ our Lord. *Amen.*

Before a Fight at Sea.

O MOST powerful and glorious Lord God, the Lord of hosts, that rulest and commandest all things: Thou sittest on the throne, judging right, and therefore we make our address to Thy divine Majesty in this our necessity, that thou wouldest take the cause into Thine own hand, and judge between us and our enemies. Stir up Thy strength, O Lord, and come and help us: for Thou givest not alway the battle to the strong, but canst save by many or by few. O let not our sins now cry against us for vengeance;

but hear us, Thy poor servants, begging mercy, and imploring Thy help, and that Thou wouldest be a defence unto us against the face of the enemy. Make it appear that Thou art our Saviour and mighty Deliverer; through Jesus Christ our Lord. Amen.

A Thanksgiving for a Safe Voyage.

MOST gracious Lord, whose mercy is over all Thy works; we praise Thy holy name, that Thou hast been pleased to conduct us in safety through the perils of the great deep, and to bring us to the end of our journey in peace. May we be duly sensible of Thy merciful providence toward us, and ever express our thankfulness by a holy trust in Thee, and obedience to Thy laws; through Jesus Christ our Lord. Amen.

A Thanksgiving for Deliverance from Storms.

O MOST merciful and mighty God, who at Thy pleasure raisest the winds and waves of the sea, or commandest them back to peace: we, Thy poor creatures, spared by Thy mercy to praise Thee, do give Thee unfeigned thanks, for that Thou heardest our cry when we were at the brink of death, and had given up all for lost, and didst not suffer us to sink in the devouring waters. And we here offer ourselves, our bodies and our souls, which Thou hast redeemed, to be a living sacrifice unto Thee of praise and thanksgiving, all the days of our lives; through Jesus Christ our Lord. Amen.

A Thanksgiving for Victory.

O Almighty God, the Sovereign Commander of all the world, in whose hands is power and might which none is able to withstand: we bless and magnify Thy great and glorious name for the happy victory wherewith Thou hast crowned our arms, and the whole glory whereof we do ascribe unto Thee, the only Giver of victory. And, we beseech Thee, give us grace to improve this great mercy to Thy glory, the honor of our country, and, as much as in us lieth, to the good of all mankind: through Christ Jesus our Lord, to whom with Thee and the Holy Spirit, as for all Thy mercies, so in particular for this, be all glory and honor, world without end. *Amen.*

BURIAL OF THE DEAD AT SEA.

The Office for the Burial of the Dead may be used, except that the following words shall be said on committing the body to the sea.

FORASMUCH as it hath pleased Almighty God, in His wise providence, to take out of this world the soul of His deceased servant, we therefore commit *his* body to the deep; looking for the general resurrection through our Lord Jesus Christ, at whose second coming in glorious majesty to judge the world, the earth and the sea shall give up their dead, according to the mighty working whereby He is able to subdue all things unto Himself.

A Prayer after Burial at Sea.

ALMIGHTY God, our heavenly Father, who in Thy perfect wisdom and mercy hast ended for Thy servant departed the voyage of this troublous life; grant, we beseech Thee, that we, who are still to continue our course, amidst earthly dangers, temptations and troubles, may evermore be protected by Thy mercy, and finally come to the haven of eternal salvation; through Jesus Christ our Lord. Amen.

PUBLIC RECEPTION OF IMMIGRANTS.

As early as convenient after the arrival of Christian brethren from a foreign land, they shall come into the Church, on the occasion of a public service, or at any other time appointed for that purpose, to render thanksgiving to God for His goodness in bringing them safely through the dangers of the sea, and that they may be publicly commended to the Christian fellowship and sympathies of the Congregation. Either at the beginning or the close of the regular service, at the discretion of the Minister, the newly-arrived brethren shall be invited to come forward and stand before the altar. Then the Minister shall announce to the Congregation their names, and at his discretion read such credentials as they may have brought from their fatherland, and give any information he may possess concerning their previous life and Christian character. Whereupon, the Congregation standing, a part of the One Hundred and Seventh Psalm shall be chanted, or said, as follows:

Minister. O that men would praise the Lord for His goodness, and for His wonderful works to the children of men!

Congregation. And let them sacrifice the sacrifices of thanksgiving, and declare His works with rejoicing.

M. They that go down to the sea in ships, that do business in great waters; these see the works of the Lord, and His wonders in the deep.

C. For He commandeth, and raiseth the stormy wind, which lifteth up the waves thereof.

M. They mount up to the heaven, they go down

again to the depths: their soul is melted because of trouble.

C. They reel to and fro, and stagger like a drunken man, and are at their wit's end.

M. Then they cry unto the Lord in their trouble, and He bringeth them out of their distresses.

C. He maketh the storm a calm, so that the waves thereof are still.

M. Then are they glad because they be quiet;
C. So He bringeth them unto their desired haven.

M. O that men would praise the Lord for His goodness, and for His wonderful works to the children of men!

C. Let them exalt Him also in the congregation of the people, and praise Him in the assembly of the elders.

Then the Minister, addressing the Congregation, shall say:

DEARLY BELOVED: Here, in the presence of the Lord, you behold Christian brethren, whom God in His merciful providence has preserved amid the perils of the great deep, and brought safely hither from a foreign land. Though strangers in the flesh, they are brethren in the spirit, fellow-citizens with the saints, and of the household of God, having obtained like precious faith with us, through the righteousness of God and our Saviour Jesus Christ.

As in the glorified Church in heaven, there are found before the throne praising God of all nations, and kindreds, and people, and tongues; so also in the Church on earth, there is no difference between one nation and another, but Christ is all, and in all. For as the body is one, and hath many members, and all the members of that one body, being many, are one body, so also is Christ. For by one spirit are we all baptized into one body, whether we be Jews or Gentiles; and have all been made to drink into one spirit. As St. Paul commended Phebe to the church at Rome, so we commend these brethren to you; and entreat, that ye receive them in the Lord, as becometh saints, and that ye assist them in whatsoever business they have need of you. Be not forgetful to entertain strangers; for thereby some have entertained angels unawares.

<small>Then the minister, addressing the Brethren at the altar, shall say:</small>

DEARLY BELOVED: Though you are no more in your earthly fatherland, you are still in the land of your Heavenly Father. All lands and all nations are His; and He is as nigh to you here, as He was in the land whence ye came. He will still be faithful to you: be ye also faithful to Him. Give unto the Lord thanksgiving, and pay your vows unto the Most High. Trust in the Lord, and do good; so shalt thou dwell in the land, and verily thou shalt be fed. Delight thyself also in the Lord; and He shall give thee the desires of thine heart. And it shall come to pass, if thou shalt hearken diligently unto the voice of the Lord thy God, to observe and to do all His commandments, that the Lord thy God will set thee on high, and all the blessings which He has promised shall come upon thee, and overtake thee, and all the people shall see that ye are called by the name of the Lord.

Then shall the Minister say:

Let us pray.

O LORD, the God of all nations, and kindreds and people, who art no respecter of persons, but rich in mercy towards all who call upon Thee, and hast united all Thy children through Jesus Christ, in one household of faith, and one communion of hope and love; we humbly commend to Thee these brethren, which have come to us from a far country, through Thy mighty hand and stretched-out arm; giving Thee most hearty thanks that Thou hast so mercifully protected them in their journey, amid perils by sea and land. Be pleased, O Lord, to give them friends and homes in this land of their choice and adoption. Bless them in basket and in store; but above all, bestow upon them freely and constantly, the richer blessings of Thy grace, that they may live in Thy fear and favor, and at last reach in safety the better country, even the eternal fatherland of the saints in heaven: through Jesus Christ our Lord, who liveth and reigneth with Thee and the Holy Ghost, ever one God, world without end. *Amen.*

Then the Minister shall bless them, saying:

The Lord bless thee, and keep thee:

The Lord make His face shine upon thee, and be gracious unto thee:

The Lord lift up His countenance upon thee, and give thee peace. *Amen.*

LAYING OF A CORNER STONE.

The people being assembled at the place where the church is to be built, the Minister, standing near the corner stone, shall say:

DEARLY BELOVED BRETHREN: It is meet and right that, in all our doings, we should beseech Almighty God for His most gracious direction and help; but, especially, as we are now assembled to begin a house, which is to be set apart for His honor and service; for the worship of His holy name, the preaching of His holy Gospel, and the administration of His holy Sacraments. Let us therefore devoutly look up to Him for assistance, protection and blessing.

Let us pray.

ALMIGHTY and everlasting God, who art always more ready to hear than we are to pray, and art wont to give more than either we desire or deserve; grant us, we beseech Thee, the fulness of Thy mercy. Prosper and bless the work which we have undertaken, that it may serve to promote Thy praise, and the honor of Thy kingdom; through Jesus Christ our Lord. *Amen.*

Then the *Ninety-Sixth Psalm* shall be chanted, or said, as follows:

Minister. O sing unto the Lord a new song: sing unto the Lord, all the earth.

Congregation. Sing unto the Lord, bless His name; show forth His salvation from day to day.

M. Declare His glory among the heathen, His wonders among all people.

C. For the Lord is great and greatly to be praised; He is to be feared above all gods.

M. For all the gods of the nations are idols; but the Lord made the heavens.

C. Honor and majesty are before Him: strength and beauty are in His sanctuary.

M. Give unto the Lord, O ye kindreds of the people, give unto the Lord glory and strength.

C. Give unto the Lord the glory due unto His name: bring an offering, and come into His courts.

M. O worship the Lord in the beauty of holiness: fear before Him, all the earth.

C. Say among the heathen that the Lord reigneth; the world also shall be established that it shall not be moved: He shall judge the people righteously.

M. Let the heavens rejoice, and let the earth be glad; let the sea roar, and the fulness thereof.

C. Let the field be joyful, and all that is therein:

then shall all the trees of the wood rejoice before the Lord.

M. For He cometh, for He cometh to judge the earth:

C. He shall judge the world with righteousness, and the people with His truth.

<small>Here, the inscription of the corner-stone being read, the Minister shall proceed to put into it the several articles which it is to contain, naming them as he does so one by one; after which, the stone being laid in its place, the service shall proceed thus:</small>

M. Our help is in the name of the Lord;
C. Who made heaven and earth.

M. Except the Lord build the house;
C. They labor in vain that build it.

<small>Placing his hand upon the stone, the Minister shall then say:</small>

I here lay the corner-stone of a house, to be erected under the name of ——— Church, and to be devoted to the worship of Almighty God. In the name of the Father, and of the Son, and of the Holy Ghost. *Amen.*

<small>Then shall the Minister say:</small>

Let us now unite in confessing our holy Catholic faith.

I BELIEVE in God the Father Almighty, Maker of heaven and earth:

And in Jesus Christ His only-begotten Son our Lord; who was conceived by the Holy Ghost, born of the Virgin Mary; suffered under Pontius Pilate, was crucified, dead, and buried; He descended into hades; the third day He rose from the dead; He ascended into heaven, and sitteth at the right hand of God the Father Almighty; from thence He shall come to judge the quick and the dead.

I believe in the Holy Ghost; the holy catholic Church; the communion of saints; the forgiveness of sins; the resurrection of the body, and the life everlasting. Amen.

Then shall he say:

Let us pray:

BLESSED be Thy name, O Lord, that it hath pleased Thee to put it into the hearts of Thy servants to commence the erection of a house, in which Thy Name is to be worshipped, the glad tidings of salvation proclaimed, and Thy holy Sacraments administered. Prosper Thou us, O Lord, in this our undertaking. Keep and preserve by Thy providence unto the end the work, which is now begun in Thy fear. Excite the skill and animate the industry of the workmen. Shield them from all accidents and dangers. And grant unto them, and all of us here present, the influences of Thy divine Spirit, so that we may become in soul and body living temples of the Holy Ghost, and be prepared for that eternal city which hath foundations, whose builder and maker is God. All which we ask through the abundant merits of our Lord and Saviour Jesus Christ, who liveth and reigneth with Thee and the Holy Ghost, ever one God, world without end. *Amen.*

LAYING OF A CORNER-STONE.

Here an address may be delivered. After which, a collection being made, the service shall be concluded with a *Hymn* and the *Apostolic Benediction*.

The grace of the Lord Jesus Christ, and the love of God, and the communion of the Holy Ghost, be with you all. *Amen.*

CONSECRATION OF A CHURCH.

The Minister, having taken his place at the altar, shall say:

GRACE be unto you, and peace from God our Father, and from the Lord Jesus Christ. *Amen.*

Then shall this *Canticle* be chanted, or said, as follows:

Minister. Arise, O Lord, into Thy rest; Thou, and the ark of Thy strength.

Congregation. Let Thy priests be clothed with righteousness; and let Thy saints shout for joy.

M. Make a joyful noise unto God, all ye lands. Serve the Lord with gladness: enter into His gates with thanksgiving, and into His courts with praise.

C. Who shall ascend into the hill of the Lord? or who shall stand in His holy place?

M. He that hath clean hands, and a pure heart; who hath not lifted up his soul unto vanity, nor sworn deceitfully.

CONSECRATION OF A CHURCH. 299

C. He shall receive the blessing from the Lord, and righteousness from the God of his salvation.

M. Lift up your heads, O ye gates; and be ye lift up, ye everlasting doors, and the King of glory shall come in.

C. Who is this King of glory? The Lord strong and mighty, the Lord mighty in battle.

M. Lift up your heads, O ye gates; even lift them up, ye everlasting doors, and the King of glory shall come in.

C. Who is this King of glory? The Lord of hosts, He is the King of glory.

Then shall the Minister say:

Let us pray.

O ETERNAL GOD, mighty in power, and of majesty incomprehensible, whom the heaven of heavens cannot contain, much less the walls of temples made with hands, to Thee alone be praise and adoration, from all the hosts of heaven and all who dwell upon the earth. With joy and gratitude we are now assembled in this house, built to the honor of Thy great name. Send down upon us, we beseech Thee, Thy Holy Spirit, that we may lift up holy hands to Thee, and worship Thee with pure hearts. O God, who art from everlasting to everlasting, hear us for the sake of Thy dear Son, Jesus Christ our Lord. *Amen.*

Here the *Scripture Lesson*, 1 Kings VIII, shall be read.

After this the *Eighty-fourth Psalm* shall be chanted, or said, as follows:

M. How amiable are Thy tabernacles, O Lord of hosts!
C. My soul longeth, yea, even fainteth for the courts of the Lord: my heart and my flesh crieth out for the living God

M. Yea, the sparrow hath found an house, and the swallow a nest for herself, where she may lay her young, even Thine altars, O Lord of hosts, my King, and my God.
C. Blessed are they that dwell in Thy house: they will be still praising Thee.

M. Blessed is the man whose strength is in Thee, in whose heart are the ways of them.
C. Who passing through the valley of Baca make it a well; the rain also filleth the pools.

M. They go from strength to strength, every one of them in Zion appeareth before God.
C. O Lord God of hosts, hear my prayer: give ear, O God of Jacob.

M. Behold, O God our shield, and look upon the face of Thine anointed.
C. For a day in Thy courts is better than a thousand. I had rather be a doorkeeper in the house of my God, than to dwell in the tents of wickedness.

M. For the Lord God is a sun and shield: the Lord will give grace and glory: no good thing will He withhold from them that walk uprightly.

C. O Lord of hosts, blessed is the man that trusteth in Thee.

Then the Minister shall say:

DEARLY BELOVED IN THE LORD: God, our heavenly Father, in all ages of the Church, has approved the acts of devout and holy men, who, moved either by His express command, or by the secret inspiration of His Spirit, have erected sanctuaries for His worship, and separated them from common use, that they might be sacred places, wholly consecrated to Himself. Animated by the pious example of those that have gone before us, sustained by the grace of God, and directed by His Spirit, we have built this house to the honor of His great name; and we are now together before God, that we may, by a solemn act of worship, devote it to its intended use.

Blessed be the Lord our God, who hath with His hand fulfilled the desires of our hearts, enabling us to build this house, where His name may be recorded, and His praise be made honorable, from generation to generation. *Amen.*

Here, the Congregation rising, the Minister shall say:

LET us now unite in confessing our holy catholic faith.

I BELIEVE in God the Father Almighty, Maker of heaven and earth:

And in Jesus Christ His only begotten Son our Lord; who was conceived by the Holy Ghost, born of the Virgin Mary; suffered under Pontius Pilate, was crucified, dead, and buried; He descended into hades; the third day He rose from the dead; He ascended into heaven, and sitteth at the right hand of God the Father Almighty; from thence He shall come to judge the quick and the dead.

I believe in the Holy Ghost; the holy catholic Church; the communion of saints; the forgiveness of sins; the resurrection of the body, and the life everlasting. Amen.

<small>The Minister shall then say:</small>

The Congregation who are here assembled, having erected this house for the worship of God, we now set it apart from all common and secular use, and, under the name of   , do hereby consecrate it to the worship of the Triune God, the Father, the Son, and the Holy Ghost. *Amēn.*

Let us pray.

O LORD OUR GOD, there is no God beside Thee. Thou alone art worthy to receive adoration and praise; for Thou art holy, and all nations shall come to worship before Thee, when they learn the joy of Thy salvation. We praise Thee, most merciful Father, for the foundation of Thy Church on earth; for Thy sacred oracles; for the ministry of Thy word; and for Thy holy sacraments. We give Thee thanks, that, by Thy providence, this house has been erected for the worship of Thy name. Accept, we beseech Thee, the work of our hands. Let this house be the house of God. Here let Thy presence dwell and Thy glory be revealed. When Thy holy word is read and preached in this place, and the holy sacraments are administered, send down upon the congregation the dews of Thy heavenly grace. When Thy people bring to Thee their thanksgiving for the gifts of Thy providence, accept their offering and bless them, that their joy may be full. And when, in seasons of calamity and distress, they humble themselves before Thee, and implore Thy mercy, hear Thou in heaven, and pity them; forgive their sins wherein they may have transgressed against Thee, and deliver them; or else comfort and support them under their trials, and sanctify unto them their affliction, that it may bring forth in them the fruits of salvation and peace.

Hear us, we beseech Thee, O God of all grace, Father of all light, and Fountain of all good. Let our prayer come up before Thee, and be acceptable, through the merit of Jesus Christ; and do unto us according to Thy great mercy and love. And unto Thee, the King eternal, immortal, and invisible; who alone art mighty, wise, and good; who dwellest in light which no man can approach unto and live; unto Thee be all glory, through Jesus Christ, in heaven and on earth, forever and ever. *Amen.*

Then shall the *Gloria in Excelsis* be chanted or said.

GLORY be to God on high, and on earth peace, good will toward men. We praise Thee, we bless Thee, we worship Thee, we glorify Thee, we give thanks to Thee for Thy great glory, O Lord God, heavenly King, God the Father Almighty.

O Lord, the only begotten Son, Jesus Christ; O Lord God, Lamb of God, Son of the Father, that takest away the sin of the world, have mercy upon us. Thou that takest away the sin of the world, have mercy upon us. Thou that takest away the sin of the world, receive our prayer. Thou that sittest at the right hand of God the Father, have mercy upon us.

For Thou only art holy; Thou only art the Lord; Thou only, O Christ, with the Holy Ghost, art most high in the glory of God the Father. *Amen.*

Then the Minister, having taken his place in the pulpit, shall deliver the *Sermon;* after which the service shall proceed as in the regular service for the Lord's Day.

CONSECRATION OF A BURIAL GROUND.

The people being assembled on the ground, the Minister shall say:

In the name of the Father, and of the Son, and of the Holy Ghost. *Amen.*

Let us pray.

O THOU ever blessed Mediator, who wast dead, but livest forever, of whom the whole family in heaven and earth is named, and who hast knit all Thy saints in one communion unto life eternal, in that mystical body of which Thou art the glorious and ever-living Head; grant us grace so to follow Thy blessed saints, who have gone before us, in the faith and fellowship of Thy holy Church, that we may come to those unspeakable joys, which Thou hast prepared for all that love Thee, from the foundation of the world. *Amen.*

The Minister shall now read the following Lessons.

The First Lesson, (*Gen.* xxiii.)

And Sarah was an hundred and seven and twenty years old: these were the years of the life of Sarah. And Sarah died in Kirjath-arba; the same is Hebron in the land of Canaan: and Abraham came to mourn for Sarah, and to weep for her. And Abraham stood up from before his dead, and spake unto the sons of Heth, saying, I am a stranger and a sojourner with you: give me a possession of a burying place with you, that I may bury my dead out of my sight. And the children of Heth answered Abraham, saying unto him, Hear us, my lord: thou art a mighty prince among us: in the choice of our sepulchres bury thy dead; none of us shall withhold from thee his sepulchre, but that thou mayest bury thy dead. And Abraham stood up, and bowed himself to the people of the land, even to the children of Heth. And he communed with them, saying, If it be your mind that I should bury my dead out of my sight, hear me, and entreat for me to Ephron the son of Zohar, that he may give me the cave of Machpelah, which he hath, which is in the end of his field; for as much money as it is worth he shall give it me for a possession of a burying place amongst you. And Ephron dwelt among the children of Heth: and Ephron the Hittite answered Abraham in the audience of the children of Heth, even of all that went in at the gate of his city, saying, Nay, my lord, hear me: the field give I thee, and the cave that is therein, I give it thee; in the presence of the sons of my people give I it thee: bury thy dead. And Abraham bowed down himself before the people of the land. And he spake unto Ephron in the audience of the people of the land, saying, But if thou wilt give it, I pray thee, hear me: I will give thee money for the field; take it of me, and I will bury my dead there. And Ephron answered Abraham, saying unto him, My lord, hearken unto me: the land is worth four hundred shekels of silver; what is that betwixt me and thee? bury therefore thy dead. And Abraham hearkened unto Ephron; and Abraham weighed to Ephron the silver, which he had named in the audience of the sons of Heth, four hundred shekels of silver, current money with the merchant. And the field of Ephron, which was in Machpelah, which was before Mamre, the field, and the cave which was therein, and all the trees that were in the field, that were in all the borders round about, were made sure unto Abraham for a possession in the presence of the children of Heth, before all that went in at the gate of his city. And after this, Abraham buried Sarah his wife in the cave of the field of Machpelah before Mamre: the same is Hebron in the land of Canaan. And the field, and the cave that is therein, were made sure unto Abraham for a burying place by the sons of Heth.

The Second Lesson, (1 *Cor.* xv., 12-26.)

Now if Christ be preached that he rose from the dead, how say some among you that there is no resurrection of the dead? But if there be no resurrection of the dead, then is Christ not risen: and if Christ be not risen, then is our preaching vain, and your faith is also vain. Yea, and we are found false witnesses of God; because we have testified of God that he raised up Christ; whom he raised not up, if so be that the dead rise not. For if the dead rise not, then is not Christ raised: and if Christ be not raised, your faith is vain; ye are yet in your sins. Then they also which are fallen asleep in Christ are perished. If in this life only we have hope in Christ, we are of all men most miserable. But now is Christ risen from the dead, and become the first fruits of them that slept.

For since by man came death, by man came also the resurrection of the dead. For as in Adam all die, even so in Christ shall all be made alive. But every man in his own order: Christ the first fruits; afterward they that are Christ's at his coming. Then cometh the end, when he shall have delivered up the kingdom to God, even the Father; when he shall have put down all rule and all authority and power. For he must reign, till he hath put all enemies under his feet. The last enemy that shall be destroyed is death.

Then the *Ninetieth Psalm* shall be chanted, or said, as follows:

Minister. Lord, Thou hast been our dwelling-place in all generations.

Congregation. Before the mountains were brought forth, or ever Thou hadst formed the earth and the world, even from everlasting to everlasting, Thou art God.

M. Thou turnest man to destruction; and sayest, Return, ye children of men.

C. For a thousand years in Thy sight are but as yesterday when it is passed, and as a watch in the night.

M. Thou carriest them away as with a flood; they are as a sleep; in the morning they are like grass which groweth up.
C. In the morning it flourisheth, and groweth up; in the evening it is cut down, and withereth.

M. For we are consumed by Thine anger, and by Thy wrath are we troubled.
C. Thou hast set our iniquities before Thee, our secret sins in the light of Thy countenance.

M. For all our days are passed away in Thy wrath; we spend our years as a tale that is told.
C. The days of our years are three score years and ten; and if by reason of strength they be fourscore years, yet is their strength labor and sorrow; for it is soon cut off, and we fly away.

M. Who knoweth the power of Thine anger? even according to Thy fear, so is Thy wrath.
C. So teach us to number our days, that we may apply our hearts unto wisdom.

Then the Minister shall say:

DEARLY BELOVED: The Holy Scriptures in divers places teach us to honor our bodies. God the Father has created them fearfully and wonderfully, and joined their destiny with that of our spirits. God the Son has honored them, by taking upon Him the form and fashion of a man in His glorious incarnation, so that His people are flesh of His flesh and bone of His bones. God the Holy Ghost honors them by dwelling in them as His temples. We are, moreover, assured that He who raised up Christ from the dead shall also quicken our mortal bodies by His Spirit that dwelleth in us; and we are encouraged to look for the Saviour, the Lord Jesus Christ, who shall change our vile body, that it may be fashioned like unto His glorious body according to the working whereby He is able even to subdue all things unto Himself.

With the whole Church of all ages, we believe in the resurrection of the body. I am the Resurrection and the Life, saith the Lord: he that believeth in Me, though he were dead, yet shall he live. Behold, saith the Apostle, I show you a mystery; we shall not all sleep, but we shall all be changed, in a moment, in the twinkling of an eye, at the last trump; for the trumpet shall sound, and the dead shall be raised incorruptible, and we shall be changed. For this corruptible must put on incorruption, and this mortal must put on immortality.

Such being the honor bestowed upon the bodies of the saints, and such the promises graciously delivered unto us concerning them, it is most meet and right that the bodies of the departed which rest in hope should also rest in honor and peace.

We are taught that the holy patriarch Abraham, the father of the faithful, when he was about to bury his dead out of his sight, bought a burying place, even the field of Machpelah. There he buried Sarah his wife: there he himself was buried: there they buried Isaac his son, and Rebecca his wife: and there afterwards they buried Jacob and Leah. We read, also, that Joseph of Arimathea, a disciple of Jesus, who waited for the kingdom of God, laid the precious body of Jesus in his own new tomb, which he had hewn out in the rock, and guarded it against desecration by rolling a great stone to the door, and setting a seal upon it.

Imitating this example of holy men, and led by the devout and tender spirit of the Church in all ages, we do now separate this ground from all common and secular use, and consecrate it under the name of ——————————————, as a place of burial and repose for the bodies of the dead, until the resurrection of the last day. In the name of the Father, and of the Son, and of the Holy Ghost. *Amen.*

Let us pray

· ALMIGHTY GOD, who by the death of Thy dear Son Jesus Christ hast destroyed death; by His rest in the tomb hast sanctified the graves of the saints; and by His glorious resurrection hast brought life and immortality to light, so that all who die in Him abide in hope as to their bodies, and in joy as to their souls: receive, we beseech Thee, our unfeigned thanks for that victory over death and the grave which He has obtained for us and for all who sleep in Him; and keep us who are still in the body, in everlasting fellowship with all that wait for Thee on earth, and with all that are around Thee in heaven, in union with Him who is the Resurrection and the Life; who liveth and reigneth with Thee and the Holy Ghost, ever one God, world without end. *Amen.*

OUR Father who art in heaven, Hallowed be Thy name. Thy kingdom come. Thy will be done in earth, as it is in heaven. Give us this day our daily bread. And forgive us our debts, as we forgive our debtors. And lead us not into temptation. But deliver us from evil. For Thine is the kingdom, and the power, and the glory, for ever. *Amen.*

After which the Minister shall close the service with this *Benediction:*

The grace of the Lord Jesus Christ, and the love of God, and the communion of the Holy Ghost, be with you all. *Amen.*

AN

ORDER OF SCRIPTURE READINGS

FOR

THE FAMILY.

FIRST WEEK IN ADVENT.

	FIRST LESSON.	SECOND LESSON.
Sunday.........	Genesis i., ii...................	Proverbs viii; John i. 1-14.
Monday.........	" iii., iv...................	Genesis ii. 4-25.
Tuesday........	" v., vi....................	Matthew xix. 1-12.
Wednesday.....	" vii., viii................	Ephesians v. 22-33.
Thursday	" ix........................	1 Corinthians vii.
Friday..........	" x.	Genesis iii.
Saturday.......	" xi........................	" viii. 15 to ix. 17.

SECOND WEEK IN ADVENT.

	FIRST LESSON.	SECOND LESSON.
Sunday.........	Genesis xii.......................	Acts xvii. 15-34.
Monday.........	" xiii.......................	Genesis xv.
Tuesday........	" xiv........................	Deuteronomy v.
Wednesday	" xv., xvi...................	Exodus xii.
Thursday	" xvii., xviii...............	Deuteronomy xxvii.
Friday..........	" xxi. 1-21..................	Romans vii.
Saturday.......	" xxii. 1-19.................	Leviticus xvi.

THIRD WEEK IN ADVENT.

	FIRST LESSON.	SECOND LESSON.
Sunday.........	Genesis xxiv., xxv. 1-11.....	Isaiah xl.; John v.
Monday.........	" xxv. 19-34, xxvi....	1 Peter i. 3-12.
Tuesday........	" xxvii., xxviii.........	2 Samuel vii.
Wednesday.....	" xxix. 1-35.............	Joel iii.
Thursday	" xxx. 25-43, xxxi.....	Jeremiah xxiii.
Friday..........	" xxxii., xxxiii.........	" xxxi.
Saturday.......	" xxxv.	Isaiah lii. 13, liii.

FOR THE FAMILY. 313

FOURTH WEEK IN ADVENT.

	FIRST LESSON.	SECOND LESSON.
Sunday.........	Genesis xxxvii................	John iii. 23–36; Lke i. 26–56.
Monday.........	" xxxix., xl............	Isaiah xlii.
Tuesday........	" xli., xlii............	" xlix.
Wednesday ...	" xliii., xliv............	" lv.
Thursday......	" xlv., xlvi.............	" lviii.
Friday..........	" xlvii., xlviii..........	" lx.
Saturday.......	" xlix. 1................	CHRISTMAS EVE: Is. xi. 1–10.

CHRISTMAS WEEK.

	FIRST LESSON.	SECOND LESSON.	
Sunday.........	Exodus i., ii................	Christmas Day,	{ Isa. ix. 2–7. Hebrews i.
Monday.........	" iii., iv................	Day after	{ Psalm ii.
Tuesday........	" v., vi. 1–13...........	Christmas.	{ " cx.
Wednesday.....	" vi. 28, vii., viii......	Sunday after Christmas.	{ Romans v. Col. i.
Thursday......	" ix., x., xi............	For the remaining days of the year.	{ Isaiah xli. " xlix. Rom. viii. 1 Cor. viii. 1–6.
Friday..........	" xii., xiii..............		
Saturday.......	" xiv., xv. 1–21........		

LAST DAY OF THE YEAR, Psalm xc. or ciii.

NEW YEAR'S WEEK.

	FIRST LESSON.	SECOND LESSON.	
Sunday..........	Exodus xv. 22, xvi., xvii....	New Year's Day,	{ 1 Pet. ii. 12–19. Luke ii. 22–40.
Monday	" xviii., xix., xx......	For the Week Days from New Year to Epiphany Sunday,	Philip. ii. 1–11. 1 Pet. iv. 12–19. Ephes. iii. Psalm xxiv., xcviii., cxlv.
Tuesday........	" xxi., xxii., xxiii.....		
Wednesday	" xxiv., xxv., xxvi...		
Thursday......	" xxvii., xxviii., xxix.		
Friday..........	" xxx., xxxi., xxxii...		
Saturday.......	" xxxiii., xxxiv........		

EPIPHANY WEEK.

	FIRST LESSON.	SECOND LESSON.
Sunday	Numbers i., ii., iii............	Luke ii. 40–52; John i. 29–34.
Monday	" iv., v., vi............	John i. 38–51.
Tuesday........	" x., xi., xii., xiii......	" ii.
Wednesday	" xiv., xv., xvi., xvii..	" iii.
Thursday......	" xx., xxi................	" iv.
Friday..........	" xxii., xxiii., xxiv....	" v.
Saturday.......	" xxxi., xxxii............	" vi. 1–25.

FIRST WEEK AFTER EPIPHANY.

	FIRST LESSON.	SECOND LESSON.
Sunday	Deuteronomy i., ii., iii.	John vi. 26–71.
Monday	" iv., v., vi.	" vii.
Tuesday	" vii., viii., ix.	" viii. 1–20.
Wednesday	" x., xi., xii.	" viii. 21–50.
Thursday	" xiii., xiv., xv.	" ix.
Friday	" xvi., xvii.	" x. 1–21.
Saturday	" xviii., xix.	" x. 22–42.

SECOND WEEK AFTER EPIPHANY.

	FIRST LESSON.	SECOND LESSON.
Sunday	Deuteronomy xxvii.	Mark i. 1–20.
Monday	" xxviii.	" i. 21–45.
Tuesday	" xxix., xxx.	" ii.
Wednesday	" xxxi.	" iii. 1–19.
Thursday	" xxxii.	" iii. 20–35.
Friday	" xxxiii.	" iv.
Saturday	" xxxiv.	" v. vi. 1–16.

THIRD WEEK AFTER EPIPHANY.

	FIRST LESSON.	SECOND LESSON.
Sunday	Joshua i., ii, iii.	Mark vi. 7–29.
Monday	" iv., v.	" vi. 30–56.
Tuesday	" vi., vii.	" vii. 1–23.
Wednesday	" viii., ix.	" vii. 24–37.
Thursday	" x., xi., xii.	" viii.
Friday	" xiii., xiv.	" ix.
Saturday	" xxiii., xxiv.	" x. 1–31.

FOURTH WEEK AFTER EPIPHANY.

	FIRST LESSON.	SECOND LESSON.
Sunday	Judges i., ii., iii.	Matthew iii.
Monday	" iv., v.	" iv. 1–22.
Tuesday	" vi., vii., viii.	" iv. 23; v. 1–12.
Wednesday	" ix., x., xi.	" v. 13–32.
Thursday	" xiii., xiv., xv., xvi.	" v. 33–48.
Friday	Ruth i., ii.	" vi.
Saturday	" iii., iv.	" vii.

FIFTH WEEK AFTER EPIPHANY.

	FIRST LESSON.	SECOND LESSON.
Sunday	1 Samuel i., ii.	Matthew viii. 1–17.
Monday	" iii., iv.	" viii. 17–34.
Tuesday	" v., vi.	" ix.
Wednesday	" vii., viii.	" x.
Thursday	" ix., x., xi.	" xi.
Friday	" xii., xiii.	" xii.
Saturday	" xiv., xv.	" xiii.

FOR THE FAMILY. 315

SIXTH WEEK AFTER EPIPHANY.

	FIRST LESSON.	SECOND LESSON.
Sunday	Job i., ii	Matthew xiv.
Monday	" iii., iv., v	" xv.
Tuesday	" vi., vii., viii	" xvi.
Wednesday	" ix., x	" xvii.
Thursday	" xi	" xviii.
Friday	" xii	" xix.
Saturday	" xiii., xiv	" xx. 1–16.

SEPTUAGESIMA WEEK.

	FIRST LESSON.	SECOND LESSON.
Sunday	Job xv	Luke iii.
Monday	" xvi	" iv.
Tuesday	" xvii	" v.
Wednesday	" xviii	" vi. 1–19.
Thursday	" xix	" vi. 20–49.
Friday	" xx	" vii.
Saturday	" xxi	" viii.

SEXAGESIMA WEEK.

	FIRST LESSON.	SECOND LESSON.
Sunday	Job xxii	Luke ix. 1–36.
Monday	" xxiii., xxiv	" ix. 37–62.
Tuesday	" xxv	" x.
Wednesday	" xxvi	" xi. 1–36.
Thursday	" xxvii., xxviii	" xi. 37—xii. 1–12.
Friday	" xxix., xxx	" xii. 13–59.
Saturday	" xxxi	" xiii. 1–21.

QUINQUAGESIMA WEEK.

	FIRST LESSON.	SECOND LESSON.
Sunday	Job xxxii., xxxiii	Luke xiii. 22–35.
Monday	" xxxiv., xxxv	" xiv.
Tuesday	" xxxvi., xxxvii	" xv.
WEDNESDAY	" xxxviii	" xvi.
Thursday	" xxxix	" xvii. 1–19.
Friday	" xl., xli	" xvii. 20–37.
Saturday	" xlii	" xviii. 1–30.

FIRST WEEK IN LENT.

	FIRST LESSON.	SECOND LESSON.
Sunday	1 Samuel xvi., xvii., xviii	John xii. 20–37; Luke xviii. 31—
Monday	" xix., xx	Luke xix.29—xx.1–18.[xix.1-28
Tuesday	" xxi., xxii	" xx. 9—xxi. 1–4.
Wednesday	" xxiii., xxiv	" xxi. 5–35.
Thursday	" xxv., xxvi., xxvii	" xxii. 1–30.
Friday	" xxviii., xxix	" xxii. 31–71.
Saturday	" xxx., xxxi	" xxiii.

SECOND WEEK IN LENT.

	FIRST LESSON.	SECOND LESSON.
Sunday	2 Samuel i., ii.	Mark x. 32–52.
Monday	" iii.	" xi.
Tuesday	" iv., v.	" xii.
Wednesday	" vi., vii., viii.	" xiii.
Thursday	" ix., x., xi.	" xiv. 1–54.
Friday	" xii.	" xiv. 55—xv. 1–15.
Saturday	" xiii., xiv.	" xv. 16–47.

THIRD WEEK IN LENT.

	FIRST LESSON.	SECOND LESSON.
Sunday	2 Samuel xv.	Matthew xx. 17–33.
Monday	" xvi., xvii.	" xxi.
Tuesday	" xviii.	" xxii.
Wednesday	" xix., xx.	" xxiii.
Thursday	" xxi., xxii.	" xxiv. 1–31.
Friday	" xxiii.	" xxiv. 32–51.
Saturday	" xxiv.	" xxv.

FOURTH WEEK IN LENT.

	FIRST LESSON.	SECOND LESSON.
Sunday	1 Kings i., ii.	Matthew xxvi. 1–13.
Monday	" iii., iv.	" xxvi. 14–35.
Tuesday	" v., vi.	" xxvi. 36–56.
Wednesday	" vii.	" xxvi. 57—xxvii.1–2.
Thursday	" viii.	" xxvii. 3–31.
Friday	" ix., x.	" xxvii. 32–50.
Saturday	" xi.	" xxvii. 51–66.

FIFTH WEEK IN LENT.

	FIRST LESSON.	SECOND LESSON.
Sunday	1 Kings xii., xiii., xiv.	John xi.
Monday	" xv., xvi.	" xii.
Tuesday	" xvii., xviii.	" xiii. 1–30.
Wednesday	" xix., xx.	" xiii. 31—xiv.
Thursday	" xxi., xxii.	" xv.
Friday	2 Kings i., ii., iii.	" xvi.
Saturday	" iv.	" xvii.

HOLY WEEK.

	FIRST LESSON.	SECOND LESSON.
Sunday	2 Kings v., vi.	Lamentations.
Monday	" vii., viii. 1–15.	Hebrews viii.
Tuesday	" viii. 16—ix., x.	" ix.
Wednesday	" xi., xii.	" x.
Thursday	" xiii., xiv.	John vi.
Friday	" xv.	Luke xxiii. 32–49.
Saturday	" xvi., xvii.	Hebrews iv.

FOR THE FAMILY.

EASTER WEEK.

	FIRST LESSON.	SECOND LESSON.
Sunday	Joel i.	Matthew xxviii.; John xx. 1–18.
Monday	" ii.	Luke xxiv. 1–12; 2 Cor. xiii.
Tuesday	" iii.	Acts ii. 22–47.
Wednesday	Jonah i.	1 Corinthians xv.
Thursday	" ii.	Romans vi.
Friday	" iii.	" viii.
Saturday	" iv.	1 Corinthians iii.

FIRST WEEK AFTER EASTER.

	FIRST LESSON.	SECOND LESSON.
Sunday	Amos i., ii.	John i.
Monday	" iii., iv.	" ii.
Tuesday	" v.	" iii.
Wednesday	" vi.	" iv.
Thursday	" vii.	" v.
Friday	" viii.	" vi. 1–40.
Saturday	" ix.	" vi. 41–71.

SECOND WEEK AFTER EASTER.

	FIRST LESSON.	SECOND LESSON.
Sunday	Hosea i., ii., iii.	John vii.
Monday	" iv., v.	" viii. 1–30.
Tuesday	" vi., vii.	" viii. 31–59.
Wednesday	" viii., ix.	" ix.
Thursday	" x., xi.	" x.
Friday	" xii.	" xi.
Saturday	" xiii., xiv.	" xii.

THIRD WEEK AFTER EASTER.

	FIRST LESSON.	SECOND LESSON.
Sunday	Zechariah ix., x.	John xiii., xiv.
Monday	" xi.	" xv.
Tuesday	Micah i., ii., iii.	" xvi., xvii.
Wednesday	" iv., v.	" xviii.
Thursday	" vi.	" xix.
Friday	" vii.	" xx.
Saturday	Nahum.	" xxi.

FOURTH WEEK AFTER EASTER.

	FIRST LESSON.	SECOND LESSON.
Sunday	2 Kings xviii.	Hebrews i., ii.
Monday	" xix.	" iii., iv.
Tuesday	2 Chronicles xxix.	" v., vi.
Wednesday	" xxx.	" vii.
Thursday	2 Kings xx., xxi.	" viii.
Friday	2 Chron. xxxiii; 2 Kings xxii.,	" ix.
Saturday	2 Kings xxiv., xxv....[xxiii.	" x.

AN ORDER OF SCRIPTURE READINGS

ASCENSION WEEK.

	FIRST LESSON.	SECOND LESSON.
Sunday	Zephaniah i.	Hebrews xi.
Monday	" ii.	" xii.
Tuesday	" iii.	" xiii.
Wednesday	Habakkuk i.	John xiv.
Thursday	" ii. 1–4.	Colossians ii.—Ephesians iv.
Friday	" ii. 5–20,	John xv.
Saturday	" iii.	" xvi.

THE WEEK BEFORE WHITSUNTIDE.

	FIRST LESSON.	SECOND LESSON.
Sunday	Zechariah xii.	1 John i.
Monday	" xiii.	" ii.
Tuesday	" xiv.	" iii.
Wednesday	Obadiah.	" iv.
Thursday	Psalm lxxvi.	" v.
Friday	" cxviii.	Joel iii.
Saturday	" cxlv.	John xvii.

WHITSUNTIDE.

	FIRST LESSON.	SECOND LESSON.
Sunday	Isaiah vi.	Exodus xix.—Gal. iii., iv. 1–7
Monday	" i.	Galatians v.—1 Corinth. xii.
Tuesday	" ii.	Romans xii.
Wednesday	" iii.	1 Corinthians xiii.
Thursday	" iv.	Romans vi. 19—vii.
Friday	" v.	" viii.
Saturday	" vii., viii. 1–8.	2 Corinthians v.

TRINITY WEEK.

	FIRST LESSON.	SECOND LESSON.
Sunday	Isaiah viii. 9—ix. 1–8.	Acts i., ii.
Monday	" ix. 9—x. 1–4.	" iii.
Tuesday	" xiv. 24—xv., xvi.	" iv.
Wednesday	" xvii., xviii.	" v.
Thursday	" xix., xx.	" vi.
Friday	" xxii.	" vii.
Saturday	" xxiii.	" viii.

FIRST WEEK AFTER TRINITY.

	FIRST LESSON.	SECOND LESSON.
Sunday	Isaiah xxiv., xxv.	1 Peter i., ii. 1–10; Acts ix.
Monday	" xxvi.	Acts x.
Tuesday	" xxvii.	" xi.
Wednesday	" xxviii.	" xii.
Thursday	" xxix.	1 Peter ii. 11—iii. 1–17.
Friday	" xxx.	" iii. 18—iv. 1–16.
Saturday	" xxxi.	" iv. 17—v.

SECOND WEEK AFTER TRINITY.

	FIRST LESSON.	SECOND LESSON.
Sunday	Isaiah xxxii.	James i.; 2 Peter i. 1–11
Monday	" xxxiii.	2 Peter i. 12, ii., iii.
Tuesday	" xxxiv.	James ii.
Wednesday	" xxxv.	" iii.
Thursday	" x. 5—xi.	" iv.
Friday	" xii.	" v.
Saturday	" xxxviii., xxxix.	Jude.

THIRD WEEK AFTER TRINITY.

	FIRST LESSON.	SECOND LESSON.
Sunday	Jeremiah i.	Acts xiii. 1–12.
Monday	" ii.	" xiii. 13–52.
Tuesday	" iii.	" xiv.
Wednesday	" iv.	" xv.
Thursday	" v.	" xvi.
Friday	" vi.	" xvii. 1–14.
Saturday	" xxii. 1–23.	" xvii. 15—xviii. 11.

FOURTH WEEK AFTER TRINITY.

	FIRST LESSON.	SECOND LESSON.
Sunday	Jeremiah vii.	1 Thessalonians i.
Monday	" viii.	" ii. 1–16.
Tuesday	" ix.	" ii. 17, iii.
Wednesday	" x.	" iv.
Thursday	" xi.	" v.
Friday	" xii.	2 Thessalonians i., ii. 1–12.
Saturday	" xiii.	" ii. 13, iii.

FIFTH WEEK AFTER TRINITY.

	FIRST LESSON.	SECOND LESSON.
Sunday	Jeremiah xiv.	Galatians i. 1–10.
Monday	" xv.	Acts xviii. 12, xix. 1–10.
Tuesday	" xvi.	Galatians i. 11, ii. 1–14.
Wednesday	" xvii.	" ii. 15, iii. 1–14.
Thursday	" xviii.	" iii. 15.
Friday	" xix.	" iv.
Saturday	" xx.	" v., vi.

SIXTH WEEK AFTER TRINITY.

	FIRST LESSON.	SECOND LESSON.
Sunday	Jeremiah xlv., xlvi.	1 Corinthians i.
Monday	" xlvii.	" ii.
Tuesday	" xlviii.	" iii., iv. 1–4.
Wednesday	" xlix.	" iv. 5, v. 1–8.
Thursday	" xxv.	" v. 9, vi.
Friday	" xxvi.	" vii.
Saturday	" xxxv., xxxvi.	" viii., ix.

SEVENTH WEEK AFTER TRINITY.

	FIRST LESSON.	SECOND LESSON.
Sunday	Jeremiah xxii., xxiii.	1 Corinthians x., to xi. 1.
Monday	" xxiv.	" xi. 2.
Tuesday	" xxix.	" xii. 1–30.
Wednesday	" xxi.	" xii. 31, xiii.
Thursday	" xxvii.	" xiv.
Friday	" xxviii.	" xv. 1–34.
Saturday	" l., li.	" xv. 35, xvi.

EIGHTH WEEK AFTER TRINITY.

	FIRST LESSON.	SECOND LESSON.
Sunday	Jeremiah xxxii.	Acts xix. 11, xx. 1.
Monday	" xxxiii.	2 Corinthians i. 1–22.
Tuesday	" xxxiv.	" i. 23, ii.
Wednesday	" xxxvii.	" iii., iv. 1–6.
Thursday	" xxxviii.	" iv. 7 to v. 10.
Friday	" xxxix.	" v. 11, vi., to vii.
Saturday	" xl., xli.	" vii. 2. [1.

NINTH WEEK AFTER TRINITY.

	FIRST LESSON.	SECOND LESSON.
Sunday	Jeremiah xlii.	2 Corinthians viii.
Monday	" xliii.	" ix.
Tuesday	" xliv.	" x.
Wednesday	" xxx., xxxi.	" xi.
Thursday	Lamentations i., ii.	" xii. 1–18.
Friday	" iii.	" xii. 19, xiii.
Saturday	" iv., v.	Acts xx. 1–3.

TENTH WEEK AFTER TRINITY.

	FIRST LESSON.	SECOND LESSON.
Sunday	Ezekiel i.	Romans i. 1–17.
Monday	" ii., iii.	" i. 18–31.
Tuesday	" iv., v.	" ii.
Wednesday	" vi., vii.	" iii.
Thursday	" viii., ix.	" iv.
Friday	" x., xi.	" v. 1–11.
Saturday	" xii.	" v. 12–21.

ELEVENTH WEEK AFTER TRINITY.

	FIRST LESSON.	SECOND LESSON.
Sunday	Ezekiel xiii., xiv.	Romans vi.
Monday	" xv., xvi.	" vii.
Tuesday	" xvii., xviii., xix.	" viii. 1–15.
Wednesday	" xx.	" viii. 16–39.
Thursday	" xxi.	" ix. 1–13.
Friday	" xxii.	" ix. 14–33.
Saturday	" xxiii.	" x.

FOR THE FAMILY. 321

TWELFTH WEEK AFTER TRINITY.

	FIRST LESSON.	SECOND LESSON.
Sunday	Ezekiel xxiv.	Romans xi.
Monday	" xxv.	" xii.
Tuesday	" xxvi., xxvii., xxviii.	" xiii.
Wednesday	" xxix.	" xiv.
Thursday	" xxx.	" xv. 1–13.
Friday	" xxxi.	" xv. 14–33.
Saturday	" xxxii.	" xvi.

THIRTEENTH WEEK AFTER TRINITY.

	FIRST LESSON.	SECOND LESSON.
Sunday	Ezekiel xxxiii.	Acts xx.
Monday	" xxxiv.	" xxi.
Tuesday	" xxxv.	" xxii., xxiii.
Wednesday	" xxxviii.	" xxiv., xxv.
Thursday	" xxxix.	" xxvi.
Friday	" xxxvi.	" xxvii.
Saturday	" xxxvii.	" xxviii.

FOURTEENTH WEEK AFTER TRINITY.

	FIRST LESSON.	SECOND LESSON.
Sunday	Isaiah xiii., xiv.	Ephesians i. 1–14.
Monday	" xxi. 1–10.	" i. 15, ii. 1–10.
Tuesday	" xl.	" ii. 11, iii.
Wednesday	" xli.	" iv. 1–17.
Thursday	" xlii.	" iv. 18.
Friday	" xliii.	" v., vi. 1–9.
Saturday	" xliv.	" vi. 10.

FIFTEENTH WEEK AFTER TRINITY.

	FIRST LESSON.	SECOND LESSON.
Sunday	Isaiah xlv., xlvi.	Colossians i.
Monday	" xlvii.	" ii., iii. 1–4.
Tuesday	" xlviii.	" iii. 5, iv.
Wednesday	" xlix. 9–13.	Philemon.
Thursday	" xlix. 14—l. 3.	Philippians i. 1–26.
Friday	" l. 4.	" i. 27, ii.
Saturday	" li., lii. 1–12.	" iii., iv.

SIXTEENTH WEEK AFTER TRINITY.

	FIRST LESSON.	SECOND LESSON.
Sunday	Isaiah lii. 13, liii.	1 Timothy i.
Monday	" liv.	" ii.
Tuesday	" lv.	" iii. 1–13.
Wednesday	" lvi. 1–8.	" iii. 14 to iv. 10.
Thursday	" lvi. 9, lvii.	" iv. 11 to v. 16.
Friday	" lviii.	" v. 17.
Saturday	" lix.	" vi.

V

SEVENTEENTH WEEK AFTER TRINITY.

	FIRST LESSON.	SECOND LESSON.
Sunday	Isaiah lx	Titus i.
Monday	" lxi	" ii.
Tuesday	" lxii., lxiii. 1–6	" iii.
Wednesday	" lxiii. 7, lxiv	2 Timothy i.
Thursday	" lxv	" ii.
Friday	" lxvi	" iii.
Saturday	Psalm cxxxvii	" iv.

EIGHTEENTH WEEK AFTER TRINITY.

	FIRST LESSON.	SECOND LESSON.
Sunday	Ezra i., ii. 64–70., iii., iv. 1–5.	Hebrews i.
Monday	" iv. 24, v., vi	" ii.
Tuesday	Haggai i., ii	" iii., iv.
Wednesday	Zechariah i., ii	" v.
Thursday	" iii., iv	" vi.
Friday	" v., vi	" vii.
Saturday	" vii., viii	" viii.

NINETEENTH WEEK AFTER TRINITY.

	FIRST LESSON.	SECOND LESSON.
Sunday	Ezra iv. 6–23, vii., viii	Hebrews ix. 1–14.
Monday	" ix., x. 1–17	" ix. 15.
Tuesday	Nehemiah i., ii., iii	" x. 1–18.
Wednesday	" iv., v., vi	" x. 19.
Thursday	" vii. 1–5, 70–73,viii	" xi.
Friday	" ix., x., xi. 1–20	" xii.
Saturday	" xii. 27, xiii	" xiii.

THE FOURTH WEEK BEFORE ADVENT.

	FIRST LESSON.	SECOND LESSON.
Sunday	Malachi i., ii. 1–16	John xxi. 1–23.
Monday	" ii. 17, iii., iv	1 John i., ii.
Tuesday	Daniel i., ii	" iii.
Wednesday	" iii., iv	" iv.
Thursday	" v., vi	" v.
Friday	" vii., viii., ix	2 John.
Saturday	" x., xi., xii	3 John.

THE THIRD WEEK BEFORE ADVENT.

	FIRST LESSON.	SECOND LESSON.
Sunday	Psalm xc., iii., iv	Revelation i.
Monday	" vii., xi	" ii.
Tuesday	" xx., xxi., xxiii., xxvii	" iii.
Wednesday	" xviii	" iv., v., vi.
Thursday	" xxiv., xcvi	" vii., viii., ix. 1–12.
Friday	" li., xxxii	" ix. 13, x., xi.
Saturday	" ii., xl., lxxii	" xii., xiii.

THE SECOND WEEK BEFORE ADVENT.

	FIRST LESSON.	SECOND LESSON.
Sunday	Psalm lxxvi., xciv............	Revelation xiv. 1–13.
Monday	" cix........................	" xiv. 14.
Tuesday	" cxl., cxli., cxlii., cxliii...	" xv.
Wednesday	" ci., cx......................	" xvi. 1–8.
Thursday	" cxx.,cxxi.,cxxii.,cxxiii	" xvi. 9.
Friday	" xci., xcii., xciii., xcv ...	" xvii.
Saturday	" xcvii., xcviii., xcix., c...	" xviii.

THE WEEK BEFORE ADVENT.

	FIRST LESSON.	SECOND LESSON.
Sunday	Psalm lxxxv., lxxxvi., lxxxvii	Revelation xix. 1–10.
Monday	" cxxxvii., cxxxviii.,	" xix. 11, xx. 1–3.
Tuesday	" cii., cv............[cxxxix.	" xx. 4.
Wednesday	" cvi.........................	" xxi. 1–8.
Thursday	" cxxiv., cxxv., cxxvi.....	" xxi. 9, xxii.
Friday	" cxxvii., cxxviii., cxxix.	Psalm xcvi.
Saturday	" cxxx., cxxxi., cxxxii., [cxxxiii.	" cxlv.

When more than 23 weeks after Trinity Week occur in any year, the Lessons for the four weeks here given may be employed. The Second Lessons can be taken from the arrangements for the weeks after Epiphany, which have not been used.

TWENTIETH WEEK AFTER TRINITY.

	FIRST LESSON.	SECOND LESSON.
Sunday	Proverbs i., ii.....................	
Monday	" iii.........................	
Tuesday	" iv........................	
Wednesday	" v., vi. 1–19...........	
Thursday	" vi. 20, vii.............	
Friday	" viii......................	
Saturday	" ix.........................	

TWENTY-FIRST WEEK AFTER TRINITY.

	FIRST LESSON.	SECOND LESSON.
Sunday	Proverbs x., xi................,	
Monday	" xii., xiii.............	
Tuesday	" xiv., xv	
Wednesday	" xvi., xvii...........	
Thursday	" xviii., xix...........	
Friday	" xx., xxi., xxii. 1–16	
Saturday	" xxii.17,xxiii.,xxiv	

TWENTY-SECOND WEEK AFTER TRINITY.

	FIRST LESSON.	SECOND LESSON.
Sunday	Proverbs xxv., xxvi............	
Monday	" xxvii..................	
Tuesday	" xxviii., xxix............	
Wednesday	" xxx., xxxi............	
Thursday	Song of Solomon i., ii., iii......	
Friday	" " iv., v.	
Saturday	" " vi., vii., viii.	

TWENTY-THIRD WEEK AFTER TRINITY.

	FIRST LESSON.	SECOND LESSON.
Sunday	Ecclesiastes i., ii..................	
Monday	" iii., iv., v., vi. 1-9.	
Tuesday	" vi.10,vii.,viii.1-15.	
Wednesday	" viii.16,ix.,x.,xi.,xii	
Thursday	Esther i., ii., iii., iv............	
Friday	" v., vi., vii., viii., ix., x.	
Saturday	Psalm ciii........................	

PRAYERS FOR THE FAMILY.

Family worship should be observed daily in every household, when the following prayers may be used in connection with the reading of a portion of Scripture. It is recommended that the Scriptures be read as directed by the Calendar, or "Order of Scripture readings for the Family."

On Sundays, after reading the Scriptures, the Family shall rise and join in saying the Creed.

Then shall be said, all kneeling, first the Sunday Collect for the week, next the Prayer for the particular day of the week, and lastly the Lord's Prayer, in which all shall join audibly.

Sunday Morning.

O LORD, merciful and gracious Father, we, Thy children, adopted in Jesus Christ, gather around the mercy-seat with humble and childlike trust in Thee. As Thou makest the outgoings of the morning to rejoice, so do Thou make glad our hearts on this day of sacred rest. Thou, O Lord, art the true and only rest of the soul, and our hearts cannot rest until they rest in Thee. Grant us this day, not only the rest of the body, but also some foretaste of that peace and joy which shall refresh us, when we, after the labors of this life, shall awake in Thy likeness, and be numbered with Thy saints in glory everlasting.

O Thou who hast made Thy Church Thy dwelling-place, and chosen it as Thy rest forever, and hast taught us in Thy word not to forsake the assembling of ourselves together; regard in special mercy, we beseech Thee, all those who meet to-day in Thy holy courts. Manifest Thyself unto them as Thou dost not unto the world. Bless unto them and us all Thine ordinances; and may our worship in the Church on earth prepare us more fully for the blessed worship of the Church in heaven.

O adorable Saviour, Head of Thy Church, who hast all power in heaven and in earth, and who dost send forth Thy servants in Thy name, to publish salvation and make disciples to Thyself; sustain the Pastors of Thy flocks at home, and in heathen lands. Give them the anointing of the Holy Ghost in their ministrations, that they may feed the flock that waiteth around Thee; comforting the distressed; instructing the ignorant; warning the careless; confirming the doubting; suiting and satisfying the wants of all from the rich treasury of Thy grace.

Be pleased, O God of compassion, whose tender mercies are over all Thy works, to remember this day all ranks and conditions of men. Succor the needy and oppressed; protect and cheer widows and orphans; restore the sick; prepare the dying for death; sanctify the merciful chastisements of Thy hand unto all who are enduring them; and grant that their afflictions may lead them to the exercise of that godly sorrow which worketh repentance unto life, and thus bring unto them, in the life to come, a far more exceeding and eternal weight of glory, through the suffering, death, resurrection, and powerful intercession of Jesus Christ our Lord.

Blessed Jesus, who in the days of Thy flesh didst take little children into Thine arms and bless them, and who hast taught us that the promise is to us and to our children, and didst command that the lambs of the flock should be fed; do Thou, this day, through Thy families, and through Thy Church, call the little children to Thyself. Cause them to be nurtured by Thy renewing grace, that out of the mouths of babes and sucklings Thy name may be glorified.

Hear our prayer, O Lord, in heaven, Thy dwelling place. Glorify Thyself in all that we do and suffer, and lead us in that way in which we shall best escape the pollutions that are in the world, and attain at last to the unspeakable joys of the life to come: and unto Thee, the Father, the Son, and the Holy Ghost, shall be all honor and glory, world without end. *Amen.*

Sunday Evening.

O LORD, our heavenly Father, we acknowledge Thy great goodness toward us, in granting us another day of holy rest. We are truly sorry for the errors and sins of this day, and of our past lives. We are grieved that we have so often forgotten Thy presence, authority, and goodness. Merciful God, pardon our offences. Especially, O Lord, forgive the iniquity of our holy things. Correct and amend what is amiss in us. Write Thy laws in our hearts; and enable us to show by holy, unblamable, and useful lives, that we have not enjoyed Thy sabbaths and Thy worship in vain. Thus prepare us ever more fully for the worship of the heavenly temple, and for the enjoyment of that eternal Sabbath which knows no setting sun.

Grant, O Lord, that every evening may remind us of the near approach of the night of death. Let a deep sense of our frailty make us careful how we live; and amid all the vanity of this present life, may we be united by a living faith, and by the power of the eternal Spirit, unto Him who is the Resurrection and the Life; so that, though we die, we may yet live, because He lives, and so escape death and the bitter pains of eternal misery.

Assist us, we beseech Thee, in carrying out the holy resolutions which we have this day formed, under the gracious movings of Thy word and Spirit.

O Thou, who hast all power in heaven and in earth, accompany the preaching of Thy word, and the administration of Thy sacraments, with the influences of Thy Holy Spirit. Continue to us, and to all Christian churches, the means of grace and salvation; and may the saving truths of the Gospel be speedily published in every land, that all the ends of the earth may hear, believe, and live forever.

Evermore keep and preserve us, O God of our salvation, in the midst of all dangers to which we are exposed, either in body or in soul; and prepare us, with meek cheerfulness and Christian resignation, to receive our sorrows as well as our joys from Thee; knowing that health and sickness, riches and poverty, yea, all things, come not by chance, but by Thy fatherly hand.

O Thou, to whom the darkness and the light are both alike, and who dost neither slumber nor sleep, defend us, we beseech Thee, from all perils and dangers of this night. Keep us as under the shadow of Thy wings; that being quiet from all fear of evil, we may be brought in peace to see the light of another day, invigorated and rightly prepared for its work.

We ask all in the name, and for the sake of Thy Son Jesus Christ. *Amen.*

Monday Morning.

O LORD, our heavenly Father, who by the rest of Thy holy day, and by the peaceful slumbers of the night, hast refreshed our bodies and souls, we give Thee hearty thanks for Thy great goodness toward us, and acknowledge Thee as the source of all our mercies. We would enter upon this new day, and upon the duties of the week, in Thy fear, and with a child-like dependence on Thee.

As Thou hast ordained that we should eat bread in the sweat of our face, we beseech Thee mercifully to prosper the work of our hands, and sanctify the fruit of our labors and cares to our good, to the good of others, and to Thy glory. Help us to carry the spirit of Thy holy day into all the business of the week; and whilst our bodies and minds are engaged in honest and useful toil, may our hearts still live and rest in

Thee. Save us from the spirit of worldliness. Suffer us not to seek our portion in this life; and having food and raiment, may we be therewith content.

O Lord God of our fathers, who dost make and keep covenant with families, and dost include parents and children in Thy most gracious promises, bless, we beseech Thee, this household dedicated to Thy holy service. Continue to provide for all our proper wants; and turn our hearts daily in gratitude and love to Thee, that being united in Thy service in this life, we may together attain to the felicity of the life everlasting, through infinite mercy and grace in Jesus Christ our Lord.

To Thy care, O Lord, we now commend ourselves for this day. Let Thy fatherly protection be over us. Preserve our feet from falling, our eyes from tears and our souls from death; and enable us to walk before thee in cheerful obedience to the end of life.

Hear, O Lord, our prayer; and grant us all things that we need, for this world and for that which is to come; since we ask in the name of our Lord and Saviour Jesus Christ. *Amen.*

Monday Evening.

ALMIGHTY God, the Father of our Lord Jesus Christ, and through Him our Father, and the source of all our mercies, blessed be Thy name for Thy gracious protection this day. Thy goodness is new every morning, and Thy faithfulness every night. O that there were such hearts in us that we might fear Thee, and keep Thy commandments always.

O Holy Spirit, proceeding from the Father and the Son, Spirit of promise and Sanctifier of them that believe, dwell Thou in us as the Spirit of holiness. Purge our hearts from all evil passions and desires, from envy, hatred, and malice: that we may never suffer the sun to go down upon our wrath, but may always seek our rest with a conscience void of offence toward Thee and toward all men.

O Lord, our heavenly Father, we beseech Thee to look graciously upon this family. Bless us in body and soul; in basket and store; in our going out and coming in, and in all that concerns us. Above all, bless us with spiritual blessings; with a pure heart and a sound mind; with contempt of the world, and a firm trust in Thee; with a grateful sense of Thy kindness, and a soul full of love; with a knowledge of Thy will, and a desire to perform it; with the assistance of Thy Spirit, and a sure and joyful hope of everlasting life, through Jesus Christ our Lord.

With these prayers in our own behalf, accept, O Lord, our hearty intercessions for all mankind. Let the light of Thy Gospel shine on all nations. Be especially gracious to the land in which we dwell. Bless all who are in authority over us. So rule their hearts, and strengthen their hands, that they may want neither will nor power to punish wickedness, and to encourage and support true piety.

O Lord, we now commit ourselves to Thy watchful care during the night. Make us to rest in safety, and to be quiet from fear of evil. Let our thoughts be serious and devout when we lie down: and when we awake may we be still with Thee. O Thou Keeper of Israel, who dost neither slumber nor sleep, be Thou evermore our guardian; and when we lie down in the grave, be Thou the comfort and strength of our hearts, and our portion forever; through the abounding mercy of Jesus Christ our Lord. *Amen.*

Tuesday Morning.

ALMIGHTY God, our heavenly Father, we acknowledge with grateful hearts Thy goodness, which is renewed unto us from day to day. When we lay in defenceless sleep thy power was beneath us, and Thy protection around us. While others have spent the night in sighs and tears, in restlessness and painful watchings, in sickness and in struggles with death, Thou hast granted unto us a comfortable and refreshing repose. Blessed be Thy name, O Lord of our life, for all Thy goodness and love toward us.

Help us with a believing heart to embrace all the sufferings and death of Christ, whereby we may obtain the forgiveness of our sins, and become more and more united to His sacred body by the Holy Ghost, who dwells both in Christ and in us. Enable us to crucify the flesh with the affections and lusts thereof, so that sin may no more have dominion over us:

and grant us grace to offer ourselves unto Him a sacrifice of thanksgiving and praise, in body and in soul, in this life, and to obtain in the world to come life everlasting.

Defend us, O Lord, this day, from all motions of sin in our own hearts, and from all hurtful influences from the world and evil spirits. In our greatest temptations be thou nearest to us by Thy sustaining and conquering power; and as Thou, blessed Saviour, didst overcome the Tempter in the wilderness, so do Thou overcome his wiles in us by thy victorious grace.

Grant us, O Lord, the spirit of cheerful resignation to Thy good and holy will, that amid all the changes of this mortal life, we may be patient in adversity, thankful in prosperity, and for what is future, have good confidence in our faithful God and Father, that no creature shall separate us from His love.

Grant us grace, we beseech Thee, to be just and upright in all our dealings; quiet and peaceable among our neighbors; full of compassion towards the needy and afflicted; and ever ready to do good to all men; that so walking faithfully before Thee all our days, and being found watching whenever our appointed time shall come, we may, from a life of grace, be tr nslated into a life of glory; through the merits and mediation of Jesus Christ our Lord. *Amen.*

Tuesday Evening.

ALMIGHTY and most merciful God, our heavenly Father, who hast brought us in safety to the close of another day; regard, we beseech Thee, our prayer, and the prayers of all Thy people, and pardon our sins, according to Thy loving-kindness and tender mercy in Jesus Christ our Lord.

Accept, O Lord, our evening sacrifice, and pour out upon us the fulness of Thy grace. Guard and defend us by Thy holy angels; preserve us from all harm and danger, both of soul and body; and give us grace, that we may spend this evening and night, and all the nights and days of our sojourn upon earth, to Thy honor and glory.

O Lord Jesus, Thou once crucified, but now exalted Saviour, we bless Thee for Thy humiliation; for Thine incarnation; for Thy life of patient suffering; for Thine agony in the garden; for Thy groans and prayers on the cross; and for Thine atoning death. We bless Thee, also, for Thy triumphant resurrection; for Thy glorious ascension into heaven; and for Thine intercession before the Father, as our Advocate and Mediator.

Let the same mind be in us, O Lord, which was also in Thee, that we may follow Thee in Thy humility; bear reproach as meekly as Thou didst bear it; and forgive our enemies, as Thou forgavest Thy murderers. When we die, may we die in Thee; commending our souls into the hands of our heavenly Father, with the full assurance of being raised up at the last day in Thine own glorious image.

O Lord, our gracious Redeemer, we now commit ourselves into Thy hands. Be with us when we lie down, and when we rise up; be with us in sickness and in health; and in the hour of death, forsake us not, O most merciful Saviour, but grant us a calm and peaceful departure out of this world, and a triumphant entrance into Thy heavenly kingdom. And all the glory shall be given to Thee, who, with the Father and the Holy Spirit, art alone worthy of all praise and glory, forever and ever. *Amen.*

Wednesday Morning.

O THOU Shepherd of Israel, who dost neither slumber nor sleep, under Thy providential care we have rested securely during another night, for which we now render Thee our humble and unfeigned thanks. We have slept and awaked, and lo! Thou art still with us; and we are yet among the living to praise Thee. Blessed be Thy holy name forever and ever. Our voice shalt Thou hear in the morning, O Lord; in the morning will we direct our prayer unto Thee, and will look up. Thou hast no pleasure in wickedness, neither can any evil dwell with Thee; but thy delight is in all that call upon Thee, and Thou wilt bless such as are of an humble and a contrite heart.

Grant us grace to begin this day in Thy fear, and to end it to Thy glory. We are weak; be Thou our strength. We are ignorant and do easily err; be Thou our light and our guide. We are prone to thoughtlessness and vanity; keep us mindful, we entreat Thee, of death and of judgment, to the end that we may live soberly, righteously, and godly in this present evil world.

O Thou omniscient and holy Lord God, we humbly confess before Thee our sins and infirmities. Though Thou didst originally create us good, after Thine own image, in righteousness and true holiness, yet has our nature fallen, and we are conceived and born in sin. Create in us, we beseech Thee, a clean heart, and renew a right spirit within us. Make us by true faith partakers of Christ and all his benefits; and grant us the Holy Ghost that He may comfort and abide with us forever.

O Lord, as thou hast called us to serve one another, and the generation in which we live, give us strength to go forth to our daily duties with cheerfulness, and in humble dependence upon Thy help. Prosper our labors, and let the work of our hands be established upon us for Thy praise.

Bless this family, and grant us grace to love and fear Thee. Bless our kindred, friends, and neighbors. Reward all that have done us good; and pardon those who have done or wished us evil. Be merciful to all who are in any trouble or affliction; and do Thou, O God of pity and compassion, grant them help and comfort according to their need, for the sake of Jesus Christ our Lord, who liveth and reigneth with Thee and the Holy Ghost, one God, world without end. *Amen.*

Wednesday Evening.

MOST gracious and merciful God, who art of purer eyes than to behold iniquity, and hast promised mercy and forgiveness to all them who confess and forsake their sins, we come before Thee with an humble sense of our own unworthiness, acknowledging our manifold transgressions of Thy righteous law, in thought, in word, and in deed. We have every day done those things which Thou hast forbidden, and left undone those things which Thou hast commanded; so that, when we look upon our past lives, and remember that Thou knowest our most secret sins, we are afraid of Thy judgments, and ashamed to lift up our eyes unto Thee. But, O gracious Father, who desirest not the death of a sinner, look upon us, we beseech Thee, in Thy Son Jesus Christ, and, for the merits of His sufferings, be merciful unto us, and grant unto us the full and free forgiveness of our sins.

May the Spirit of Christ ever rule and live in us, inspiring our hearts with a sincere love of Thee, O God; with an earnest desire to please Thee, and with a dread of offending Thee. Sanctify us wholly, we beseech Thee, that our souls and bodies may be preserved blameless unto the coming of our Lord Jesus Christ.

Help us, O Lord, to possess our souls in patience

amidst all the changes of this mortal life. Give us a cheerful faith, a joyful hope, and a peaceful love. From gloominess of mind, from repinings, from dejection of spirit, from distrust of Thy mercies, and from fear of death, good Lord, deliver us.

We humbly pray for all mankind, especially for our kindred and friends, that they may receive mercies suitable to their wants. If any are estranged from Thee, draw them to Thyself by Thy good Spirit and grace, that as they share in Thy goodness here, they may partake also of Thy glory hereafter, through the great mercy of Jesus Christ our Lord.

Bless, O Lord, the poor and needy, the sick and afflicted, the wretched and distressed. Have compassion upon all ranks and conditions of men. Sanctify the afflictions of Thy hand unto those who endure them, and in Thine own good time turn their sorrow into joy.

We beseech Thee, O Lord, to continue Thy gracious protection to us this night. Into Thy hands we commend ourselves, and all things that belong to us. Be pleased to watch over us, O Thou who dost neither slumber nor sleep. Defend us from danger and mischief, and from the dread and fear of evil: to the end that we may enjoy such quiet and refreshing sleep as may fit us for the duties of the coming day.

O Lord, make us ever mindful of that time when we shall lie down in the dust; and grant us grace always so to live, that we may never be afraid to die; but that, whether we live we may live unto Thee, and whether we die we may die unto Thee; that so living and dying, we may be Thine, through the merits and satisfaction of Thy Son Jesus Christ our Lord. *Amen.*

Thursday Morning.

O GOD, our God, early will we seek Thee. Thy mercies are new unto us every morning, and call for new expressions of gratitude to Thee, the Giver of all good. For the rest of the night, for the light of another day, and for the comforts which now surround us, we praise Thee, O Lord our God. Help us to feel more deeply that we owe our life and all its blessings to Thy fatherly love and care.

We come unto Thee as Thy children. O give us the spirit of adoption whereby we may cry, Abba Father; and loving Thee, who hast first loved us, may have grace to dedicate ourselves anew to Thy blessed service, in body and in soul.

O Holy Saviour, who hast redeemed and delivered us from our sins, renew us also by the Holy Ghost after Thine own image: that so we may testify, by our whole life, our gratitude to Thee for Thy great love and mercy to us; that every one of us may be assured in ourselves of our faith, by the fruits thereof; and that, by godly walk and conversation, we may win others also unto Christ.

Grant us grace, O Lord, to flee from every temptation that may this day assail us, and to overcome the power of sin in our hearts. May we rightly acknowledge Thee, the only true God; trust in Thee alone;

with humility and patience expect all good from Thee only: love, fear, and honor Thee with our whole heart: so as rather to renounce all creatures than do the least thing against Thy will.

Bestow upon us, O most merciful Father, what is needful for us, and give us grace not to abuse Thy favors. Give us, we beseech Thee, contented minds, and help us to regard with compassion the wants and sorrows of others.

O God, our Saviour, who art the hope of all the ends of the earth, remember, we beseech Thee, the children of affliction and sorrow. Heal the sick; provide for the poor; befriend the forsaken; and be a helper to the helpless.

We now resign ourselves, Almighty Father, into Thy hands. Let Thy mercy be upon us according as we hope in Thee. Guide us by Thy counsel while we live, and afterwards receive us to Thy heavenly glory, through infinite riches of grace in Christ Jesus our Lord. *Amen.*

Thursday Evening.

MOST merciful God, from heaven, the habitation of Thy holiness, look down upon us and accept the confession of our sins, with our evening sacrifice of thanksgiving and praise. We acknowledge our unworthiness, and the frailty and perverseness of our corrupt nature, through which we daily transgress Thy just and holy laws. Have mercy upon us, O Lord, and pardon us, for the sake of Jesus Christ, who is our advocate with Thee. Wash our souls from the defilements of this day in His most precious blood, that we may go to our rest, comforted by Thy grace, and sanctified by Thy Holy Spirit.

Kind and gracious Father, we give Thee unfeigned thanks, for all Thy mercies bestowed upon us : for our being; for our powers of mind and body; for health, friends, food, and raiment; for Thy patience with us, notwithstanding our many and great provocations; for the direction, assistance, and comfort of Thy Holy Spirit; for Thy continual care and watchful providence over us, through the whole course of our lives ; and particularly for the favors and benefits of the past day. We beseech Thee, continue these blessings to us, and enable us to show forth our gratitude for them, by sincere obedience to Thy holy laws, and entire devotion to Thee, through Jesus Christ our Lord.

O Lord, take away from us all ignorance, hardness of heart, and undue carefulness for the things of this life. Help us as a household to fear Thee, sincerely to seek Thy glory, and to put our whole trust in Thy mercy.

Make us mindful that as we have now come to the end of another day, so the end of life is at hand; and as we know neither the day nor the hour of our Master's coming, grant us grace so to live, that, when Thou shalt call us hence, we may not be afraid to die ; but stand prepared always to meet Thee in peace.

Be pleased to watch over us this night, and spread the wings of Thy protection around our resting place.

Preserve us from sin and harm, and from the malice of the spirits of darkness. Visit us with refreshing sleep; cause us to rest safely in the arms of Thy love; and raise us up again in health and peace. Thus may all our days and nights be spent with Thee in Thy blessed service, till we awake in Thy likeness and reign with Thee in everlasting joy; through Jesus Christ our Lord. *Amen.*

Friday Morning.

ALMIGHTY and everlasting God, in whom we live, and move, and have our being, we render thanks unto Thee, for Thy kind care over us during the night that is past. Since of Thy great mercy another day has dawned upon us, we once more consecrate ourselves in soul and body to Thy service. We renounce the works of darkness: cause us to walk in the light of Thy countenance. We renounce the vanities of the world: help us to seek after the enduring substance that is laid up with Thee in heaven. We renounce the sinful lusts of the flesh: enable us to walk in the Spirit. In these desires and purposes, do Thou, most merciful God, confirm and strengthen us by Thine ever present grace.

We humbly confess before Thee, O Lord, our guilt, and beseech Thee to pardon our sins and transgressions. Create in us a clean heart, and renew a right spirit within us, that we may have power to serve Thee in righteousness and true holiness all our days.

Give us, O Lord, an abiding sense of the vanity and shortness of this mortal life. Seeing that the Son of man cometh at an hour when we think not, may we be always ready; that so the dread summons may not come upon us unawares; but that, having our loins girt about, and our lamps burning, we may be like those that wait for their Lord.

Accept, O Lord, our earnest intercessions for all mankind. Cause Thy glorious Gospel to be proclaimed among all nations. Bless Thy Church, purchased with Thine own most precious blood. Clothe her ministers with salvation; and may earth's millions of sinning, sorrowing, and suffering souls, find their home and their rest in her bosom.

Bless our kindred and friends: those who are in sin, O Lord, convert; strengthen and confirm those who are in grace. Unite us to one another by mutual love, and to Thyself, by continual piety and faith, through the merits of Thy blessed Son, our Saviour.

Be merciful to those who are in any trouble or affliction in mind, body, or outward estate. Raise up helpers to such as are in want; and administer grace and comfort to all, according to their several necessities, for the sake of Jesus Christ our Lord. *Amen.*

Friday Evening.

ETERNAL and infinitely glorious God, the great Creator, gracious Preserver, and wise Governor of the world, we, Thy sinful and unworthy servants, bow before Thee at this time to present our prayers and supplications at the throne of Thy heavenly grace.

Thou, Lord, art never weary in doing us good; but alas! we acknowledge with shame that we have been guilty of great ingratitude towards Thee. We have been unprofitable servants: we have neglected much of our duty; we have followed too often the inclinations of our corrupt nature; and instead of loving Thee, and delighting in Thee, we have been too eagerly and fondly pursuing the things of this world. Enter not into judgment with us, O Lord, whom Thou hast redeemed with Thy most precious blood. Let Thy goodness and forbearance lead us to repentance; and of Thy great mercy, O Lord, deliver us not into the bitter pains of eternal death. Spare us, good Lord, spare Thy servants, and be not angry with us for ever.

O Lord, enlighten our understandings, that we may know Thee; sanctify our affections, that we may love Thee: and put Thy fear into our hearts, that we may dread to offend Thee. Convince us thoroughly, we beseech Thee, of the great evil of sin, that we may hate it, and endeavor in all things to obey Thy blessed will, and to walk before Thee in holiness and righteousness all our days.

Impress us, O Lord, with a lively and abiding sense of the frailty of our lives, the certainty of judgment, the unspeakable glories of heaven, and the most dreadful torments of hell; that we may be moved in good earnest to lay hold of salvation, and never be so foolish as to prefer the pleasures of sin, which are but for a season, to that everlasting fulness of joy, which is in Thy presence for evermore.

Establish, O Lord, and greatly enlarge, the borders of Thy Church; and grant that the knowledge of Thy name, and the consolations of Thy grace, may soon fill every land and all hearts. Let the wickedness of the wicked come to an end, and do Thou establish and increase the just.

We humbly commend ourselves this night to Thy blessing and protection. Give us, O Lord, the comfortable refreshment of a quiet and undisturbed sleep. Defend us from evil, and from all fear and dread. Preserve us especially from the evil of sin, and from the assaults of our spiritual enemies; and let Thy goodness and mercy follow us all the days of our life; for the sake of Jesus Christ our Lord. *Amen.*

Saturday Morning.

O GOD, by whom the whole world is governed and preserved, we give Thee humble thanks for Thy fatherly care over us, in preserving us from the dangers of the night which is past, and in bringing us safely to the beginning of another day.

We gratefully acknowledge our dependence on Thee for the necessities, conveniences, and comforts of our daily life; for the means of our well-being in this world; and for the hope of everlasting happiness in the world to come.

We give Thee thanks for the gift of Thy Son, our Saviour; for the gift of Thy Holy Spirit, our Sanctifier and Comforter; for the institution of Thy Church, the mother of us all; for the light of Thy glorious Gospel, and the helps of Thy grace; and for the precious promises of pardon, through Thy Son Christ Jesus, in whose blood we have the atonement.

Give us always, we beseech Thee, such a tender sense of Thy mercies, that we may be truly thankful for them. Save us from hardness of heart, and from blindness of mind, that we may never neglect or abuse Thy grace. Enable us honestly to improve all the talents which Thou hast committed to our trust; and let no worldly business, nor love of pleasure, draw our minds or hearts from the solemn concerns of the life to come.

Let Thy blessing, O Lord, be upon our persons, upon our labors, upon our substance, and upon all that belongs to us. In prosperity may we not forget Thee, and in adversity may we still trust in Thy wisdom, mercy, and love; assured that whatever evils Thou dost send upon us in this vale of tears, Thou wilt turn them to our good.

Defend us, O Lord, and those who are near and dear to us, against the assaults of our enemies. Grant that this day we fall into no sin, neither run into any kind of danger. May all our doings be ordered by Thee, and meet with Thy favor and blessing; that so we may walk, O Lord, in the light of Thy countenance.

Into Thy hands, gracious Father, we now commend ourselves for this day, and for all coming time. Glorify Thyself in all that we do and suffer; and grant us, we beseech Thee, in this world knowledge of Thy truth, and in the world to come life everlasting; through the mercy and mediation of Jesus Christ our Lord, to whom, with Thee and the Holy Ghost, one God, be all honor and glory, as it was in the beginning, is now, and ever shall be, world without end. Amen.

Saturday Evening.

O LORD GOD, our Heavenly Father, who hast brought us safely through another day, and to the close of another week, unto Thee we render our humble and hearty thanks. Give us, we beseech Thee, a due sense of the manifold favors Thou hast bestowed upon us through life; and especially teach us to value, as we ought, Thy great mercy in Christ Jesus our Lord, through whom alone we enjoy the means of grace, and the hope of glory.

We confess, O Lord, that we have not served Thee according to the measure of our knowledge and ability. We have again and again broken Thy laws and commandments; we have too much neglected Thy warnings; we have resisted the quiet influences of Thy Holy Spirit; and we have just cause to fear Thy righteous judgments. We acknowledge and bewail our unworthiness. O merciful Father, accept our penitence, and give us the comforting assurance of pardon. By Thy manifold and great mercies; by the all-sufficient merits of Thy blessed Son, Jesus Christ; by His agony and bloody sweat; by His bitter cross and passion; by His glorious resurrection and ascension; by His continual intercession for us at Thy right hand; and by the grace and comforts of the Holy Ghost, good Lord, deliver us.

In all the changes and trials of this mortal life; in all time of our prosperity and in all time of our adversity: in the hour of death and in the day of judgment, good Lord, deliver us.

We beseech Thee, O Lord, extend Thy mercy to the whole race of mankind. Have pity upon the nations that know Thee not; cause the light of Thy glorious gospel to shine among them, and visit them with Thy salvation.

Look with pity and compassion, O Lord, upon those who are in affliction and temptation; upon the poor, the sick, and the dying; strengthen and support them, and give them in Thine own good time a happy issue out of all their sufferings.

Be merciful and gracious, O God, to our kindred and friends; forgive our enemies; reward our benefactors; and grant that we, with all Thy people every where, may have grace to serve Thee with full purpose of heart, and so be made partakers at last of eternal bliss in Thy presence in heaven.

And now, most gracious Father, who hast delivered our eyes from tears, our feet from falling, and our souls from death, take us, we entreat Thee, under Thy watchful care this night; guard us from all evil and harm, and bring us to the light, and prepare us for the duties of the coming Sabbath; and we will praise Thee, the Father; Son, and Holy Ghost, ever one God, world without end. *Amen.*

PRAYERS FOR SPECIAL OCCASIONS IN THE FAMILY.

A Morning Litany.

REMEMBER not, O Lord, our offences, nor the offences of our forefathers; neither take Thou vengeance of our sins. Spare us, good Lord; spare Thy servants, whom Thou hast redeemed with Thy most precious blood, and be not angry with us forever.

Spare us, O Lord.

From the guilt and burden of our sins; from the stings and terrors of conscience; from the illusions and assaults of the enemy; and from the bitter pains of eternal death;

Deliver us, O Lord.

From all impatience under Thy chastisements; from dejection of spirit and distrust of Thy mercies; from the fear of death; and from the terrors of judgment;

Deliver us, O Lord.

By Thy manifold and great mercies; by the all-

sufficient merits of Thy blessed Son Jesus Christ; by His agony and bloody sweat; by His bitter cross and passion; by His glorious resurrection and ascension; by His continual intercession for us at Thy right hand; and by the graces and comforts of the Holy Ghost;
Deliver us, O Lord.

In all the changes and trials of this mortal life; in all time of our tribulation, and in all time of our wealth; in the hour of death, and in the day of judgment;
Deliver us, O Lord.

We wretched sinners do beseech Thee to hear us, O Lord;
Son of God, we beseech Thee to hear us.

That it may please Thee to look upon us with the eye of Thy mercy, to give us a hearty faith and confidence in Thee, and in all our dangers and adversities to stretch forth the right hand of Thy majesty to help and defend us in perpetual peace and safety;
We beseech Thee to hear us, O Lord.

That it may please Thee to remember us with Thy favor, and to give us grace so to follow the good examples of Thy servants, who have departed this life in Thy faith and fear, that with them we may become partakers of Thy heavenly kingdom;
We beseech Thee to hear us, O Lord.

That it may please Thee to give us an entire re-

signation to Thy holy will; to wean our affection from things below; to fill us with ardent desires after heaven; and finally to make us partakers of all Thy blessings and promises in Christ Jesus;
We beseech Thee to hear us, O Lord.

That it may please Thee to fill our souls with the peace and love of God, that when Thou shalt call us to walk through the valley and shadow of death, we may fear no evil, but fall gently asleep in Jesus, and awake up in the glory of Thy presence;
We beseech Thee to hear us, O Lord.

Son of God, we beseech Thee to hear us.
We beseech Thee to hear us, O Lord.

O Lamb of God, that takest away the sin of the world;
Have mercy upon us.

O Christ, hear us.
Lord, have mercy upon us.

Christ, have mercy upon us.
Lord, have mercy upon us, and grant us Thy peace.

Almighty God, who dost accept the penitence and confession of the contrite, that they may share in Thy mercy and live; be merciful and gracious unto us, absolve us from all sin, establish us in Thy grace, grant us the comforts of the Holy Ghost, and bring us to life everlasting, through Jesus Christ our Lord. *Amen.*

An Evening Litany.

Lord, have mercy upon us.
Have mercy upon us.

Christ, have mercy upon us.
Have mercy upon us.

Christ, hear us and grant us Thy peace.
Hear us and grant us Thy peace.

Jesus, the Son of the living God, the eternal Word, the brightness of the Father's glory, and express image of his person;
Have mercy upon us.

Jesus, the Son of Man, conceived by the Holy Ghost, born of the Virgin Mary, meek and humble of heart, obedient unto death, the example of all virtues, the way, the truth, and the life;
Have mercy upon us.

Jesus, the author of life, the Captain of salvation, the eternal high-priest, the prince of peace;
Have mercy upon us.

Jesus, the joy of angels, the hope of the patriarchs, the inspirer of the prophets, the teacher of the apostles, the strength of martyrs, the king of saints;
Have mercy upon us.

From all sin and evil, from death and hell;
Deliver us, O Lord Jesus.

By Thy holy nativity and circumcision; by Thy holy words and deeds; by Thine agony and bloody sweat; by Thy bitter cross and passion; by Thy death and burial; by Thy glorious resurrection and ascension; by thy sitting at the right hand of the Father Almighty; and by Thy return to judge the quick and the dead;

Deliver us, O Lord Jesus.

Lamb of God that takest away the sin of the world;

Have mercy upon us.

Lamb of God that takest away the sin of the world;

Hear our prayers.

Lamb of God that takest away the sin of the world;

Grant us Thy peace.

Almighty God, who dost accept the penitence and confession of the contrite that they may share in Thy mercy and live; be merciful and gracious unto us, absolve us from all sin, establish us in Thy grace, grant us the comforts of the Holy Ghost, and bring us to life everlasting, through Jesus Christ our Lord. *Amen.*

A Morning Prayer.

ALMIGHTY GOD, Father of our Lord Jesus Christ, we approach to the throne of grace this morning with reverence and holy fear, begging of Thee mercy and peace, pardon and salvation. Thou art holy, and justly offended with us; but yet Thou art our gracious Lord and merciful Father in Christ Jesus. Be pleased, we beseech Thee, to blot out our sins from Thy remembrance, and heal our souls, that we may sin no more against Thee. Open our eyes, that we may see and amend our own infirmities and follies; and give us perfect understanding in the way of godliness, that we may walk in it all the days of our pilgrimage. Give us a spirit diligent in the works of our calling, cheerful and zealous in religion, fervent and frequent in prayer, charitable and useful in conversation. Give us a healthful and chaste body, a pure and holy soul, a sanctified and humble spirit; and preserve our body, soul, and spirit, blameless to the coming of our Lord Jesus Christ.

Blessed be Thy name, O God of all mercies, who hast preserved us through the past night from sickness and sorrow, from sad chances and a violent death, from the malice of the Devil, and the evil effects of our own corrupt nature and infirmity. The outgoings of the morning and evening shall praise Thee, and Thy servants shall rejoice in giving Thee glory and thanks for all Thy wonderful dealings with the children of men, and with the members of Thy Church.

Let Thy providence and care watch over us this day, and all the days of our life, that we may never sin against Thee by idleness or folly, by evil company or private sins, by word or deed, by thought or desire. Enable us so to spend the day that it may be profitable to us and to others, and leave no sorrows, or the remembrance of an evil conscience, at night; and so conduct us through life by Thy Holy Spirit, that when the days of our short abode on earth are done, and the shadow is departed, we may die in Thy fear and favor, and rest in a holy hope, and at last return to the joys of a blessed resurrection, through Jesus Christ our Lord. *Amen.*

An Evening Prayer.

The day is gone, and we give Thee thanks, O Lord. The evening has come; make it bright unto us. As day has its evening, so also has life; abide with us Lord, for it is toward evening, and the day is far spent of this fretful life. Let Thy strength be made perfect in our weakness. We beseech of Thee for the close of our life, that Thou wouldest direct it in peace, gathering us together in the repose of Thy saints, when Thou wilt, and as Thou wilt, only without shame and sin.

As long as we live will we magnify Thee, O Lord, and lift up our hands in Thy name. Let our prayer be set forth before Thee as incense, and the lifting up of our hands as an evening sacrifice. Blessed art Thou, O Lord, our God, the God of our fathers, who hast created the changes of days and nights, who givest songs in the night, who hast not cut off like a weaver our life, nor from day even to night made an end of us.

Lord, as we add day to day, so do we add sin to sin. But we turn with groans from our evil ways, and we return into our heart, and with all our heart we turn to Thee, O God of penitents and Saviour of sinners. We have sinned, O Lord, against Thee; heavily against Thee. We repent; spare us, O Lord: we repent; help Thou our impenitence. Have mercy upon us, O Lord, after Thy great goodness; according to the multitude of Thy mercies, do away our offences. O bring Thou us out of our trouble. Cleanse Thou us from secret faults; keep back Thy servants also from presumptuous sins. Our wanderings of mind and idle talking, lay not to our charge. Deal not with us after our sins, neither reward us after our iniquities. Look mercifully upon our infirmities; and for the glory of Thy holy name, turn from us those ills and miseries, which for our sins, are by us most righteously deserved.

To our weariness, O Lord, vouchsafe Thou rest; to our exhaustion renew Thou strength. O Keeper of Israel, who neither slumberest nor sleepest, guard us this night from all evil; guard our souls, O Lord. Visit us with the sleep of those who rest in Thy love; reveal to us wisdom in the visions of the night; or if not, for we are not worthy, at least let sleep be to us a breathing time as from toil, so from sin. Yea, O Lord, let us not in our dreams imagine what may anger Thee, what may defile us. Lord, Thou knowest how sleepless are our unseen foes, and how feeble is our wretched flesh. O shelter us, we pray Thee, with the wing of Thy pity. Awake us at the fitting time;

and bring us to seek Thee early, for Thy glory, and for Thy service.

O Thou who art the hope of all the ends of the earth, remember Thy whole creation for good, visit the world in Thy compassion.

O God of grace and truth, establish all who stand in truth and grace; restore all who are sick with heresies and sins.

O wholesome defence of Thine anointed, remember Thy Church which Thou hast purchased and redeemed of old; O grant to all believers one heart and one soul.

O Thou by whom are ordained the powers that be, grant to those who are chief in authority over us, to be chief in virtue and Thy fear; grant to the National Congress Thy holy wisdom; and to our great men to do nothing against, but for the truth.

O Helper of the helpless, seasonable aid in affliction, remember all who are in necessity, and need Thy succor. Have mercy on them, as on us also, when in extremities. Remember, Lord, infants and children, orphans and widows, foreigners, travellers and voyagers, the sick in soul or body, all in extreme age and weakness, all in prison and chains, all in bitter servitude, or in loneliness. Thou, Lord, preservest both man and beast; how excellent is Thy loving-kindness, O God; therefore the children of men put their trust under the shadow of Thy wings.

The Lord bless us, and keep us, and show the light of His countenance upon us, and be merciful unto us; the Lord lift up His countenance upon us, and give us peace. *Amen.*

THE CANTICLES,

PSALMS AND ANCIENT HYMNS,

POINTED FOR CHANTING.

1.   *The Nicene Creed.*

1. We believe in one God, the | Father Al'mighty, || Maker of heaven and earth, and of all things | visi- ble | and in-| visible:
2. And in one Lord | Jesus | Christ, || the only begotten Son of God, begotten of the Father be-|fore = | all = | worlds.
3. God of God, Light of Light, very God of | ve ry | God;|| be| gotten | not = | made;
4. Of one substance | with the | Father, || by | whom all | things were | made;
5. Who, for us men, and for our salvation came | down from | heaven, || and was incarnate by the Holy Ghost | of the | Virgin | Mary,
6. And was | made = | man: || who was also crucified for us | under | Pontius | Pilate,
7. And suffered, and was buried; and the third day | rose a-| gain || according to the Scriptures: and as-| cended | into | heaven,
8. And sitteth at the right hand | of the | Father; || and shall come again with glory to judge the quick and the dead; of whose | kingdom there | shall be no | end.

9. And we believe in the Holy Ghost, the Lord, the | Giver of |
life, || who proceedeth from the | Father | and the | Son,
10. Who, with the Father and the Son together, is worshipped
and | glo-ri-| fied, || who | spake = | by the | prophets;
11. In one holy catholic and apos-| tolic | Church. || We confess
one baptism | for the re-| mission of | sins.
12. We look for the resurrection | of the |dead, || and the | life of
the | world to | come. || Amen.

2. *The Advent Canticle.*

1. Sing unto the Lord a new song; and His praise from the | end
of the | earth, || ye that go down to the sea, and | all that |
is there-| in.
2. Let the wilderness and the cities thereof lift | up their | voice; ||
let the inhabitants of the rock sing, let them shout | from
the | tops of the | mountains.
3. Let them give glory unto the Lord, and declare His praise |
among the | heathen. || The Lord hath | com- forted | His=|
people;
4. He hath made bare His holy arm in the eyes of | all = | na-
tions: || and all the ends of the earth shall see the sal-|
vation | of our | God.
5. Say to the Daughter of Zion, behold, thy sal-| vation | cometh; ||
behold, His reward is with Him, | and His | work be-| fore
Him.
6. Fear thou not; for | I am | with thee; || be not dismayed; for |
I am | thy = | God:
7. I will strengthen thee; yea, I will | help = | thee. || Unto you
that fear my name shall the Sun of righteousness arise with |
healing | in His | wings!
8. The glory of the Lord shall be revealed, and | all flesh shall |
see it. || Death shall be swallowed up in victory, and God
will wipe away | all tears | from our | eyes.
9. And it shall be said in that day, Lo! | this is our | God; || we
have waited for Him, | and = | He will | save us:

10. This is the Lord; we have | waited for | Him, || we will be glad and re-| joice in | His sal-| vation.

11. Sanctify and prepare yourselves to look upon the glory of our God; for the | Lord = | cometh. || Prepare ye the way of the Lord and | make His | paths = | straight.

12. Let us serve Him with gladness, and come before His | presence with | singing! || Blessed is He that cometh in the| name = | of the | Lord!

Glory be to the Father, | and to the | Son, || and | to the | Holy | Ghost:

As it was in the beginning, is now, and | ever shall | be, || world without | end. = | A = | men.

3. *The Christmas Canticle.*

1. Behold, I bring you good tidings of | great = | joy; || for unto you is born this day a Saviour, | which is | Christ the | Lord!

2. Glory to God | in the | highest, || and on earth, peace, | good = | will toward | men!

3. The Lord hath remembered His | cov- e-|nant || and sent sal-| vation | to His | people.

4. Israel is saved | by the | Lord || with an | ever-|lasting sal-| vation.

5. This is the Lord's doing, and marvellous | in our | eyes. || This is the day the Lord hath made; we will rejoice | and be | glad in | it.

6. Let the voice of rejoicing and sal-|vation be | heard, || in the taber-|na- cles | of the | righteous.

7. Blessed is He that cometh in the name | of the | Lord! || Blessed be the kingdom of our Father David! Ho-|sanna | in the | highest!

8. Open to me the gates of | righteous-|ness, || I will enter in and | praise = | the = | Lord.

THE CANTICLES, PSALMS AND ANCIENT HYMNS. 361

9. Say among the heathen, that the | Lord = | reigneth. || Let the multitudes of the isles be glad thereof: let the heavens rejoice, and | let the | earth be | glad.
10. He shall judge the world with | righteous-|ness; || and the | people | with His | truth.
11. Blessed be His glorious Name for | ever and | ever: || and let the whole earth be | filled | with His | glory.

Glory be to the Father, | and to the | Son, || and | to the | Holy | Ghost:
As it was in the beginning, is now, and | ever shall | be, || world without | end. = | A = | men.

4. *The Good Friday Canticle.*

1. Christ our Passover was offered for us | on this | day. || He was delivered for | our of-| fen = | ces.
2. He bore our sins in His own body | on the | tree, || and the Lord hath laid on Him the in-| iquity of | us = | all.
3. He hath trodden the wine-| press a-| lone, || and of the people | there was | none with | Him.
4. He was taken from prison | and from | judgment; || He was cut off out | of the land | of the | living.
5. Thou wast slain, and hast re-| deemed | us || out of every kindred, and tongue, and | people, | and = | nation;
6. Thou hast loved us, and washed us from our sins in | Thine own | blood; || and hast made us unto our God, | kings = | and = | priests.
7. Worthy is the Lamb | that was | slain || to receive power, and riches, and wisdom, and strength, and honor, and glory, for-| ever and | ev = | er.
8. Now is come sal | vation and | strength, || and the kingdom of our God, and the | power of | His = | Christ.
9. Death shall be swallowed | up in | victory, || and God shall wipe away all | tears = | from our | eyes.

Glory be to the Father, | and to the | Son, || and | to the | Holy | Ghost:

As it was in the beginning, is now, and | ever shall | be, |, world without | end. = | A = | men.

5.   The Easter Canticle.

1. Christ our Passover | has = risen. || He was dead, and behold He is alive for evermore, and hath the keys of | hell = | and of | death.

2. Christ our Passover was dead, a sacrifice | for our | sins. || He was put to death in the flesh, but was | quickened | by the | Spirit.

3. Christ is risen from the dead, and henceforth | dieth no | more; || death hath no more do-| minion | over | Him.

4. He died unto sin once, but now He liveth | unto | God; || the Prince of Life could not be | holden | of = | death.

5. God did not leave His soul | in the | grave, || nor suffer His Holy one to | see = | cor- = | ruption.

6. Christ is risen, the first fruits of | them that | slept. || Since by man came death, by man came also the resur-| rection | of the | dead.

7. Death is swallowed | up for | ever! || O Death, | where = | is thy | sting?

8. O Grave, | where is thy | victory? || Thanks be unto God, which giveth us the victory, | through our Lord | Jesus | Christ.

Glory be to the Father, | and to the | Son, || and | to the | Holy | Ghost:

As it was in the beginning, is now, and | ever shall | be, || world without | end. = | A = | men.

6.   The Ascension Day Canticle.

1. O clap your hands, | all ye | people. || Shout unto God with the | voice = | of =: | triumph!

2. God is gone up with a shout, the Lord with the sound | of a | trumpet. || Lift up your heads, O ye gates, and be ye lifted up, ye everlasting doors, and the King of | glory | shall come | in!
3. Who is this | king of | glory? || The Lord, strong and mighty; | He is the | king of | glory.
4. Sing praises to God, and unto our King! | Sing = | praises! || For He is the | King of | all the | earth.
5. God reigneth | over the | heathen; || He sitteth upon the | throne of | His = | holiness.
6. Let all the world bow | down be-| fore Him, || and all the angels of | God = | worship | Him!
7. Thy throne, O God, is for | ever and | ever; || the sceptre of Thy kingdom | is a | right = | sceptre.
8. Thou lovest righteousness and | hatest | wickedness; || therefore God, Thy God, hath anointed Thee with the oil of | gladness a-| bove Thy | fellows.
9. Thou hast as-| cended on | high; || Thou hast led cap-| tiv-i-| ty = | captive.
10. Thou has received | gifts for | men. || Thou hast entered into Thy Father's house, to pre-| pare a | mansion for | us.
11. Thou hast prepared Thy throne | in the | heavens; || and Thy kingdom | ruleth | over | all.
Glory be to the Father, | and to the | Son, || and | to the | Holy | Ghost:
As it was in the beginning, is now, and | ever shall | be, || world without | end. = | A = | men.

7. *The Whitsunday Canticle.*

1. Let us praise the Lord, and ex-| alt His | goodness. || Let us come before him with songs of | praise, and | hymns of thanks-| giving.
2. God hath raised up His holy Child Jesus, who, being by His right hand exalted, shed forth the promise of the Holy Ghost up-| on the Ap-| ostles, || so that they spake with new tongues, and wrought signs and | wonders | in His | name.

3. He gave power to the testimony | of His | servants. || The kingdoms of the earth, the people and | nations have | heard His | voice,

4. And have rendered obedience | unto our | Lord, || and | to = | His = | Christ.

5. We render thanks unto | Thee, O | Lord, || who art the Alpha and Omega, the | first = | and the | last,

6. That thou hast re-| vealed Thy | power, || and entered | upon | Thy = | kingdom.

7. Thou hast sent unto | us the | Comforter, || even the Spirit of truth, that he may a-| bide with | us for-| ever.

8. Thou hast sent the Spirit of Thy Son into our hearts, whereby we cry unto Thee: | Abba, | Father. || It is the Spirit, which witnesseth with our spirits, that | we are the | children of | God.

9. The Spirit also helpeth | our in-| firmities, || and with groanings, which cannot be uttered, | maketh inter-| cession | for us.

10. We wait for the redemption | of our | body, || and for the manifestation of the glorious liberty | of the | sons of | God.

11. The Spirit is the earnest and pledge of | our in-| heritance; || whereby also we are sealed | unto the | day of re-| demption.

12. O Lord, we praise Thee, and | render Thee | thanks, || that Thou hast | given | us the | Spirit.

Glory be to the Father, | and to the | Son, || and | to the | Holy Ghost:

As it was in the beginning, is now, and | ever shall | be, || world without | end. = | A = | men.

8. *The Trinity Sunday Canticle.*

The proper Canticle for this Day is the Ambrosian Hymn, Te Deum Laudamus, No. 44.

9. Psalm XXIII.

1. The Lord | is my | Shepherd; || I | shall = | not = | want.
2. He maketh me to lie down in | green = | pastures: || He leadeth me be-| side the | still = | waters.
3. He re-|storeth my | soul: || He leadeth me in the paths of righteousness for | His = | name's = | sake.
4. Yea, though I walk through the valley of the shadow of death, I will | fear no | evil: || for Thou art with me; Thy rod and Thy | staff they | comfort | me.
5. Thou preparest a table before me in the presence of | mine = | enemies: || Thou anointest my head with | oil; my | cup runneth | over.
6. Surely goodness and mercy shall follow me all the days | of my | life: || and I will dwell in the house | of the | Lord for-| ever.

10. Psalm XLVI.

1. God is our | refuge and | strength, || a very | present | help in | trouble.
2. Therefore will not we fear, though the | earth be | removed, || and though the mountains be carried into the | midst = | of the | sea.
3. Though the waters thereof | roar and | be troubled, || though the mountains shake | with the | swelling there-| of.
4. There is a river, the streams whereof shall make glad the | city of | God, || the holy place of the tabernacles | of the | most = | High.
5. God is in the midst of her; she shall | not be | moved: || God shall help her, | and = | that right | early.
6. The heathen raged, the kingdoms | were = | moved: || He uttered His | voice, = | the earth | melted.
7. The Lord of | hosts is | with us; || the God of | Jacob | is our | refuge.
8. Come, behold the works | of the | Lord, || what desolations He hath | made = | in the | earth.

31*

9. He maketh wars to cease unto the end | of the | earth; || He breaketh the bow, and cutteth the spear in sunder; He burneth the | chariot | in the | fire.

10. Be still, and know that | I am | God: || I will be exalted among the heathen, I will be ex-| alted | in the | earth.

11. The Lord of | hosts is | with us; || the God of | Jacob | is our | refuge.

11.   *Psalm XLVII.*

1. O CLAP your hands, | all ye | people; || shout unto | God with the | voice of | triumph.
2. For the Lord most | High is | terrible; || He is a great | King over | all the | earth.
3. He shall subdue the people | under | us, || and the | nations | under our | feet.
4. He shall choose our in-| heri-tance | for us, || the excellency of | Jacob | whom He | loved.
5. God is gone | up with a | shout, || the Lord with the | sound = | of a | trumpet.
6. Sing praises to | God, sing | praises: || sing praises | unto our | King, sing | praises.
7. For God is the King of | all the | earth: || sing ye | praises with | under- | standing.
8. God reigneth | over the | heathen: || God sitteth upon the | throne = | of His | holiness.
9. The princes of the people are | gathered to-| gether, || even the people of the | God of | A-bra-| ham:
10. For the shields of the earth belong | unto | God: || He is | great = | ly ex-| alted.

12.   *Psalm LI.*

1. Have mercy upon me, | O = | God, || according to || Thy = | loving- | kindness:

2. According unto the multitude of Thy | tender | mercies || blot | out = | my trans- | gressions.
3. Wash me throughly | from mine | iniquity, || and | cleanse me | from my | sin.
4. For I acknowledge | my trans-| gressions: || and my sin is | ever be-| fore = | me.
5. Against Thee, Thee only, have I sinned, and done this evil | in Thy | sight: || that Thou mightest be justified when Thou speakest, and be | clear when | Thou judg-| est.
6. Behold, I was | shapen in | iniquity; || and in sin did my | mother con-| ceive = | me.
7. Behold, Thou desirest truth in the | inward | parts: || and in the hidden part Thou shalt | make me | to know wis-| dom.
8. Purge me with hyssop, and I | shall be | clean: || wash me, and I shall be | whi- = | ter than | snow.
9. Make me to hear | joy and | gladness; || that the bones which Thou hast | broken | may re-| joice.
10. Hide Thy face | from my | sins, || and blot | out all | mine in- iquities.
11. Create in me a clean | heart, O | God; || and renew a right | spirit with-| in = | me.
12. Cast me not away | from Thy | presence; || and take not Thy | Holy | Spirit | from me.
13. Restore unto me the joy of | Thy sal-| vation; || and uphold me | with Thy | free = | Spirit.
14. Then will I teach transgressors | Thy | ways; || and sinners shall be con-| verted | unto | Thee.
15. Deliver me from blood-guiltiness, O God, Thou God of | my sal-| vation; || and my tongue shall sing aloud | of Thy | righteous-| ness.
16. O Lord, open | Thou my | lips; || and my mouth shall | shew forth | Thy = | praise.
17. For Thou desirest not sacrifice; else | would I | give it: || Thou delightest | not in | burnt = | offering.

18. The sacrifices of God are a | broken | spirit: || a broken and a contrite heart, O God, | Thou wilt | not de-| spise.
19. Do good in Thy good pleasure | unto | Zion: || build Thou the walls | of Je-| rusa-| lem.
20. Then shalt Thou be pleased with the sacrifices of righteousness, with burnt offering and | whole burnt | offering: || then shall they offer bullocks | upon | Thine = | altar.

13. Psalm LXVII.

1. God be merciful unto | us, and | bless us; || and cause His | face to | shine up-| on us.
2. That Thy way may be | known upon | earth, || Thy saving | health a-| mong all | nations.
3. Let the people praise | Thee, O | God; || let | all the | people | praise Thee.
4. O let the nations be glad and | sing for | joy: || for Thou shalt judge the people righteously, and govern the | nations | up- on | earth.
5. Let the people praise | Thee, O | God; || let | all the | people | praise Thee.
6. Then shall the earth | yield her | increase; || and God, even our own | God, = | shall = | bless us.
7. God | shall = | bless us; || and all the ends of the | earth shall | fear = | Him.

14. Psalm LXXXIV.

1. How amiable are Thy | taber-| nacles, || O | Lord = | of = | hosts!
2. My soul longeth, yea, even fainteth for the courts | of the | Lord: || my heart and my flesh crieth out | for the | living | God.
3. Yea, the sparrow hath found an house, and the swallow a nest for herself, where she may | lay her | young, || even Thine altars; O Lord of hosts, my | king = | and my | God.

4. Blessed are they that dwell | in Thy | house: || they will be | still = | praising | Thee.
5. Blessed is the man whose strength | is in | Thee; || in whose heart | are = | the ways | of them.
6. Who, passing through the valley of Baca, make | it a | well; || the rain also | fill = | eth the | pools.
7. They go from | strength to | strength, || every one of them in Zion ap-| peareth | before | God.
8. O Lord God of hosts, | hear my | prayer: || give ear | O = | God of | Jacob.
9. Behold, O | God our | shield, || and look upon the | face of | Thine a-| nointed.
10. For a day in Thy courts is better | than a | thousand. || I had rather be a doorkeeper in the house of my God, than to dwell in the | tents of | wicked-| ness.
11. For the Lord God is a | sun and | shield: || the Lord will give grace and glory: no good thing will He withhold from | them = | that walk | uprightly.
12. O | Lord of | hosts, || blessed is the | man that | trusteth in | Thee.

15.   *Psalm CX.*

1. Lord, Thou hast been our | dwelling-| place || in | all gene-| ra = | tions.
2. Before the mountains were brought forth, or ever Thou hadst formed the earth | and the | world, || even from everlasting to ever-| lasting, | Thou art | God.
3. Thou turnest man | to de-| struction; || and sayest, Re-| turn, ye | children of | men.
4. For a thousand years in Thy sight are but as | yester-| day || when it is past, and as a | watch = | in the | night.
5. Thou carriest them away as with a flood; they are | as a | sleep: || in the morning they are like | grass which | grow-eth | up.
6. In the morning it flourisheth, and | groweth | up; || in the evening it is cut | down, and | wither-| eth.

Y

7. For we are consumed by | Thine = | anger, || and by | Thy wrath | are we | troubled.
8. Thou hast set our iniquities be-| fore = | Thee, || our secret sins in the light | of Thy | counte-| nance.
9. For all our days are passed away | in Thy | wrath: || we spend our years as a | tale = | that is | told.
10. The days of our years are three-score years and ten; and if by reason of strength they be | four-score | years, || yet is their strength labor and sorrow; for it is soon cut off, | and we | fly a-| way.
11. Who knoweth the power of | Thine = | anger? || even according to Thy fear, | so is | Thy = | wrath.
12. So teach us to number | our = | days, || that we may apply our | hearts = | unto | wisdom.

16. *Psalm XCI.*

1. He that dwelleth in the secret place of the | most = | High || shall abide under the shadow of | the Al-| migh = | ty.
2. I will say of the Lord, He is my refuge and | my = | fortress: || my God; in | Him = | will I | trust.
3. Surely He shall deliver Thee from the snare | of the | fowler, || and from the | noisome | pesti-| lence.
4. He shall cover Thee with His feathers, and under His wings | shalt thou | trust: || His truth shall | be thy | shield and | buckler.
5. Thou shalt not be afraid for the | terror by | night; || nor for the | arrow that | flieth by | day.
6. Nor for the pestilence that walketh in | dark = | ness; || nor for the destruction that | wasteth | at = | noonday.
7. A thousand shall fall at thy side, and ten thousand at | thy right | hand; || but it shall | not come | nigh = | thee.
8. Only with thine eyes shalt | thou be-| hold || and see the re-| ward = | of the | wicked.
9. Because thou hast made the Lord which | is my | refuge, || even the most | High, thy | habi-| tation,

10. There shall no evil be-| fall = | thee, || neither shall any | plague come | nigh thy | dwelling.
11. For He shall give His angels charge | over | thee, || to keep | thee in | all thy | ways.
12. They shall bear thee up | in their | hands, || lest thou dash thy | foot a-| gainst a | stone.
13. Thou shalt tread upon the | lion and | adder: || the young lion and the dragon shalt | thou trample | under | feet.
14. Because he hath set his love upon Me, therefore will I de-| li- ver | him: || I will set him on high, because | he hath | known My | Name.
15. He shall call upon Me, and I will | answer | him: || I will be with him in trouble; I will deliver | him, and | honor | him.
16. With long life will I | satis-| fy him, || and | shew him | My sal-| vation.

17. *Psalm XCII.*

1. It is a good thing to give thanks un-| to the | Lord, || and to sing praises unto Thy | name, = | O most | High:
2. To shew forth Thy loving kindness | in the | morning, | and Thy | faithful-| ness every | night,
3. Upon an instrument of ten strings, and up-| on the | psaltery; || upon the harp | with a | solemn | sound.
4. For Thou, Lord, hast made me glad | through Thy | work: || I will triumph in the | works of | Thy = | hands.
5. O Lord, how great | are Thy | works! || and Thy | thoughts are | very | deep.
6. A brutish man | knoweth | not; || neither doth a | fool = | under-| stand this.
7. When the wicked spring as the grass, and when all the workers of iniquity do | flour = | ish; || it is that they shall be de- stroyed for ever: but Thou, Lord, art most | High for | ever-| more.
8. For, lo, Thine enemies, O Lord, for, lo, Thine enemies shall | per = | ish; || all the works of iniquity | shall = | be scat-| tered.

9. But my horn shalt Thou exalt like the horn of an | uni-| corn: ||
I shall be a-| nointed | with fresh | oil.
10. Mine eye also shall see my desire on mine | ene-| mies, || and
mine ears shall hear my desire of the wicked that | rise = |
up a-| gainst me.
11 The righteous shall flourish like the | palm = | tree: || he shall
grow like a | cedar in | Leba-| non.
12. Those that be planted in the house | of the | Lord || shall flourish in the | courts = | of our | God.
13. They shall still bring forth fruit | in old | age; || they shall be |
fat and | flourish-| ing;
14. To shew that the Lord is | up = | right; || He is my rock, and
there is no un-| righteous-| ness in | Him.

18.   *Psalm XCV.*

1. O come, let us sing un-| to the | Lord: || let us make a joyful
noise to the | Rock of | our sal-| vation.
2. Let us come before His presence | with thanks-| giving, | and
make a joyful noise | unto | Him with | psalms.
3. For the Lord is a | great = | God, || and a great | King a-| bove
all | gods.
4. In His hand are the deep places | of the | earth: || the strength
of the | hills is | His = | also.
5. The sea is His, | and He | made it: || and His hands | formed
the | dry = | land.
6. O come, let us worship | and bow | down: || let us kneel be-|
fore the | Lord our | Maker.
7. For He | is our | God; || and we are the people of His pasture, |
and the | sheep of His | hand.

19.   *Psalm XCVI.*

1. O sing unto the Lord a | new = | song: || sing unto the |
Lord, = | all the | earth.
2. Sing unto the Lord, | bless His | name; || shew forth His sal-|
vation from | day to | day.

3. Declare His glory a-| mong the | heathen, || His wonders | a- mong | all = | people.
4. For the Lord is great, and greatly to be | prais- = | ed: || He is to be | feared | above all | gods.
5. For all the gods of the nations | are = | idols: || but the | Lord = | made the | heavens.
6. Honor and majesty are be-| fore = | Him: || strength and beauty are | in His | sanctu-| ary.
7. Give unto the Lord, O ye kindreds | of the | people, || give unto the | Lord = | glory and | strength.
8. Give unto the Lord the glory due un-| to His | Name: || bring an offering, and | come in-| to His | courts.
9. O worship the Lord in the beauty of | holi-| ness: || fear be-| fore Him, | all the | earth.
10. Say among the heathen that the | Lord = | reigneth: || the world also shall be established that it shall not be moved: He shall judge the | people | righteous-| ly.
11. Let the heavens rejoice, and let the | earth be | glad; || let the sea | roar, and | the fulness there-| of.
12. Let the field be joyful, and all that | is there-| in: || then shall all the trees of the wood re-| joice be-| fore the | Lord:
13. For | He = | cometh, || for He | cometh to | judge the | earth:
14. He shall judge the | world with | righteousness, || and the | people | with His | truth.

20. *Psalm XCVIII.*

1. O sing unto the Lord a | new = | song; || for He hath | done = | marvellous | things.
2. His right hand, and His | holy | arm, || hath | gotten | Him the | victory.
3. The Lord hath made known | His sal-| vation: || His righteousness hath He openly shewed in the | sight = | of the | heathen.

4. He hath remembered His mercy and His truth toward the | house of | Israel: || all the ends of the earth have seen the sal-| vation | of our | God.
5. Make a joyful noise unto the Lord, | all the | earth: || make a loud noise, and re-| joice, = | and sing | praise.
6. Sing unto the Lord | with the | harp; || with the harp, and the | voice = | of a | psalm.
7. With trumpets and | sound of | cornet || make a joyful noise be-| fore the | Lord, the | King.
8. Let the sea roar, and the | fulness there-| of; || the world, and | they that | dwell there-| in.
9. Let the floods clap their hands: let the hills be joyful together be-| fore the | Lord; || for He | cometh to | judge the | earth:
10. With righteousness shall He | judge the | world, || and the | people | with = | equity.

21. *Psalm C.*

1. Make a joyful noise unto the Lord, | all ye | lands. || Serve the Lord with gladness: come before His | presence | with = | singing.
2 Know ye that the Lord | He is | God: || it is He that hath made us, and not we ourselves; we are His people, | and the | sheep of His | pasture.
3. Enter into His gates with thanksgiving, and into His | courts with | praise: || be thankful unto Him, and | bless = | His = | Name.
4. For the Lord is good; His mercy is | ev-er-| lasting; || and His truth endureth | to all | gene-| rations.

22. *Psalm CIII.*

1. Bless the Lord, | O my | soul: || and all that is within me, | bless His | holy | Name.
2 Bless the Lord, | O my | soul, || and for-| get not | all His | benefits :

3. Who forgiveth all | thine in-| iquities; || who healeth | all = | thy dis-| eases;
4. Who redeemeth thy life | from de-| struction; || who crowneth thee with loving-| kindness and | tender | mercies.
5. Who satisfieth thy mouth | with good | things; || so that thy youth is re-| newed | like the | eagle's.
6. The Lord executeth righteousness and | judg = | ment || for | all that | are op-| pressed.
7. He made known His ways | unto | Moses, || His acts unto the | children of | Isra-| el.
8. The Lord is merciful and | gra- = | cious, || slow to anger, and | plen = | teous in | mercy.
9. The mercy of the Lord is from everlasting to everlasting upon them that | fear = | Him, || and His righteousness unto | children's | chil = | dren.
10. To such as | keep His | covenant, || and to those that remember His com-| mand = | ments to | do them.
11. The Lord hath prepared His throne | in the | heavens; || and His kingdom | ruleth | over | all.
12. Bless the Lord, ye His angels, that ex-| cel in | strength, || that do His commandments, hearkening unto the | voice = | of His | word.
13. Bless ye the Lord, all | ye His | hosts; || ye ministers of | His, that | do His | pleasure.
14. Bless the Lord, all His works in all places of | His do-| minion: || bless the | Lord, = | O my | soul.

23.   *Psalm CVII.*

1. O that men would praise the Lord | for His | goodness, || and for His wonderful works | to the | children of | men!
2. And let them sacrifice the sacrifices of | thanks = | giving, || and declare | His works | with re-| joicing.
3. They that go down to the | sea in | ships, || that do business in great waters; these see the works of the Lord, and His | wonders | in the | deep.

4 For He commandeth, and raiseth the | stormy | wind, || which lifteth | up the | waves there-| of.

5. They mount up to the heaven, they go down again | to the | depths: || their soul is melted | be = | cause of | trouble.

6. They reel to and fro, and stagger like a | drunken | man, || and | are at | their wit's | end.

7. Then they cry unto the Lord | in their | trouble, || and He bringeth them | out of | their dis-| tresses.

8. He maketh the | storm a | calm, || so that the | waves there-| of are | still.

9. Then | are they | glad || be-| cause = | they be | quiet;

10. So He | bringeth | them || unto | their = | desired | haven.

11. O that men would praise the Lord | for His | goodness, || and for His wonderful works | to the | children of | men.

12. Let them exalt Him also in the congregation | of the | people, || and praise Him in the as-| sembly | of the | elders.

24. Psalm CXI.

1. I will praise the Lord with | my whole | heart, || in the assembly of the upright, and | in the | congre-| gation.

2. The works of the | Lord are | great, || sought out of all them that have | pleas =| ure there-| in.

3. His work is honorable | and glo-| rious: || and His righteousness en-| dur = | eth for | ever.

4. He hath made His wonderful works to | be re-| membered: || the Lord is gracious and | full = | of com-| passion.

5. He hath given meat unto them that | fear = | Him: || He will ever be mindful | of His | cove-| nant.

6. He hath shewed His people the power | of His | works, || that He may give them the | heritage | of the | heathen.

7. The works of His hands are verity and | judg = | ment; || all His com-| mand- = | ments are | sure.

8. They stand fast for | ever and | ever, || and are done in | truth and | upright-| ness.

9. He sent redemption un-| to His | people: || He hath command-
ed His covenant for ever: holy and | reverend | is His |
Name.

10. The fear of the Lord is the be-| ginning of | wisdom: || a good
understanding have all they that do His commandments:
His praise en-| dur = | eth for | ever.

25. Psalm CXXI.

1. I will lift up mine eyes un-| to the | hills, || from | whence com-|
eth my | help.
2. My help cometh | from the | Lord, || which | made = | heaven
and | earth
3. He will not suffer thy foot | to be | moved: || He that | keepeth
thee | will not | slumber.
4. Behold, He that keepeth | Isra-| el || shall neither | slum = |
ber nor | sleep.
5. The Lord | is thy | Keeper: || the Lord is thy shade up-| on
thy | right = | hand.
6. The sun shall not smite | thee by | day, || nor the | moon = |
by = | night.
7. The Lord shall preserve thee | from all | evil: || He shall pre-|
serve = | thy = | soul.
8. The Lord shall preserve thy going out and thy | coming | in ||
from this time forth, and | even for | ever | more.

26. Psalm CXXII.

1. I was glad when they said | unto | me, || Let us go into the |
house = | of the | Lord.
2. Our feet shall stand with-| in thy | gates, || O Je-| ru = |
sa = | lem.
3. Jerusalem is builded | as a | city || that | is com-| pact to-|
gether.

4. Whither the tribes go up, the tribes | of the | Lord, || unto the testimony of Israel, to give thanks unto the | Name = | of the | Lord.

5. For there are set | thrones of | judgment, || the thrones | of the | house of | David.

6. Pray for the peace of Je-| rusa-| lem: || they shall | prosper | that love | thee.

7. Peace be with-| in thy | walls, || and prosperity with-| in thy | pala-| ces.

8. For my brethren and com-| panions' | sakes, || I will now say, | Peace be | within | thee.

9. Because of the house of the | Lord our | God, || I will | seek = | thy = | good.

27.   *Psalm CXXX.*

1 Out of the depths have I cried unto | Thee, O | Lord. || Lord, | hear = | my = | voice:

2. Let Thine ears | be at-| tentive || to the | voice of my | suppli-| cations.

3. If Thou, Lord, shouldest | mark in-| iquities, || O | Lord, = | who shall | stand?

4. But there is for-| giveness | with Thee, || that | Thou = | mayest be | feared.

5. I wait for the Lord, my | soul doth | wait, || and in His | word = | do I | hope.

6 My soul waiteth for the Lord more than they that watch | for the | morning: || I say, more than they | that watch | for the | morning.

7. Let Israel hope in tne Lord: for with the Lord | there is | mercy, || and with | Him is | plenteous re-| demption.

8. And He shall re-| deem = | Israel || from | all = | his in-| iquities.

28. Selected from Psalm CXXXII and XXIV.

1. Arise, O Lord, in-| to Thy | rest; || Thou, and the | ark = | of Thy strength.
2. Let Thy priests be clothed with | righteous-| ness; || and let Thy | saints = | shout for | joy.
3. Make a joyful noise unto God, | all ye | lands. || Serve the Lord with gladness: enter into His gates with thanksgiving, and in-| to His | courts with | praise.
4. Who shall ascend into the hill | of the | Lord? || or who shall stand | in His | holy | place?
5. He that hath clean hands, and a | pure = | heart; || who hath not lifted up his soul unto vanity, nor | sworn de-| ceitful-| ly,
6. He shall receive the blessing | from the | Lord, || and righteousness from the | God of | his sal-| vation.
7. Lift up your heads, O ye gates; and be ye lift up, ye ever-| lasting | doors; || and the King of | glory | shall come | in.
8. Who is this | King of | glory? || The Lord, strong and mighty, the | Lord = | mighty in | battle.
9. Lift up your heads, O ye gates; even lift them up, ye ever-| lasting | doors, || and the King of | glory | shall come | in.
10. Who is this | King of | glory? || The Lord of hosts, He is the | King of | glo = | ry.

29. Psalm CXXXIII.

1. Behold, how good and how pleasant it | is for | brethren || to dwell to-| gether in | uni-| ty.
2. It is like the precious ointment upon the head, that ran down up-| on the | beard, || even Aaron's beard: that went down to the | skirts = | of his | garments;
3. As the | dew of | Hermon, || and as the dew that descended up-| on the | mountains of | Zion:
4. For there the Lord com-| manded the | blessing, || even | life for | ever-| more.

30. Psalm CXLVI.

1. Praise | ye the | Lord. || Praise the | Lord, = | O my | soul.

2. While I live will I | praise the | Lord: || I will sing praises unto my God | while I | have any | being.

3. Put not your trust in princes, nor in the | son of | man, || in | whom there | is no | help.

4. His breath goeth forth, he returneth | to his | earth; || in that very day | his = | thoughts = | perish.

5. Happy is he that hath the God of Jacob | for his | help, || whose hope is | in the | Lord his | God.

6. Who made heaven, and earth, the sea, and all that | therein | is: || which | keepeth | truth for-| ever.

7. Which executeth judgment | for the | oppressed: || which giveth | food = | to the | hungry.

8. The Lord looseth the prisoners: the Lord openeth the eyes | of the | blind: || the Lord raiseth them that are bowed down: the Lord | lov =| eth the | righteous.

9. The Lord preserveth the strangers; He relieveth the fatherless and | wid = | ow: but the way of the wicked He | turneth | upside | down.

10. The Lord shall reign forever, even thy God, O Zion, unto | all gene-| rations. || Praise | ye = | the = | Lord.

31. Psalm CXLVIII.

1. Praise | ye the | Lord. || Praise ye the Lord from the heavens: | praise Him | in the | heights.

2. Praise ye Him, | all His | angels: || praise | ye Him, | all His | hosts.

3. Praise ye Him, | sun and | moon: || praise Him, | all ye | stars of | light.

4. Praise Him, ye | heavens of | heavens, || and ye waters that be a-| bove = | the = | heavens.

5. Let them praise the | name of the | Lord: || for He command-
ed, | and they | were cre-| ated.
6. He hath also stablished them for-| ever and | ever: || He hath
made a decree | which shall | not = | pass.
7. Praise the Lord from the earth, ye dragons, | and all | deeps: |
Fire and hail; snow and vapors; stormy | wind ful-| filling
His | word:
8. Mountains, | and all | hills; || fruitful | trees = | and all | ce-
dars:
9. Beasts, | and all | cattle; || creeping things | and = | flying |
fowl:
10. Kings of the earth, | and all | people; || princes, and all |
judges | of the | earth.
11. Both young men, and maidens; | old men, and | children: || let
them praise the | name = | of the | Lord:
12. For His name a-| lone is | excellent; || His glory is a-| bove the |
earth and | heaven.
13. He also exalteth the horn | of His | people, || the | praise of |
all His | saints;
14. Even of the | children of | Israel; || a people near unto Him. |
Praise = | ye the | Lord.

32. *Psalm CXLIX.*

1. Sing unto the Lord a | new = | song, || and his praise in the
congre-| gation | of = | saints.
2. Let Israel rejoice in | Him that | made him: || let the children
of Zion be | joyful | in their | King.
3. Let them praise His name | in the | dance: || let them sing
praises unto | him with the | timbrel and | harp.
4. For the Lord taketh pleasure | in His | people: ||He will beau-
tify the | meek with | sal = | vation.
5. Let the saints be | joyful in | glory: || let them sing a-| loud
up-| on their | beds.
6. Let the high praises of God be | in their | mouth, || and a two-
edged | sword = | in their | hand;

7. To execute vengeance upon the heathen, and punishments up-on the | people; || to bind their kings with chains, and their | nobles with | fetters of | iron.

8. To execute upon them the | judgment | written: || this honor have all His saints. |Praise = | ye the | Lord.

33. Psalm CL.

1. Praise ye the Lord. Praise God | in His | sanctuary: || praise Him in the | firmament | of His | power.

2. Praise Him for His | mighty | acts: || praise Him according | to His | ex- cellent | greatness.

3. Praise Him with the | sound of the | trumpet: || praise Him | with the | psaltery and | harp.

4. Praise Him with the | timbrel and | dance: || praise Him | with stringed | instruments and | organs.

5. Praise Him upon the | loud = | cymbals: || praise Him up-| on the | high-sounding | cymbals.

6. Let every thing | that hath | breath || praise the Lord. | Praise = | ye the | Lord.

34. Isaiah LII, 7-9.

1. How beautiful up-| on the | mountains || are the feet of Him that bringeth good tidings, | that = | pub- lisheth | peace;

2. That bringeth good tidings of good, that publisheth | sal = | vation; || that saith unto Zion, | Thy = | God = | reign-eth!

3. Thy watchmen shall lift | up the | voice; || with the voice to-| gether| shall they | sing:

4. For they shall see | eye to | eye, || when the Lord shall | bring a-| gain = | Zion.

5. Break forth into joy, sing together, ye waste places | of Je-| rusalem: || for the Lord hath comforted His people, He | hath re-| deemed Je-| rusalem.

6. The Lord hath made bare His holy arm in the eyes of | all the | nations; || and all the ends of the earth shall see the sal-| vation | of our | God.

35.   1 Cor. XV, 51-58.

1. We shall not | all = | sleep, || but we | shall = | all be | changed,
2. In a moment, in the twinkling of an eye, | at the last | trump: || for the trumpet shall sound, and the dead shall be raised incorruptible, | and we | shall be | changed.
3. For this corruptible must put on | incor- | ruption, || and this mortal must | put on | immor-| tality.
4. So when this corruptible shall have put on | in- cor-| ruption, || and this mortal shall have | put on | immor-| tality,
5. Then shall be brought to pass the saying | that is | written, || Death is | swallowed | up in | victory.
6. O Death, | where is thy | sting? || O | Grave, where | is thy | victory?
7. The sting of | death is | sin; || and the | strength of | sin is the | law.
8. But | thanks be to | God, || which giveth us the victory through our | Lord = | Jesus | Christ.

36.   Baptismal Chant.

1. The mercy of the Lord is from everlasting to everlasting upon | them that | fear Him, || and His righteousness | unto | children's | children.
2. To such as | keep His | covenant; || and to those that remember His com- | mandments to | do = | them.
3. Suffer little children to come unto me, and for-| bid them | not: || for of | such is the | kingdom of | heaven.

(After the Baptism.)

4. I will pour My Spirit up-| on thy | seed, || and My | blessing up-| on thine | offspring.

5. And they shall spring up as a-| mong the | grass, || as | willows by the | water-| courses.
6. For the promise is unto you, and | to your | children; || and to all that are afar off, even as many as the |· Lord our |· God shall | call.

37. Isaiah LIII, 5--9.

1. He was wounded for | our trans-| gressions, || He was | bruised for | our in-| iquities.
2. The chastisement of our peace | was upon | Him; || and with His | stripes $=$ | we are | healed.
3. All we like sheep have | gone a-| stray; || we have turned every | one to | his own | way;
4. And the Lord hath | laid on | Him || the in-| iquity | of us | all.
5. He was oppressed, and He | was af-| flicted, || yet He | opened | not His | mouth:
6. He is brought as a lamb to the slaughter, and as a sheep before her | shearers is | dumb, || so He | openeth | not His | mouth.
7. He was taken from prison | and from | judgment: || and who shall de-| clare His | gene-| ration?
8. For He was cut off out of the land | of the | living: || for the transgression of my |· people | was He |· stricken.
9. And He made His grave with the wicked, and with the rich | in His | death; || because He had done no violence, neither was any de-| ceit $=$ | in His | mouth.

38. Magnificat.

1. My soul doth magni-| fy the | Lord, || and my spirit hath re-| joiced in | God my | Saviour.
2. For He | hath re-| garded || the low | estate of | His hand-| maiden:
3. For, behold, | from hence-| forth || all gene-| rations shall | call me | blessed.

4. For He | that is | mighty, || hath done to me great things; and | holy | is His | name.
5. And His mercy is on them | that fear | Him || from gene-| ration | to gene-| ration.
6. He hath shewed strength | with His | arm; || He hath scattered the proud in the imagi-| nation | of their | hearts.
7. He hath put down the mighty | from their | seats, || and exalted | them of | low = | degree.
8. He hath filled the hungry | with good | things; || and the rich He | hath sent | empty a-| way.
9. He hath holpen His | servant | Israel, || in remem-| brance of | His = | mercy;
10. As He spake | to our | fathers, || to Abraham, and | his = | seed for-| ever.

39.   Benedictus.

1. Blessed be the Lord | God of | Israel; || for He hath visited | and re-| deemed His | people,
2. And hath raised up a horn of sal-| vation | for us || in the house | of His | servant | David;
3. As He spake by the mouth of His | holy | prophets, || which have been | since the | world be-| gan:
4. That we should be saved | from our | enemies, || and from the | hand of | all that | hate us;
5. To perform the mercy promised | to our | fathers, || and to remember | His holy | cov-e-| nant;
6. The oath | which He | sware || to our | father | A-bra-| ham,
7. That He would grant unto us, that we being delivered out of the hand | of our | enemies || might | serve Him | without | fear.
8. In holiness and righteousness be-| fore = | Him, || all the | days = | of our | life.
9. And Thou, Child, shalt be called the prophet | of the | Highest: || for Thou shalt go before the face of the Lord to pre-| pare = | His = | ways;
10. To give knowledge of salvation | unto His | people || by the re-| mission | of their | sins,

33

11. Through the tender mercy | of our | God; || whereby the dayspring from on | high hath | visited | us,
12. To give light to them that sit in darkness, and in the | shadow of | death, || to guide our feet | into the | way of | peace.

40. Nunc Dimittis.

1. Lord, now lettest Thou Thy servant de-| part in | peace, || ac-| cording | to Thy | word:
2. For | mine = | eyes || have | seen = | Thy sal-| vation,
3. Which Thou | hast pre-| pared || before the | face of | all = | people;
4. A light to | lighten the | Gentiles, || and the glory | of Thy | people | Israel.

41. The Seraphic Hymn.

1. Holy, Holy, Holy, Lord | God of | Sabaoth; || heaven and earth are full of the | majesty | of Thy | glory.
2. Hosanna | in the | highest! || Blessed is He that cometh in the name of the Lord. Ho-| sanna | in the | highest!

42. Gloria Patri.

1. Glory be to the Father | and to the | Son, || and | to the | Holy | Ghost:
2 As it was in the beginning, is now, and | ever shall | be, || world without | end. = | A = | men.

43. Gloria in Excelsis.

1. Glory be to | God on | high, || and on earth | peace, good | will toward | men.
2. We praise Thee, we bless Thee, we | worship | Thee, || we glorify Thee, we give thanks to | Thee for | Thy great | glory,
3. O Lord God, | heavenly | King, || God the | Father | Al=| mighty.

4. O Lord, the only begotten Son, | Jesus | Christ; || O Lord| God, Lamb of God, | Son = | of the | Father,
5. That takest away the | sin of the | world, || have | mercy up-| on = | us.
6. Thou that takest away the | sin of the | world, || have | mercy up-| on = | us.
7. Thou that takest away the | sin of the | world, || re-| ceive = | our = | prayer.
8. Thou that sittest at the right hand of | God the | Father, || have | mercy up-| on = | us.
9. For Thou only | art = | holy; || Thou | only | art the | Lord;
10. Thou only, O Christ, with the | Holy | Ghost, || art most high in the | glory of | God the | Father. || Amen.

44. *Te Deum Laudamus.*

1. We praise | Thee, O | God; || We acknowledge | Thee to | be the | Lord.
2. All the earth doth | worship | Thee, || the | Father | ever-| lasting.
3. To Thee all angels | cry a-| loud: || the heavens and | all the | powers there-| in.
4. To Thee cherubim and | seraph-| im || con-|tinual-| ly do | cry,
5. Holy, Holy, Holy, Lord | God of | Sabaoth. || Heaven and earth are full of the | majesty | of Thy | glory.
6. The glorious company of the apostles | praise = | Thee : || The goodly fellowship of the | prophets | praise = | Thee,
7 The noble army of martyrs | praise = | Thee: || The holy Church throughout all the world | doth ac-| knowledge | Thee,
8. The | Fa = | ther, || of an | infinite | Majes-| ty;
9. Thine adorable, true. and | only | Son: || Also, the | Holy | Ghost, the | Comforter.
10. Thou art the king of glory, | O = | Christ: || Thou art the ever-lasting | Son = | of the | Father.
11. When Thou. tookest upon Thee to de-| liver | man, || Thou didst humble Thyself to be | born = | of a | Virgin.

12. When Thou hadst overcome the | sharpness of | death, || Thou didst open the kingdom of | heaven to | all be | lievers.
13. Thou sittest at the right | hand of | God, || in the | glory | of the | Father.
14. We believe that Thou shalt come to | be our | Judge: || We therefore pray Thee, help Thy servants, whom Thou hast redeemed | with Thy | precious | blood.
15. Make them to be numbered | with Thy | saints, || in | glory | ever-| lasting.
16. O Lord, | save Thy | people, || and | bless = | Thy = | heritage.
17. Gov-| ern = | them, || and | lift them | up for | ever.
18. Day by day we | magnify | Thee: And we worship Thy name ever | world with-| out = | end.
19. Vouch-| safe, O | Lord, || to keep us this | day with-| out = | sin.
20. O Lord, have | mercy up-| on us, || have | mer = | cy up-| on us.
21. O Lord, let Thy mercy | be up-| on us, || as our | trust, is | in = | Thee.
22. O Lord, in Thee | have I | trusted: |, let me | never | be confounded.

www.ingramcontent.com/pod-product-compliance
Lightning Source LLC
Chambersburg PA
CBHW032027220426
43664CB00006B/389